Foreign Trade Regimes and Economic Development:
COLOMBIA

Foreign Trade Regimes and Economic Development:

*A Special Conference Series
on Foreign Trade Regimes
and Economic Development*

VOLUME IX

NATIONAL BUREAU OF ECONOMIC RESEARCH
New York   *1976*

COLOMBIA

by **Carlos F. Díaz-Alejandro**

YALE UNIVERSITY

DISTRIBUTED BY Colombia University Press
New York and London

NATIONAL BUREAU OF ECONOMIC RESEARCH

A Special Conference Series on Foreign Trade Regimes and Economic Development

Library of Congress Card Number: 75–24035
ISBN for the series: 0–87014–500–2
ISBN for this volume: 0–87014–509–6

Printed in the United States of America
DESIGNED BY JEFFREY M. BARRIE

Para Luisa y Rodrigo

Contents

Tables

xiv

Figure

Charts

Co-Directors' Foreword

This volume is one of a series resulting from the research project on Exchange Control, Liberalization, and Economic Development sponsored by the National Bureau of Economic Research, the name of the project having been subsequently broadened to Foreign Trade Regimes and Economic Development. Underlying the project was the belief by all participants that the phenomena of exchange control and liberalization in less developed countries require careful and detailed analysis within a sound theoretical framework, and that the effects of individual policies and restrictions cannot be analyzed without consideration of both the nature of their administration and the economic environment within which they are adopted as determined by the domestic economic policy and structure of the particular country.

The research has thus had three aspects: (1) development of an analytical framework for handling exchange control and liberalization; (2) within that framework, research on individual countries, undertaken independently by senior scholars; and (3) analysis of the results of these independent efforts with a view to identifying those empirical generalizations that appear to emerge from the experience of the countries studied.

The analytical framework developed in the first stage was extensively commented upon by those responsible for the research on individual countries, and was then revised to the satisfaction of all participants. That framework, serving as the common basis upon which the country studies were undertaken, is further reflected in the syntheses reporting on the third aspect of the research.

The analytical framework pinpointed these three principal areas of research which all participants undertook to analyze for their own countries. Subject to a common focus on these three areas, each participant enjoyed maximum latitude to develop the analysis of his country's experience in the way he deemed appropriate. Comparison of the country volumes will indicate that this freedom was indeed utilized, and we believe that it has paid handsome dividends. The three areas singled out for in-depth analysis in the country studies are:

1. *The anatomy of exchange control:* The economic efficiency and distributional implications of alternative methods of exchange control in each country were to be examined and analyzed. Every method of exchange control differs analytically in its effects from every other. In each country study care has been taken to bring out the implications of the particular methods of control used. We consider it to be one of the major results of the project that these effects have been brought out systematically and clearly in analysis of the individual countries' experience.

2. *The liberalization episode:* Another major area for research was to be a detailed analysis of attempts to liberalize the payments regime. In the analytical framework, devaluation and liberalization were carefully distinguished, and concepts for quantifying the extent of devaluation and of liberalization were developed. It was hoped that careful analysis of individual devaluation and liberalization attempts, both successful and unsuccessful, would permit identification of the political and economic ingredients of an effective effort in that direction.

3. *Growth relationships:* Finally, the relationship of the exchange control regime to growth via static-efficiency and other factors was to be investigated. In this regard, the possible effects on savings, investment allocation, research and development, and entrepreneurship were to be highlighted.

In addition to identifying the three principal areas to be investigated, the analytical framework provided a common set of concepts to be used in the studies and distinguished various phases regarded as useful in tracing the experience of the individual countries and in assuring comparability of the analyses. The concepts are defined and the phases delineated in Appendix F.

The country studies undertaken within this project and their authors are as follows:

Brazil	Albert Fishlow, University of California, Berkeley
Chile	Jere R. Behrman, University of Pennsylvania
Colombia	Carlos F. Díaz-Alejandro, Yale University
Egypt	Bent Hansen, University of California, Berkeley, and Karim Nashashibi, International Monetary Fund
Ghana	J. Clark Leith, University of Western Ontario

India   Jagdish N. Bhagwati, Massachusetts Institute of Technol-
              ogy, and T. N. Srinivasan, Indian Statistical Institute
Israel   Michael Michaely, The Hebrew University of Jerusalem
Philippines   Robert E. Baldwin, University of Wisconsin
South Korea   Charles R. Frank, Jr., Princeton University and The
              Brookings Institution; Kwang Suk Kim, Korea Develop-
              ment Institute, Republic of Korea; and Larry E. Westphal,
              Northwestern University
Turkey   Anne O. Krueger, University of Minnesota

The principal results of the different country studies are brought together
in our overall syntheses. Each of the country studies, however, has been
made self-contained, so that readers interested in only certain of these studies
will not be handicapped.

In undertaking this project and bringing it to successful completion, the
authors of the individual country studies have contributed substantially to the
progress of the whole endeavor, over and above their individual research.
Each has commented upon the research findings of other participants, and has
made numerous suggestions which have improved the overall design and
execution of the project. The country authors who have collaborated with us
constitute an exceptionally able group of development economists, and we
wish to thank all of them for their cooperation and participation in the project.

We must also thank the National Bureau of Economic Research for its
sponsorship of the project and its assistance with many of the arrangements
necessary in an undertaking of this magnitude. Hal B. Lary, Vice President-
Research (retired), most energetically and efficiently provided both intellectual
and administrative input into the project over a three-year period. We would
also like to express our gratitude to the Agency for International Development
for having financed the National Bureau in undertaking this project. Michael
Roemer and Constantine Michalopoulos particularly deserve our sincere
thanks.

JAGDISH N. BHAGWATI
Massachusetts Institute of Technology

ANNE O. KRUEGER
University of Minnesota

Preface

Much has been written during the last few years on the international trade and financial policies of developing countries. As Colombia has received a good share of this attention, and as most authors in the field are eager to protest that trade policies are only part (and perhaps not the most important part) of a well-balanced development plan, the reader may wonder why I seek to lure him or her into looking at yet one more book on Colombian trade and development.

My basic motivation in writing this volume has been straightforward: since 1962, when I became acquainted at firsthand with Colombia, which contains the strengths as well as the problems and contradictions of Latin America, I have wanted to study its import and exchange control system, and more generally, its trade and payments policies. My pre-1959 Caribbean background had not prepared me for exposure to large numbers of public figures who, whether wise or misguided in their economic policymaking, made decisions on the basis of considerations excluding personal monetary gain. Surely this species of ruling group deserved a closer look.

Since the difficult mid-1960s, particularly since 1967, the Colombian economy has expanded at an impressive although characteristically unspectacular rate. We thus have the opportunity to begin studying the extent to which a return to export-led growth can help or hinder the achievement of the several Colombian development targets, an opportunity not available to those writing in the 1960s.

This new stage in Colombian development is still in its infancy. There is some reason to wonder whether it will have a chance to reach adulthood. I began this study in about July 1971, shortly before the world boom of 1972–73. As I write these lines, in the first week of 1975, each new forecast about the world economy is gloomier than the preceding one.

Yet, whatever happens in the nonsocialist part of the world economy, Colombia, and most of the rest of Latin America as well, have considerable grounds for optimism. The country and the region have second lines of defense against a world depression not available in the 1930s, when their performance was far from catastrophic. The forces searching for growth, national affirmation, and social justice cannot be stopped for very long, not even by a world depression. Indeed, Albert O. Hirschman has taught us that the optimal mix of external circumstances for a Latin American type of developing country may involve a spasmodic sequence of positive and negative stimuli. The historical challenge of Latin American integration and the bountiful natural resources of the region constitute key reserves against turbulence emanating from outside the area.

My book is focused on the 1950–72 period. Inevitably I also make some incursions into earlier economic history (but not enough) and spotty references to post-1972 policy changes. I do not attempt to be completely up-to-date even though many interesting changes in the trade and payments system have occurred during the last few years. Casual references, but no more, are made to economic policies not included under the trade and payments label. For these and other limitations it is up to the reader, particularly the Colombian reader, to decide whether or not to absolve me.

Two omissions should be highlighted. I hardly discuss coffee, and I can imagine a reviewer making references to Hamlet without the Prince. But all I need here is the Coffee Ghost; the Prince of this story is the nontraditional export sector. Excellent and up-to-date studies of Colombian coffee policy are available, the most recent one by Roberto Junguito, director of FEDESARROLLO. The special characteristics of the Colombian oil industry have also been neglected, an omission which has become more obvious since October 1973, shortly before Colombia became an oil importer. But FEDESARROLLO has also published a recent study on that subject.

During the preparation of this volume I received much help from many individuals and institutions. My greatest debt is to Rodrigo and Luisa Botero; without their support and fraternal aid my work would have suffered grievously. This book is dedicated to them.

The following persons have contributed to the preparation of one or several chapters or have commented on earlier drafts: Lillian Barros, Jere Behrman, Albert Berry, Guillermo Calvo, César Cardozo, Benjamin I. Cohen, Richard N. Cooper, Mary K. Downey, Jonathan Eaton, Albert Fishlow, Hernando Gomez Otálora, Gerald K. Helleiner, Eduardo del Hierro, Juan Carlos Jaramillo, Stephen Kadish, Robert E. Lipsey, Herminia Martinez

Neufeld, José Antonio Ocampo, Francisco Ortega, Gustav Ranis, Carlos Sansón, Eduardo Sarmiento, Francisco Thoumi, and Miguel Urrutia. They all have my gratitude.

Intrepid and cheerful assistance was provided by José Francisco Escandón in Bogotá and by Van Whiting in New Haven. Christina Lanfer was in this project from beginning to end, in New Haven and in Bogotá, always the helpful queen of Colombian sources and the resourceful intermediary with the computer.

The detailed and massive comments by Hal Lary on earlier drafts of this study frequently, and at first sight, threatened to push me into the abyss of insanity. Calmer reflection has shown me how very useful his comments have been in improving those drafts. The co-directors of this project, Anne O. Krueger and Jagdish N. Bhagwati, also deserve special thanks for their many good comments and suggestions. Together with other colleagues in the project, they made our occasional seminars fruitful events from which this work benefited greatly. Masterful editing by Ester Moskowitz is gratefully acknowledged. I also thank H. Irving Forman for his expert drawing of the charts and figure.

FEDESARROLLO in Bogotá provided a congenial and stimulating base, first during July and August of 1971, and many times since then. Fellow research workers there contributed their good advice and many ideas; in addition to those already mentioned I wish to express my gratitude to Haroldo Calvo, Roberto Junguito, Guillermo Perry, and Daniel Vargas.

INCOMEX officials in Bogotá, who had good reason to suspect my a priori hostility to the import control system they were running, were remarkably open and cooperative. Without their generous help I could not have produced Chapter 6, which is my favorite in this book. Criticisms in this volume directed toward the import control system must be clearly separated from judgments regarding how this group of unusually hardworking, dedicated, and public spirited officials carry out their tasks.

Seminars at CEDE, at the Universidad de los Andes, and conversations with many Colombian businessmen and public officials outside INCOMEX also provided many valuable insights.

Impersonal but sincere thanks are due to three other institutions which provided the material base for this project: the National Bureau of Economic Research, the National Science Foundation, and the Yale Economic Growth Center.

Finally, my brother and closest companion-in-arms, José Ramón Díaz-Alejandro, has kindly provided the frontispiece.

Ever since the railroad had been officially inaugurated and had begun to arrive with regularity on Wednesdays at eleven o'clock and the primitive wooden station with a desk, a telephone, and a ticket window had been built, on the streets of Macondo men and women were seen who had adopted everyday and normal customs and manners but who really looked like people out of a circus. In a town that had chafed under the tricks of the gypsies there was no future for those ambulatory acrobats of commerce who with equal effrontery offered a whistling kettle and a daily regime that would assure the salvation of the soul on the seventh day; but from those who let themselves be convinced out of fatigue and the ones who were always unwary, they reaped stupendous benefits. Among those theatrical creatures, wearing riding breeches and leggings, a pith helmet and steel-rimmed glasses, with topaz eyes and the skin of a thin rooster, there arrived in Macondo on one of so many Wednesdays the chubby and smiling Mr. Herbert, who ate at the house.

Gabriel García Márquez,
One Hundred Years of Solitude

Foreign Trade Regimes
and Economic Development:
COLOMBIA

Chapter 1

Trends and Phases in the Colombian Economy and Its Foreign Trade and Payments, 1950-72

In this chapter, major trends in Colombian foreign trade and payments occurring mainly between 1950 and 1972 will be reviewed, with sporadic discussion of events occurring before and after that period. Contemporary developments in the rest of the economy will also be discussed, but more selectively. Breaking a sector away and analyzing it apart from its proper general-equilibrium setting is no less arbitrary than cutting off the historical flow with starting and finishing dates for the study. But both prunings will, it is hoped, help yield richer fruit.

Possible subdivisions of the 1950–72 years will also be examined here. In the Colombian setting, one scheme of division readily suggests itself, based on the behavior of the dollar coffee price which, simplifying somewhat, may be taken as exogenously given to the country. The discussion of trade and payments policies can also be organized around four-year presidential terms, which since 1958 have followed the constitutional pattern foreseen in the National Front political agreement between the Conservative and Liberal parties. Finally, changes in foreign economic policy can be traced with the help of the phases devised by Jagdish N. Bhagwati and Anne O. Krueger and described in Appendix A. Each of these schemes will be used here, and their interconnections will be explored.

AN OVER-ALL VIEW: GROSS DOMESTIC PRODUCT AND ITS DISTRIBUTION

The postwar growth of the Colombian economy, while not spectacular, has been respectable. Table 1-1 shows one measure of long-term growth, yielding

1

TABLE 1-1

Average Annual Growth Rates and Standard Errors of Key Colombian Domestic Variables, Selected Periods,[a] 1950–72

(per cent; figures in parentheses are standard errors)

	1950–72	1950–56	1956–67	1967–72
Real gross domestic product at	4.75	5.23	4.57	6.08
market prices	(0.07)	(0.22)	(0.09)	(0.06)
Primary production	3.36	2.86	3.06	3.84
	(0.05)	(0.21)	(0.12)	(0.29)
Manufacturing	6.11	7.25	5.68	7.62
	(0.08)	(0.33)	(0.10)	(0.24)
Construction (value added)	5.72	12.85	3.21	6.29
	(0.41)	(1.88)	(0.75)	(0.68)
Services, Type I	5.48	7.43	5.64	7.58
	(0.16)	(0.68)	(0.33)	(0.16)
Services, Type II	5.00	4.26	5.22	5.98
	(0.07)	(0.14)	(0.10)	(0.15)
Real gross domestic fixed capital	3.61	11.41	2.64	7.52
formation	(0.47)	(1.97)	(0.90)	(0.85)
Volume of capital goods	0.76	13.32	0.60	8.01
imports (BdlR)	(0.81)	(2.89)	(1.93)	(2.03)
Production of manufactured	14.25	17.25	12.88	19.55
capital goods	(0.49)	(1.31)	(0.98)	(2.39)
Construction and building	4.87	9.44	2.99	5.37
(investment)	(0.32)	(1.89)	(0.57)	(0.66)
All investment in machinery	2.36	13.10	2.40	10.41
and equipment	(0.74)	(2.67)	(1.72)	(1.66)

SOURCE: Data obtained from BdlR-CN (see Appendix C for explanation of abbreviations used in this book). "Primary production" includes agriculture, livestock, fishing and hunting, forestry, and mining. Services, Type I includes commerce, transport, communications, electricity, gas and water, and banking and insurance. Services, Type II includes housing, government, and personal services.

METHOD: Growth rates were estimated by fitting a regression of the form $\log Xt = a + bt$ to the basic data, where Xt refers to the relevant variable, and t to a time trend. The coefficient b yields the growth rate; its standard error provides a measure of instability for different variables covering the same period of time. Note that the subperiods overlap one year, e.g., 1956 and 1967 observations appear twice in the subperiod regressions, but only once in the regression for the whole period 1950–72. This and other reasons, related to sharp breaks in trends, imply that growth rates for the whole period need not fall within the range of growth rates obtained for the subperiods, although that is usually the case.

Measures of instability, other than the standard error of the trend coefficient, are of course possible and can yield different instability rankings. For example, the standard deviation of year-to-year growth rates will be larger, and in different proportions for different variables, than the measure shown in this table.

a. Unless otherwise indicated, all dates in this volume are inclusive.

an expansion of real GDP of 4.8 per cent per year for 1950–72 (all dates are inclusive unless otherwise indicated). Such expansion was far from smooth, as can be seen in charts 1-1 and 1-2; consequently, different estimates for the growth of GDP and of other macroeconomic variables shown in Table 1-1 are

CHART 1-1

Rates of Growth of Colombian Gross Domestic Product and Gross Fixed Capital Formation, 1952–71

(centered three-year moving averages)

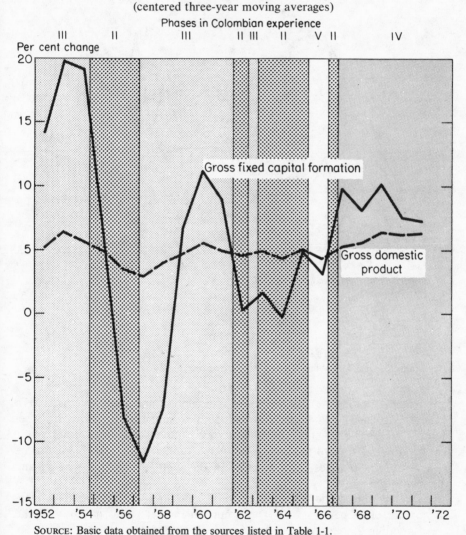

SOURCE: Basic data obtained from the sources listed in Table 1-1.

CHART 1-2

Merchandise Imports, Exports, and Coffee Prices, 1948–72

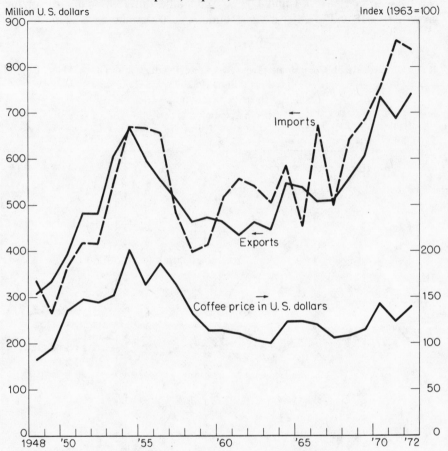

SOURCE: Basic data obtained from the sources listed in Table 1-2.

possible, depending on the method of calculation and the years used. For example, for just 1972 compared with 1950, the annual GDP growth is 5.0 per cent. Between those years, population grew at about 3.0 per cent per year.[1] Per capita GDP toward the end of the period under study is estimated to be U.S. $380 in 1970 prices, somewhat below the average for Latin America and the Caribbean.

Primary production, including rural activities, fishing, and mining, accounted for 28 per cent of GDP at current market prices in 1971–72; the corresponding amount was 39 per cent in 1950–51. The real output of this sector as a whole grew at a rate not much above that of population. In spite of massive rural-urban migrations, by 1970 about 59 per cent of the total population still lived outside the thirty principal urban conglomerations defined as having at least 50,000 inhabitants. These thirty urban centers grew during the period under study at the remarkable annual rate of 6.5 per cent. Of the economically active population, it has been estimated that 43 per cent could be regarded as engaged in rural activities.

Value added by the rural coffee sector alone amounted to 8 per cent of GDP in 1950–51 at current prices; by 1971–72 that percentage had declined to an estimated 4 per cent. Were Colombian output to be measured at "world prices," those percentages would undoubtedly be higher, inter alia because coffee output is valued at (after-tax) prices received by producers. Coffee output has expanded at an annual rate of 1.7 per cent, not far ahead of the growth of the volume of coffee exported (1.0 per cent per annum). In other words, the performance of the primary sector excluding coffee is significantly superior to that suggested by Table 1-1.

Measured at current prices, the manufacturing share of GDP in 1971–72 was 20 per cent, compared with 17 per cent in 1950–51; a moderate decline in the relative implicit prices for manufacturing was registered between these two periods. Measured in real terms, manufacturing annual growth was 1.3 times that of GDP as shown in Table 1-1. Manufacturing employment, however, appears to have expanded at a rate similar to that of over-all population, and thus lower than the growth of city dwellers.

The GDP share of construction and those services more closely linked to commodity production and distribution (Type I in Table 1-1) expanded from 26 per cent in 1950–51 to 33 per cent in 1971–72. This upward trend has been stimulated by the urbanization and modernization that have been taking place in Colombia between those years, and probably absorbed a large share of the increments to the urban labor force. But these services grew less than did manufacturing. The GDP share of Type II services, closer to pure "home goods" or nontradables, remained at about 19 per cent between 1950–51 and 1971–72, growing only slightly faster than GDP.

Evidence on the distribution as compared with the sectoral composition of output is scarce. The most thorough study on Colombian income distribution concludes that over-all distribution has probably not improved over the last thirty or forty years. It is likely that the so-called middle class, which can be placed in the eighth and ninth deciles of the income distribution, has benefited most from the growth of those years. As of 1964, the Gini coefficient for the distribution of personal income was 0.57, ranking Colombia, among the countries for which such estimates are available, as one of those with a most unequal distribution. Between the 1930s and mid-1950s, income distribution worsened in both urban and rural areas. Between the mid-1950s and mid-1960s the evidence indicates an improvement in urban distribution, a continued worsening of that in agriculture, and a moderate global improvement.[2]

AN OVER-ALL VIEW: FOREIGN TRADE

Even measured at current-dollar values, total merchandise imports and exports as well as international reserves show trend growth rates for 1948–72 below those of real GDP, manufacturing, and even primary production and population, as may be seen in Table 1-2. No long-term leading sector can be detected here. Indeed, many authors have identified the sluggish expansion of Colombia's postwar capacity to import as the major brake on growth.[3]

During 1948, 1949, and 1950, coffee accounted for 75 per cent of all registered merchandise exports; petroleum accounted for an additional 16 per cent. For both commodities, export dollar values had little to do with domestic policy and much to do with luck in world markets or in exploration. Colombian policy has had *some* influence on the behavior of the world coffee market and on the extent of oil exploration, but room for maneuvering has been small. Thus, from the viewpoint of Colombian policymakers, the meager 1948–72 growth rates shown in Table 1-2 for coffee and petroleum can be taken, in a first approximation, as exogenous parameters. Perhaps little more need be said to define Colombia's postwar foreign trade plight than to indicate that the two commodities accounting for 91 per cent of the export bill during 1948, 1949, and 1950 showed no sustained significant long-term upward trend in their dollar earnings.

Colombian coffee policy has sought higher and more stable dollar prices, if necessary by restricting sales and output in cooperation with other coffee-exporting countries. Internal coffee price policy has aimed at keeping real returns to growers at a stable level, too, but below that justified by dollar prices. The Colombian share in world coffee exports measured in physical units rose from 13.9 per cent in 1934–38 to 16.8 per cent during 1950–54, declining steadily since then to 11.6 per cent in 1971–72. The Colombian share in the value of world exports is higher (13.8 per cent in 1971–72) because of the quality of Colombian coffee, but has declined during recent years at a steeper rate than her share in physical units. Colombian policymakers regard these trends as an inevitable consequence of the rise of new producers, particularly in Africa, and changes in consumer tastes.

During the 1960s declining international oil prices coupled with relatively high Colombian costs for extraction and exploration led to the observed shrinkage in oil exports. An increasing share of oil output was used domestically. Domestic oil policy, which involved cumbersome regulations, special exchange rates, and specific price controls, seems to have had no major

TABLE 1-2

Average Annual Growth Rates and Standard Errors of Key Colombian Foreign Trade Variables, Selected Periods, 1948–72

(per cent; figures in parentheses are standard errors)

	1948–72	1948–56	1956–67	1967–72
Merchandise exports, current	1.85	8.94	0.30	7.69
dollars	(0.48)	(1.69)	(0.71)	(1.48)
Coffee exports, current dollars	0.57	10.01	−1.51	6.14
	(0.57)	(2.12)	(0.73)	(2.34)
Dollar price of coffee per pound	−0.40	9.58	−3.33	6.11
	(0.60)	(1.82)	(1.24)	(1.88)
Volume of coffee exports	1.04	1.21	1.34	0.98
	(0.24)	(1.57)	(0.71)	(0.63)
Registered "minor" exports,	8.89	7.37	9.02	14.15
current dollars	(0.77)	(3.34)	(1.95)	(1.95)
Registered crude petroleum	−1.13	3.90	0.05	−6.77
exports, current dollars	(0.65)	(1.81)	(0.95)	(6.82)
Merchandise imports, c.i.f.,	2.85	11.58	0.85	10.18
current dollars	(0.57)	(1.64)	(1.40)	(1.79)
Volume of merchandise imports	1.92^a	10.49	0.69	13.72^b
	(0.70)	(1.54)	(1.70)	(2.10)
Gross international reserves,	0.88	5.96	−7.14	20.67
current dollars	(1.08)	(3.52)	(1.88)	(6.18)

SOURCE: Data obtained from IMF-IFS: growth rates estimated as in Table 1-1.
a. Refers to 1948–70 only.
b. Refers to 1967–70 only.

discouraging effect on oil output during those years. More recently, however, Colombian oil policy has not reflected changes in the international oil market: prices for local consumers and producers are substantially below world prices, discouraging exploration and intensive exploitation of old fields and encouraging consumption of oil products. The state oil enterprise, ECOPETROL, has devoted its efforts toward refining and petrochemicals, neglecting exploration. Noticing the ample oil deposits found in neighboring Venezuela, Perú, and Ecuador, some Colombians may fret and wonder why only relatively poor deposits have been discovered thus far in their own country.

Hope for a vigorous and diversified export sector had to focus on exports of goods other than coffee and oil, still referred to in Colombia as "minor" or nontraditional exports. It will be seen in Chapter 2 that domestic policy can be said to have much to do with their behavior, but only fairly recently has pessimism regarding the competitive strength and growth of these exports been decisively routed in Colombia. In Table 1-2 an impressive long-term growth rate is shown for these exports; their starting base, however, was so small that until recently the impact of their expansion on the over-all export growth rate was modest. Nevertheless, these exports, which represented only 9 per cent of export earnings in 1948–50, were responsible for 56 per cent of the net increase in export earnings between those years and 1970–72.

High targets for GNP growth, sluggish expansion in traditional exports, and nontraditional exports still in their infancy provided the setting for policies encouraging import substitution, particularly in the industrial sector. As in other countries, both short-run balance-of-payments difficulties and a long-run desire for industrialization buttressed by export pessimism provided the rationale for protectionist policies to be discussed in chapters 3–6.

The fluctuations in Colombian postwar foreign trade have been particularly severe, and if just the years 1970–72 are compared with 1948–50, export growth rates are obtained that differ substantially from the trend estimates of Table 1-2, in which every year is taken into account. There is, of course, no "right" or "wrong" way to handle these ambiguities. For 1970–72 compared with 1948–50, the annual growth rate for minor exports is 9.8 per cent, and for coffee plus petroleum it is 1.9 per cent. It is an encouraging reflection on the progress already achieved by Colombia that if identical growth rates for traditional and nontraditional exports are projected for twenty-two years into the future, the over-all export growth rate turns out to be a healthy 6.7 per cent per year, almost double that achieved between 1948–50 and 1970–72 (3.4 per cent). Minor exports had reached 34 per cent of total export revenues by 1970–72, and would reach 63 per cent at the end of the following twenty-two years if the indicated past growth rates hold.

EXTERNAL AND INTERNAL INSTABILITY

Colombia has been one of the classic examples of an export economy that relies on a major staple whose price is subject to considerable fluctuation in world markets. But even during the early 1950s, exports of goods and services did not exceed l6 per cent of GDP at current prices. The corresponding figure for 1972 was l4 per cent. (It will be seen later that sharp fluctuations took place during the period under study in the price of tradable goods relative to those of nontradables.)

The data in the first column of Table 1-2 show that two pieces of conventional wisdom regarding the typical Latin American export economy hold up reasonably well for the Colombia of 1948–72. The terms of trade of its major staple declined, with dollar coffee prices showing no trend while dollar import prices crept steadily upward (compare lines 7 and 8 and disregard quality complications). The dollar coffee price registered substantial instability, as measured by the standard error of the estimated annual rate of change; contrary to what has been argued for other countries,[4] the expansion of the volume of coffee exports shows a much smaller standard error. The fluctuations registered in the growth of dollar earnings of coffee exports can then be properly blamed mostly on price fluctuations. Indeed, for 1948–72, the correlation between (the logarithm of) the dollar value of coffee exports and (the logarithm of) the dollar price index of coffee yields a coefficient of determination R^2 of 0.74; a similar correlation between the value and volume of coffee exports yields an R^2 of 0.11. Instability in coffee export earnings was reduced in some years because of the inverse relation between price and quantity, but for the whole period the price-quantity correlation was weak, as reflected by a negative R of only 0.18 between the logarithms of price and quantity.

It is less well recognized that import instability during 1948–72 was as high or higher than export instability,[5] whether measured in dollars or in physical units. Clearly, such instability cannot be blamed solely on external circumstances: domestic policies play a prominent part in the explanation of this peculiar fact. More on this in later chapters.

Given the stress in the literature on the dependence of the Colombian domestic economy on foreign trade, and the confirmation of the instability of imports and exports, it is surprising to find that the standard error of real GDP growth is only 0.07 (first column of Table 1-1). Had I used a macroeconomic measure embodying term-of-trade effects (which the GDP does not), the instability would of course be higher, but it is nevertheless notable that small echoes of fluctuations in exports and imports may be found in short-run GDP expansion. Even more striking, in view of all the literature stressing rigid links, is the steadiness found in manufacturing growth for the whole period. Which is the most unstable component of GDP? It is construction, which presumably is one of the least import- (or export-) intensive sectors of the economy![6]

Fluctuations in trade, especially imports, are so much larger than those of GDP that it could be argued, in a reversal of the chain of causation, that we are looking at an economy where slight adjustments in GDP expansion, perhaps brought about by monetary and fiscal policies, are highly successful in correcting payments imbalances. Additional knowledge permits us to discard this argument, applicable to economies with relatively unrestricted trade and payments systems, in the Colombian case. But it serves to emphasize the apparently marginal influence of Colombian foreign trade on GDP growth in the short run.

Another remarkable (negative) result involves the lack of correlation between real GDP growth for a given year t and the growth in exports, deflated by import price indices (or an approximation to the growth of "capacity to import"), during t, $t - 1$, $t - 2$, and $t - 3$. Even when a trend term was added to the regression, the results were insignificant, showing no link, both for the period 1950–68, and for 1929–68.[7]

For *any given year* it appears that above a certain minimum, which was in fact available to Colombia during almost all the years under study, few *imports* are indeed absolutely essential for the maintenance of economic activity. Imports of capital goods for expansion of capacity, as well as those of durable and nondurable consumer goods, can of course be postponed without much loss of that year's GDP. It is more difficult to cope with fluctuations in the supply of intermediate and raw material inputs, spare parts, etc. However, in an ongoing economic system, especially one in which people are accustomed to import controls, fluctuations in import availability can be partly absorbed in the short run through changes in inventories as well as use of more imaginative expedients, thus decreasing (but not eliminating) the negative impact of the fluctuations on GDP.

It should also be recalled that primary production still represents a substantial share of Colombian GDP. Much of it has only tenuous links with foreign trade and with economic activity in the rest of the country. By combining many services and even segments of manufacturing, especially crafts, a robust nontradables sector can be put together, the hard core of it located among the small cities and towns scattered amidst the abrupt Colombian mountains (see Figure 1-1). In this sense, the Colombian economy can be said to retain widespread "duality," or structural heterogeneity.

The above considerations help to explain why on the basis of year-to-year changes the link between foreign trade and GDP growth in Colombia has been relatively weak. But the foregoing factors are less informative regarding longer-term links.

CAPITAL FORMATION AND FOREIGN TRADE

Trend growth of real fixed capital formation during 1950–72 was lower than that of GDP. Domestic production of machinery and equipment, like minor exports, expanded at a rapid clip, but from a low base. Construction experienced a trend growth similar to GDP. The growth of total capital formation was dragged down by the sluggish expansion of capital goods imports, as may be seen in Table 1-1. As imports accounted for 93 per cent of capital formation in the form of machinery and equipment in 1950, and for 67 per cent as late as 1972 (magnitudes measured in 1958 prices), the failure of import capacity to

FIGURE 1-1

Topographical Map of Colombia

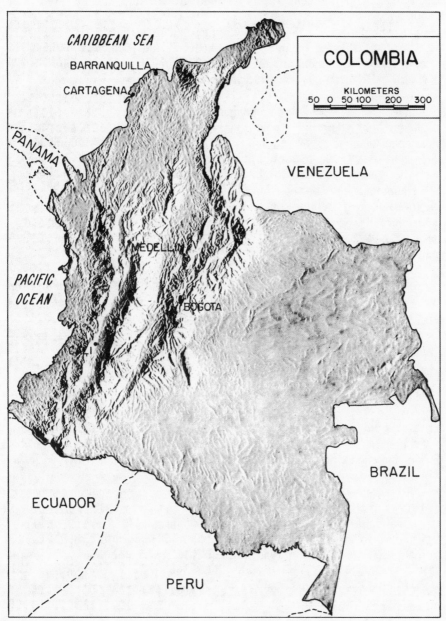

rise over the long run seriously limited investment and probably important aspects of technical change. Note that in Table 1-1 capital formation in all machinery and equipment shows a trend growth rate inferior to that of population.

The standard errors for the growth rates in all investment components are high, as old-fashioned business cycle theory would predict. But those for machinery and equipment and for capital goods imports are the highest. Here is where trade instability and stagnation take their sharpest bite. As will be seen in Chapter 3, there is in fact a very close correlation in Colombia between capital formation, especially in machinery and equipment and imports. This is surprising only insofar as it includes construction, given the weakness of the Colombian machinery and equipment industry. Under these circumstances, the export sector is the major (indirect) supplier of machinery and equipment.[8]

The relative prices of capital goods in Colombia, especially machinery and equipment, have on the whole followed the acute gyrations of the prices for tradable goods relative to nontradables. So while the share of all gross investment in GNP measured at current prices was 17 per cent in 1950 and 21 per cent in 1972, the corresponding figures in constant 1958 prices are 22 per cent and 20 per cent.

While the link between Colombian foreign trade and capital formation has been strong, variations in the marginal capital-output ratio, even for a medium run of several years, considerably loosen the connection between capital goods imports and growth. In the last chapter, I will discuss possible explanations for the variations in the marginal capital-output ratio, which include direct and indirect effects of Colombian foreign trade policies.

COFFEE AND PHASES

The years 1948 through 1972 cover a variety of trade and domestic experiences that clearly deserve separate treatment. The fundamental nature of the Colombian economic system remained unchanged, but dollar coffee prices as well as domestic policies differed substantially from phase to phase.

A first subdivision, based mainly on the world coffee market, is easy to make: before 1956, from 1956 through 1967, and since 1967. Coffee prices showed an impressive upward trend from 1948 through 1956, pulling up export and import dollar values, the physical volume of imports, and fixed capital formation. GDP rose from 1950 through 1956 at a faster than average (for 1950–72) rate, but the gap between the booming trade and investment variables and the unspectacular GDP performance looks puzzling. At least part of the answer to this contrast can be found in the divergence in sectoral growth rates. On the whole, urban (and especially big-city) activities such as manufacturing and construction boomed, while the important rural sector made slow progress. During 1948–56, a good part of rural Colombia was in the midst of social turmoil or bloody civil war. Another name for growth and development, or for favorable terms of trade, is not always peace, as this experience shows. A good share of investment during those years went into social overhead facilities, as well as spectacular projects with debatable social returns.

The trend of coffee prices from 1956 through 1967 was downward; attempts of the Colombia government to cope with that situation make up much of the substance of later chapters. While the annual growth in the volume of merchandise imports dropped dramatically, from 10.5 per cent to 0.7 per cent (Table 1-2), GDP growth sagged by less than a percentage point, from 5.2 to 4.6 per cent, as shown in tables 1-1 and 1-2. The slowdown in manufacturing expansion was larger, from 7.3 to 5.7 per cent per year, although far less spectacular than the drop in the growth rate of construction (value added), in spite of the latter's relative independence from imported inputs. Capital formation, especially in machinery and equipment, behaved more like the trade variables than like GDP, manufacturing, or primary production (the latter growing quite steadily in spite of unsteady weather). The slowdown in the expansion of domestic production of capital goods is notable, suggesting that while this activity is aimed at import substitution, it maintains complementary links with imported inputs. It may be added that the Colombian social and political picture was quieter and more peaceful during 1956–67 than it was before.

Dollar coffee prices did not change abruptly after 1967, as they had done after 1956. As will be seen below, the claim that 1967 was a turning point in Colombian economic history rests primarily on domestic policy accomplishments. Nevertheless, after a dip in 1967, dollar coffee prices tended to rise; their average for 1971–72 was still below that for 1955–56, but by 1973 that postwar high had been surpassed. As shown in Table 1-2, from 1967 through 1972 coffee earnings grew at 6 per cent per year, a healthy rate, but outpaced by the 10 per cent rate registered from 1948 through 1956. The most significant feature of the post-1967 years was the remarkable 14 per cent annual growth in minor exports, which was double the rate for 1948–56, in spite of its having started from a larger base. Supported by an expanded capacity to import, which even discounting inflation in dollar prices rose remarkably after 1967, the GDP grew faster and in a more balanced fashion than during 1950–56. In Chapter 8, I will examine in detail several characteristics of the post-1967 growth path. Here it is sufficient to note that by 1973 such growth had left the Colombian economy in a much better position to withstand external shocks than it was in 1956.

POLICY AND SUBPHASES

Before the Fall.

While trends in dollar coffee prices provide the critical 1956 watershed in Colombian postwar economic history, and 1967 provides, ex post, another clear turning point, policy hesitations and coffee price instability hinder neat and simple further subdivisions of the period under study. Appendix B contains a detailed list of principal postwar economic events related mainly to Colombian foreign trade and payments. A close look at policy shifts reflected there will show that they were influenced by at least the following major factors: cyclical fluctuations in the ex ante demand for imports and foreign exchange; dissatisfaction with the mechanisms used to repress such demand; the search for ways to stimulate minor exports; general political events, which since 1958 have followed a four-year presidential cycle; pressures from international and bilateral creditors, mainly the IMF, the IBRD, and the United States government; and, of course, the short-run gyrations of coffee prices.

Subdivision into phases is naturally somewhat arbitrary, but it is hoped that those suggested in Table 1-3 will on balance add more clarity than confusion. The last four follow, as well as calendar years and data allow, the post-1958 terms of the National Front presidents. They are preceded by two biennial transitional subphases (1957–58 and 1955–56), and by 1950–54. The following brief sketch of the characteristics of each of these subphases and their relation to the Bhagwati-Krueger phases (see Appendix A) is intended to place later discussion in perspective.

As in many Latin American countries, the great depression of the 1930s put an end to an era of relative economic liberalism in Colombia; in terms of the Bhagwati-Krueger scheme, Colombia went from Phase V to Phase I. Key import duties were raised, and widespread exchange and import controls were introduced in 1931; they have not been fully abandoned since. It should be noted, however, that quantitative restrictions were not the only response to the crisis; the Colombian exchange rate went from 1.03 pesos per U.S. dollar in 1929 to 1.78 pesos in 1935. An index (1963 = 100) of the purchasing-power-parity exchange rate, adjusted for price-level changes both in Colombia and the United States, rose from 56 in 1929 to 101 in 1935 when GDP deflators are used as proxies for "the price level," and from 70 in 1929 to 103 in 1935 when cost-of-living indices are used.[9] Such real devaluation foreshadowed the one following the post-1956 drop in the price of coffee. Indeed, the index for the real exchange rate for imports was not to reach the 1935 level again until 1958. As in the cases of Argentina and Brazil, the real devaluation helped Colombia weather the Great Depression surprisingly well, and stimulated industrialization.

Coffee recovery and the threat of war, then the Second World War, and later the circumstances of postwar European reconstruction appear to have induced the authorities to leave exchange rates alone. At any rate, between 1935 and 1948 the nominal exchange rate hardly moved, and Phase I controls became an established feature of the trade and payments system. The index for the purchasing-power-parity import exchange rate, which stood at 101 in 1935, dropped to 80 in 1939, to 63 in 1945, and to 59 in 1948 (similar results are obtained using cost-of-living deflators). In spite of some adjustment in the nominal rate, the index fell further, to 54 in 1950, roughly the 1929 level. As was the case in some other Latin American countries, the 1950s opened with exchange rates which had gradually, almost imperceptibly, become overvalued during the 1940s as nominal rates remained frozen while domestic inflation advanced faster (but not that much faster in any given year) than in the United States, the major participant in the world market.

The adjective "overvalued" is one to be used with care at all times, but particularly so in Colombia. There is probably no exchange rate observed in Colombia during 1925–72 which could not have been turned into an "equilibrium" one at some dollar coffee price, even if the possible choices were limited to the range of prices actually observed during the same period. The instability and unpredictability of world coffee prices thus has discouraged exchange authorities from seeking such an "equilibrium" rate, and has provided a major rationalization for import and exchange control.[10] For the 1930–68 period, there has been in fact a significant negative correlation between the purchasing-power-parity import exchange rate and the terms of trade as well as a significant upward trend in the real import exchange rate. The same results are obtained if just the 1950–68 years are analyzed. While on the subject of (very) long-term trends, it may be noted that although the Colombian coffee terms of trade (international) declined when the years 1948–72 are considered as a whole, they show a significant *positive* trend, or at worst no trend, when all of the years since 1925 are taken into account.[11]

The early postwar years, through 1954, are generally regarded as prosperous ones. While comprehensive national accounts are available starting only in 1950, earlier estimates of UNECLA put the annual growth of real GDP during 1945–50 at 5.2 per cent. The corresponding figure for 1925–45 is 4.1 per cent, at a time when population was expanding at an annual rate of about 2.1 per cent. As current-dollar coffee prices tripled between 1945 and 1950, the expansion of consumption plus investment (absorption) must have been higher than real GDP growth. By the late 1940s and during 1950 dissatisfaction with import and exchange controls rose, in spite of tinkering with the system.

TABLE 1-3

Major Colombian Economic Indicators, 1950–72

(annual averages)

	1950–54	1955 and 1956	1957 and 1958	1959–62	1963–66	1967–70	1971 and 1972
Foreign trade indices (averages for 1950–54 = 100)							
Merchandise exports, current dollars	100	109	92	87	97	114	136
Coffee plus oil exports, current dollars	100	105	90	83	86	87	93
Other (minor) exports, current dollars	100	156	121	146	244	483	698
Dollar price of coffee per pound	100	112	94	71	74	75	85
Volume of coffee exports	100	103	97	115	112	120	122
Merchandise imports, current dollars	100	137	91	105	115	133	175
Volume of merchandise imports	100	132	85	92	96	101	n.a.
GDP and its components (average annual percentage growth rates)							
GDP	5.6	4.0	2.3	5.5	4.6	5.9	6.1
Primary production	2.9	3.2	4.5	3.1	2.7	4.8	3.2
Manufacturing	7.1	7.0	4.5	6.8	5.5	6.4	8.8
Construction	13.6	5.5	-4.2	6.2	2.3	11.1	4.5
Services, Type I	9.1	2.4	-2.3	8.2	5.9	6.4	7.5
Services, Type II	4.1	5.0	3.8	5.2	5.7	5.6	6.1

Fixed capital formation as per cent of GNP (1958 prices)	21.2	25.1	17.1	18.1	16.4	17.7	18.3
In building and construction	9.3	10.9	10.0	9.8	8.6	10.3	10.1
In machinery and equipment	12.0	14.2	7.1	8.3	7.8	7.3	8.3
Over-all marginal fixed capital-output ratio, with capital formation leading by one year	3.9	9.2	3.4	4.3	3.4	3.0	2.7[a]
Purchasing-power-parity exchange rates, 1963 prices (pesos per dollar)							
Effective coffee rate	4.83	5.15	6.10	5.99	5.45	5.78	6.13
Average nominal import rate	6.08	5.58	9.19	9.11	8.44	10.34	11.45
Effective minor-export rate	7.96	9.78	9.76	11.19	11.39	12.35	13.58
Annual percentage rate of change in price indices							
Wholesale prices	6.6	4.7	20.8	5.8	17.4	6.8	14.9
Consumer prices	10.6	−1.2	14.9	5.6	18.3	7.7	11.7

n.a. = not available.

SOURCE: Basic trade and national accounts data obtained as in tables 1-1 and 1-2. GDP and GNP estimates, and those for their components, are at 1958 market prices. Foreign trade data refer to registered transactions. Effective coffee rate calculated by comparing peso prices in Colombia with dollar prices in New York, taking into account estimated transport costs and quality differences. Price data obtained from IMF-IFS. Import and minor-export exchange rates are taken from chapters 2 and 4.

a. Includes an estimated GNP growth rate of 7 per cent for 1973.

During those years Colombia could be said to be in Phase II of the Bhagwati-Krueger scheme.

The export-led or coffee-fueled prosperity, aided by the quietest and least expected postwar devaluation, in March 1951 (which led to a 28 per cent increase in the nominal peso price of the U.S. dollar), was accompanied by a relaxation of exchange and import controls inherited from the war and the Great Depression. Consequently, in the first half of 1954, in spite of an import exchange rate which in purchasing-power-parity terms was still substantially cheaper than the rates of the 1930s, the prohibited import list was eliminated and the most liberal import regime witnessed in Colombia since 1929 was instituted. It appears, however, that import controls and regulations were used even during those years for specific, ad hoc protective purposes. Nevertheless, 1951–52 can be considered to mark the first Phase III liberalization episode in Colombian postwar history, with movement toward Phase IV taking place during 1953 and early 1954.

Coffee prices dropped sharply in mid-1954 from the astronomical levels reached earlier that year, but remained at historically high levels through 1956. A booming demand for imports and exchange (merchandise imports during 1954 reached $672 million, a level not surpassed until 1966) led to growing payments arrears, which piled up during 1955 and 1956 as pending requests to the Exchange Control Office. Import and payments liberalization began to be reversed late in 1954, and controls once again tightened, with the authorities reluctant to devalue across the board.

During early 1955 stamp taxes were imposed on imports, graduated according to the degree of their "essentiality." In May, a free market was introduced, where exchange for the less essential imports and most invisibles was to be purchased. Most minor exports also benefited from the new free-market rate. A large gap appeared between the free and official rates, and the free rate fluctuated considerably. Throughout 1955 and 1956 the control regime grew in complexity and, it is said, in arbitrariness of administration. Colombia was back to Phase II.

It may be seen in Table 1-3 that although exports and imports remained at high levels during 1955–56, GDP growth slowed down. The 1955–56 rate of capital formation, buttressed by massive imports, reached 25 per cent of GNP (at 1958 prices), the highest average for the period under study, and the growth rate of manufacturing held up. The investment rate in machinery and equipment is particularly noteworthy. It can also be seen in the table that in spite of the creation of a free market for some imports, the purchasing-power-parity import rate declined during 1955–56 relative to 1950–54. The effective purchasing-power-parity rate applicable to minor exports, however, improved. Finally, the table shows that large imports did a fine job in keeping down price rises.

The 1957–58 Crisis.

Economic conditions during early 1957 were of a sort to inspire journalists and unsympathetic critics of those then in power to use lively, descriptive words such as "chaos" and "bankruptcy." The bad news included growing payments arrears, capital flight, tightening import restrictions, increasing use of bank credit to finance public deficits, as well as a generally expansive credit policy, growing inflationary pressures, a rising black-market peso rate, stagnant real output, and, last but not least, a falling dollar coffee price. In May 1957 a provisional military government took power from General Rojas Pinilla, and the next month a stabilization program was undertaken. A new Phase III had begun.

The June 1957 program simplified the multiple exchange-rate structure which had developed during previous years, replacing it with two fluctuating peso rates. The new certificate market,[12] however, was to cover most merchandise transactions, including minor exports, and some invisibles; the free market was limited to unregistered capital and most invisibles. Various export taxes were also introduced. This was the second time during the 1950s that simplification of the multiple rate system led to a lower nominal rate for (most) minor exports. Before the March 1951 exchange reform and devaluation, minor exports (excluding hides, gold, and bananas) received the fluctuating nominal exchange certificate rate, which at the end of 1950 stood at 3.2 pesos. After the March 1951 measures, the nominal rate applicable to minor exports was reduced to 2.5 pesos, until export vouchers were introduced, in August 1952. In a similar fashion, before the June 1957 reforms most minor exports received the free rate, whose nominal value reached 7.0 pesos in April 1957. By July 1957 the rate applicable to minor exports was the certificate rate, which stood at 4.8 pesos. The effective change against minor exports was even higher, not only because of the acceleration of Colombian inflation but also because of the imposition of emergency export taxes to finance the servicing of the foreign debt that had piled up during 1955 and 1956.

It appears from these and later events that the quest for simplicity and stability in the Colombian exchange-rate structure was often carried out at the expense of incentives for minor exports. A somewhat rigid interpretation of the letter of the Bretton Woods agreements was frequently invoked during the 1950s and early 1960s both to close the gap between favorable rates applied to minor exports and the coffee-influenced major rates, as well as to eliminate free fluctuations in the rate applicable to minor exports. In practice, both of these policies led to less favorable rates for minor exports, as politically it was much easier to lower those rates than to raise the ones corresponding to imports and coffee. The Colombian and international civil servants who maintained such legally admirable but economically faulty adherence to Bretton Woods also expressed concern from time to time that excessive rates for minor exports would breed inefficiency, even as protection against imports was kept at high levels and the foreign-exchange shortage persisted.

The stabilization efforts that began in June 1957 also highlighted a policy problem which persisted, although in a reduced way, until 1973. It was urgent for the authorities to get control of and slow down the expansion in domestic credit. This was done only with difficulty, as at that time the government did not even fully control the bank of issue, the Banco de la República. Powerful private banking groups, as well as the Coffee Growers' Federation, were able, at least within certain limits, to circumvent the government's desire to tighten up credit. Under these circumstances, after June 1957 increasing use was made of import prior-deposit requirements not only as a way of reducing import demand, but also of controlling the growth in the money supply. As those deposits grew, the authorities found themselves increasingly locked into a rigid and cumbersome situation.

Pressure from the politically powerful coffee growers resulted in an increase in the purchasing-power-parity de facto coffee exchange rate of about 18 per cent between 1955–56 and 1957–58 despite gloomy prospects in the world coffee market. This experience illustrates the political difficulties which traditionally have limited the freedom of the Colombian policymaker to raise exchange rates applicable to imports and minor exports while trying not to touch, or to lower, the de facto coffee rate. Coupled with the relatively easy access coffee growers have had to central-bank credit to finance their price-supported crop, this limitation on policy flexibility has accounted for a good share of the headaches of those in charge of coordinating Colombian short-run policies during the years under study. It may be seen in Table 1-3 that only after 1959–62 has there been a sustained increase in the gap between the effective exchange rate applied to minor exports and that applied to coffee. The relationship between these two rates fluctuated around 1.7 throughout 1950–62, rising to about 2.0 since then.

In spite of the difficulties and ambiguities, and in spite of dollar coffee prices which during 1957–58 were 16 per cent below those for 1955–56, the stabilization plan was successful in clearing up many of the short-term economic problems in time for the inauguration of a new constitutional President in August 1958. This, incidentally, contrasts with the luck of the next two Colombian presidents, who during their early months in office faced serious short-term crises. Only President Pastrana Borrero, inaugurated in August 1970, was to inherit, as President Lleras Camargo did in 1958, a smoothly going concern.

The stabilization plan could not stave off an average annual rate of inflation of around 15 to 21 per cent during 1957–58. Given the magnitude of the gross devaluation of the average import rate, as well as the clumsiness of the monetary policy tools and the degree of adjustment sought in the economy, these rates do not appear unreasonable and were clearly on the decline when the new President was inaugurated. The average purchasing-power-parity import rate rose by an impressive 65 per cent between 1955–56 and 1957–58, as shown in Table 1-3, and import and exchange controls were rationalized, but remained very tight. The austerity policy on imports drove their average dollar value during 1957–58 to one-third below their level of 1955–56; restrictions on capital goods imports appear to have been unusually severe, and the rate of capital formation in machinery and equipment, measured as a percentage of GNP at 1958 prices, was *halved* between 1955–56 and 1957–58.

Given these circumstances, it is not surprising to find GDP growth falling below that of population during 1957–58. Indeed, the surprise is that it did not fall more.[13] Construction and some services performed more poorly than import-intensive manufacturing. Luckily, the crops appear to have been good during the period of the stabilization plan.

The commercial arrears accumulated during 1955–56, the immediate cause of the payments crisis, had been either paid off or refinanced by the time of the inauguration of the new President. In spite of lower coffee earnings during 1957–58, a current account surplus was generated which, together with official short-term borrowing, went to pay for the arrears as well as to finance private capital outflows. This can be seen in Table 1-4, which summarizes the Colombian balance of payments since 1957 (earlier years are not available in this format). Such a dramatic belt tightening earned Colombia the respect of international creditors, and prepared the scenario for making Colombia a "showcase of the Alliance of Progress."

Four Presidencies.

Dramatic developments in Colombian foreign trade and payments, comparable to those just discussed, came again in 1962 and reached their peak of excitement during 1965–66. These episodes deserve a special chapter, as they illustrate the difficulties of a transition from Phase III to Phase IV; so in this section I will limit myself to discussing a few key trends and themes of policy during the four presidencies of the National Front, touching upon those dramatic events only lightly.

Especially until March 1967, most policymakers involved with Colombian international trade and payments appeared to have had the following major objectives, often difficult to reconcile:

a. Import liberalization, in the sense of meeting all "reasonable" requests for imported capital, intermediate goods, and raw materials. The notion of

TABLE 1-4

Colombian Balance of Payments, 1957–71
(annual averages in millions of current U.S. dollars)

	1957 and 1958	1959–62	1963–66	1967–70	1971 and 1972
Coffee exports	378	317	366	380	416
Exports of petroleum products	69	70	79	53	39
Nonmonetary and monetized gold	—	—	11	7	7
Other merchandise exports including nonregistered	124	107	106	217	356
Merchandise exports, f.o.b.	570	494	562	657	818
Merchandise imports, f.o.b.	−418	−492	−537	−632	−825
Trade balance	153	2	25	25	−7
Transport receipts	n.a.	n.a.	58	82	102
Travel receipts	n.a.	n.a.	26	48	67
Other receipts from services and transfers	n.a.	n.a.	41	79	82
Transportation payments	n.a.	n.a.	−85	−120	−188
Travel payments	n.a.	n.a.	−46	−61	−73
Other payments for services and transfers excluding investment income	n.a.	n.a.	−85	−111	−133
Net services excluding investment income	−38	−41	−91	−83	−143
Net payments for investment income	−44	−47	−80	−144	−189
Balance on current and transfer account	71	−85	−146	−202	−339
Net long-term private capital	−13	29	107	98	106
Net short-term private capital	−8	5	12	−2	23
Private commercial arrears and net credit from commercial banks	−104	4	19	36	40
Net grants and official capital	—	25	44	113	137
Errors and omissions	−34	16	−42	0	84
Net "autonomous" capital	−159	79	140	245	390
Net loans and credits received by BdlR	97	−18	8	−21	19
Net IMF account and net SDRs	3	8	3	5	−19
BdlR gold and foreign exchange net of payment agreements liability	−12	17	−4	−28	−52
Net "compensatory" capital	88	7	7	−44	−52

Notes to Table 1-4

    n.a. = data not available in directly comparable form.

    SDRs = special drawing rights.

    SOURCE: Adapted from IMF-BOPY, various issues, analytic presentation. Negative signs denote debits; all other figures are credits. Therefore, for BdlR gold and foreign exchange, a negative sign indicates a buildup of reserves. Note that net long-term private capital includes loans received by the Colombian private sector from institutions such as IBRD, IABD, and USAID. Merchandise trade includes adjustments for coverage and timing; so the figures differ from those in trade returns.

allowing imports of goods that competed with local production, or imports of "luxury" goods, even with stiff tariffs but without prior import permits, was seldom popular and even more rarely became a policy objective.

b. Stable, "noninflationary," "nonspeculative" exchange rates.

c. Sharply growing minor exports.

d. Substantial inflows of concessional long-term capital, particularly from the IBRD, the IADB, and the U.S. government, as well as ready access to short-term international credit, especially from the IMF, U.S. commercial banks, and suppliers of imports.

e. Keeping down the de facto coffee exchange rate, to reduce excessive domestic coffee stocks and promote agricultural diversification, while increasing public revenues and dampening inflationary credit requests from the Coffee Growers' Federation.

f. Maintenance of exchange controls, particularly over capital outflows and service payments, and over inflows of direct foreign investments.

    The coordination of just the various policy instruments relevant to the balance of payments was a difficult task during most of the years under study, since frequently each policy instrument was jealously guarded by a separate bureaucratic unit. Unless the President himself kept a firm grip on the policy package, the likely result was contradictory and unstable policies.

    The coordination between foreign trade and payments policies, on the one hand, and more general growth and development policies, on the other, was of course even trickier. The first Colombian development plan was completed during the last year of the Lleras Camargo administration (1961–62). It was analyzed and reported on by the Committee of Nine of the Alliance for Progress in July 1962.[14] It was quietly ignored by the Valencia administration which took power a month later. Serious, comprehensive, long-term planning was not again undertaken until 1966.

    Although the country has been governed by constitutional civilian regimes since 1958, and although before 1953 the country had a long tradition of civilian, constitutional governments, its political system has been aptly described as "elitist rule" by Albert Berry,[15] even though the "elitism" gradually declined throughout the 1960s and early 1970s. As noted earlier, income distribution is sharply skewed. Furthermore, in 1962 only 34 per cent of children aged 5 to 19 were in primary and secondary schools (though that was some improvement over the corresponding figure of 24 per cent in 1950). Other social indicators confirm the picture of inequality, severe poverty, and nonparticipation in public affairs of families at the bottom 50 per cent of the income scale.

It appears that the poorest half of the population has shared to some extent in the increases registered in Colombian per capita income over the last two or three decades. So they cannot be said to be totally indifferent to what goes on in the economy as a whole. But it should be borne in mind that, especially in the short and medium run, many of the policies discussed in these and later chapters touch only marginally upon the welfare of large parts of the Colombian masses. And it is not always clear whether policies desirable on grounds of growth and efficiency positively or negatively affect the welfare of those people in the short and medium run. At any rate, their opinions in these matters are unlikely to carry much weight among the politicians, the national and international civil servants, and the private pressure groups, including local and foreign businessmen, some trade union leaders, and the Coffee Growers' Federation, who have the most to say on these issues and have the most to gain or lose from the way they are settled.

THE LLERAS CAMARGO PRESIDENCY.

This presidency opened not only with considerable national and international goodwill, but also with short-run trade and payments well under control, thanks to the austerity program of 1957–58. There was an understandable eagerness to return to higher growth rates and to more relaxed import and credit controls. Circumstances appeared propitious for a smooth transition to Phase IV. As shown in Table 1-3, higher GDP growth rates were indeed achieved, and merchandise imports, although still below the 1955–56 levels, rose sharply above the depressed 1957–58 figures and were comparable to those registered during 1950–54. Coffee prices, however, continued their decline; their average for 1959–62 was 37 per cent below their 1955–56 levels. Some contribution toward equilibrium in the balance of payments was made by the start of Alliance for Progress disbursements during 1961 and 1962, recorded in Table 1-4 both under net grants and official capital and under net long-term private capital.

The more generous granting of import licenses, started in 1959, was accompanied by a stickiness in the nominal import exchange rate, which was to prove fatal to the hope of a smooth transition into Phase IV. Earlier plans gradually to adjust that rate, aimed at an eventual unification of the free market with the certificate market, in which exchange for imports was obtained, were quietly dropped under circumstances to be explored in Chapter 7. An opportunity to adopt the crawling peg, which proved successful after 1967, was missed. The purchasing-power-parity average import rate in 1963 prices dropped from 11.2 pesos in 1958, to 9.9 pesos in 1959, to 9.2 pesos in 1960, and to 8.7 pesos in 1961. The 1958 rate was not to be reached again until the last quarter of 1970. Fears of reviving inflationary pressures blocked a more vigorous adjustment of the import rate. Inflation was in fact kept to an annual rate of less than 6 per cent from 1959 through 1962.

The effective exchange rate applicable to minor exports, however, remained at levels above those of 1950–58, reaching quite a high level late in 1962. Systematic use began to be made during this period of powerful tax incentives to exporting firms, while crop-specific promotion programs originally undertaken to replace imports, and which featured credit and tax concessions, began to pay off also in terms of new exports, as in the case of cotton. Exports of sugar and tobacco also received a boost, accepted but not celebrated by sensitive Colombians, from the blockade imposed on Cuban exports by most countries of the Western Hemisphere. A more positive source of improved Colombian export prospects was the creation of the Latin American Free Trade Association in 1960.

The more favorable exchange rate applied to minor exports came about from its identification with the free-market rate, beginning in January 1959, after the former had been associated with the pegged certificate rate during most of 1958. The free market, however, remained thin and fluctuated a fair amount; the average quarter-to-quarter (absolute) change in the nominal free-market rate during the sixteen quarters of 1959–62 was about 6 per cent. Neither the extent nor the contribution toward stability, if any, of sporadic central-bank intervention in the free market during this period is clear.

By early 1962 the pressures on the balance of payments were becoming quite severe, a fact not unrelated to the rapid Colombian presentation of its first development plan to Alliance for Progress experts. But the expansion of aid and of minor exports was insufficient to meet growing import demands, and the dreary process of denials, heroics, and increased Bogotá-Washington shuttles clearly pointed to an impending devaluation of the major import rate. The trend toward some liberalization of import licensing observed from 1959 through 1961 was reversed early in 1962, and the restrictions gathered force throughout the year. Matters were complicated by the inauguration in August 1962 of a new administration, headed by President Guillermo León Valencia, a remarkable man of talent and courage, but not particularly interested in economics, just at a time when the inherited situation called for a chief executive with an appetite for financial matters.

THE VALENCIA PRESIDENCY.

On November 7, 1962, all imports were placed on the prohibited list, and licensing was suspended for about a month. On November 20, the exchange rate applicable to most imports was allowed to move from 6.7 to 9.0 pesos per U.S. dollar. Memories of this devaluation, undertaken in the midst of financial disorder and without a comprehensive political-economic program, were to play an important role during the following years, hindering liberalization efforts. Reasons for the failure of this devaluation will be discussed in Chapter 7. It is enough to point out here that a sharp domestic inflation during the early part of 1963 wiped out practically all the incentive effects of the devaluation; as a result, the purchasing-power-parity average import exchange rate for 1963 was only 4 per cent higher than that for 1962 and was, of course, below the 1958–60 levels. The gloomiest predictions of devaluation opponents had come to pass. Furthermore, in January 1963, in a misguided search for stability, the central bank began to peg the free rate, applicable to minor exports, at 10 pesos, or below the December 1962 level, which had averaged 11.1 pesos during the last two weeks of that year. As a result, the effective exchange rate applicable to minor exports during 1963 was 13 per cent below what it had been during 1962.

Under these circumstances, expected postdevaluation import liberalization moves remained feeble, and it was not long before rumors of a new devaluation began to circulate. Colombia was once again in Phase II. In October 1964, almost two years after devaluation, the central bank, short of reserves, ceased pegging the free-market rate. Import licensing became progressively tighter; and on December 1, 1964, the import free list was suspended for ninety days (except for imports from LAFTA). The President, however, burned by the devaluation of November 1962 and in a difficult political position, would not hear about any new major devaluation of the basic import rate. The Colombian image as the "showcase of the Alliance for Progress" became tarnished, and aid disbursements for 1964 and 1965 fell below the 1963 level.

Throughout the first half of 1965 import restrictions continued to tighten. New lists of prohibited imports were issued, and on May 5 even imports from LAFTA countries were included in the prior license list. The free-market rate climbed steadily from 10 pesos in October 1964 to nearly 19 pesos in June 1965. Once again the authorities deemed this to be an excessive reward for minor exports, whose rate was pegged on June 30 at 13.5 pesos.

Once established, the figure of 13.5 took on some magic. It is said that the President was persuaded that a gradual transfer of imports from the ("preferential") rate of 9 pesos to the new ("intermediate") rate of 13.5 pesos could be interpreted as a *revaluation* relative to the free rate, which went beyond 19 pesos during July and August of 1965, as devaluation rumors became wide-spread.

Be that as it may, in September 1965, that plan was announced, and the rate of 13.5 pesos began to be applied not only to minor exports, but to a growing list of imports, which at the same time were freed from license requirements. This was indeed the beginning of the most ambitious liberalization attempt of Colombia's postwar economic history, a leap toward Phase V which ended in a dramatic confrontation between a new Colombian government and foreign creditors in November 1966. The import liberalization program advanced boldly, with the result that by September 1966 practically all imports had been transferred to the 13.5-peso rate and had been freed from licensing requirements. Many tariff rates were adjusted, mainly upward, to take into account the new situation, almost unique in Colombia's post-1929 economic history and comparable only to the early 1954 liberalization. The Valencia administration, which opened with a devaluation bang, and went through a variety of moods in trade policy, ended up with an import boom.

During the years 1963–66 taken as a whole, GDP growth slowed down, as shown in Table 1-3, with the rates of expansion of manufacturing, construction, and type I services showing the most significant declines, even though both the value of exports and of imports recovered somewhat from the depressed levels of 1959–62. In spite of the hesitations over incentives, minor exports continued to grow. The rate of capital formation declined, but more in construction than in machinery and equipment. The average rate of inflation for the whole period was about three times that registered during the previous four years, mainly reflecting the 1963 experience. Although hiding many gyrations, the exchange rates for coffee, imports, and minor exports during 1963–66 were fairly close to those of 1959–62.

THE LLERAS RESTREPO PRESIDENCY.

The administration of President Carlos Lleras Restrepo, inaugurated in August 1966, at first continued the inherited import liberalization program. Indeed, during the first half of 1966 the Colombian balance of payments, bolstered by new aid commitments from foreign creditors delighted with the liberalization program, appeared to be in reasonable shape. The free-market rate declined from 19.2 pesos in August 1965 to 16.0 pesos in July 1966. But toward the end of the third quarter of 1966 a new fall in dollar coffee prices, growing nervousness about the high import levels and a decline in the growth rate of minor exports, coupled with preoccupation with the thinness of foreign-exchange reserves, led to a questioning of the viability of the existing pattern of exchange rates and import freedom. Some influential foreign creditors argued that a new devaluation was required. They claimed that at the start of the liberalization program in 1965 the Colombian government had committed itself to further devaluations if certain targets, mainly related to the level of exchange reserves, were not met and that such a failure had been registered in September 1966. At any rate, they first hinted and later made clear that aid would be held up unless a further devaluation was forthcoming.

The new Colombian government pleaded for time so as first to get a firm grip on monetary and fiscal policy, pointing out the circumstantial nature of the fall in export earnings, while forecasting that import demand was likely to decline after its postliberalization boom. Aid, it added, was supposed to help out precisely in times such as those, and no simple quantitative trigger should provoke a major devaluation. The memory of the 1962 devaluation, of its loose or nonexistent coordination with fiscal, monetary, and wage policy, and of its politically disastrous effects was of course very much in the mind of the new government. More will be said on these matters in Chapter 7. Here it will be sufficient to note that in an extraordinary television appearance on November 29, 1966, President Lleras Restrepo announced to the nation a rejection of the demands of the by then united foreign creditors and termination of the import liberalization program and of operations in the free exchange market. Rigorous exchange and price controls were also announced. The speech came almost exactly four years after the traumatic November 1962 devaluation.

The President and his economic team, a sophisticated and capable group indeed, immediately turned their full attention to the preparation of what was to become Law 444 of March 22, 1967. The President took a direct role in the economic discussions; ministers not involved with the economy could hardly see him between November 1966 and March 1967. Law 444 restructured the whole Colombian trade and payments system, and has remained the key piece of legislation in that field to this day, giving the country its longest postwar period of policy stability. A vital element in the package was the establishment of small, frequent devaluations, or a controlled "crawling peg," for the major certificate market, avoiding the twin dangers of stickiness in the major rates and volatility in the free-market rate. Past stickiness in the major rates had eventually led to balance-of-payments crises and to large, traumatic devaluations; the volatility of the free-market rate had led to real or imagined instability and distortions. The free market was substituted for a pegged capital market rate, set at 16.3 pesos. When the upward-crawling certificate rate reached that level, in June 1968, the two markets were unified, i.e., the capital market was abolished. Special exchange regulations for the petroleum and mining industries as well as for some other minor items were maintained by Law 444, which, however, introduced a subtle but important change in the treatment of coffee exports. Earnings from coffee were to receive the same major fluctuating certificate rate paid by importers and received by minor exporters, *minus* an ad valorem tax, first set at 23 per cent and later lowered to 20 per cent. Previously, coffee exports received a special fixed exchange rate. In other words, after March 1967 coffee exporters acquired a vested interest in the continuation of the upward crawl of the certificate rate, while before they had been primarily interested in just a favorable coffee rate.

Law 444 replaced previous fiscal incentives for minor exports, under which proceeds from these exports could be used to reduce the income tax liability (Law 81 of 1960), with the simpler and more general tax credit certificate (*certificado de abono tributario*, CAT). The CAT given to minor exporters was set at 15 per cent of the export value, and could be used in payment of taxes one year after its date of issue. Those certificates were to be freely negotiable, and were exempt from all taxes. More will be said about them and their changing features in the next chapter. The new law also created the Export Promotion Fund (PROEXPO), with wide powers and functions.

In the field of exchange and import controls Law 444 reorganized previous regulations, maintaining and often strengthening restrictive mechanisms. Stringent rules for the negotiation and holding of foreign currencies and gold were set up; controls over direct foreign investors and over royalties and payments for patents foreshadowed, and in some respects inspired, the tough rules adopted by the Andean Common Market since 1970.

Simultaneously with the preparation of Law 444, the Lleras Restrepo administration struggled to get a firm and integrated grasp on fiscal, monetary, and wage policy, and on the whole succeeded. So March 1967 opened a new chapter in Colombian economic history and, paradoxically, the stormy and interventionist events of November 1966–March 1967 set the stage for a gradual liberalization trend which continued at least until mid-1974.

The new Phase IV, starting from a quite restrictive situation, has not been free of hesitations, especially regarding the proper pace for the "crawl" in the exchange rate. The year 1967 was a difficult one for the Colombian economy, and import restrictions were applied rigorously. Only in May 1968 did the free import list regain some significance, when some essential products, corresponding to 150 tariff positions, were exempted from import licensing. Throughout 1968 previous import deposit rates were lowered, but licensing remained tight. A sharp upswing in coffee prices, starting late in 1969, gave further impetus to liberalization which had also been encouraged by the resumption of large aid commitments in 1967, once foreign creditors became adjusted to the new Colombian administration. By the end of that administration, in August 1970, the import system remained more restrictive than it had been at the time of its inauguration in August 1966, but expectations of sudden and disruptive changes in policies had declined considerably. How the restrictive system looked in 1970 and 1971 will be discussed in later chapters.

During 1967–70 the GDP growth rate, as shown in Table 1-3, exceeded even the 1950–54 levels, and the growth profile by sectors appeared more balanced than in earlier years. The 1967–70 aggregate marginal capital-output ratio was the lowest recorded up to that time.

Dollar coffee prices in 1967–70 were on average not much higher than during 1963–66. The dollar value of minor exports, however, about *doubled* between these two periods. Helped by minor exports and capital inflow, merchandise imports approached the average dollar values reached during 1955–56. As shown in Table 1-4, expansion this time was accompanied by a sizable growth in central-bank gross gold and foreign-exchange reserves, as well as net repayments of credits received by the central bank during earlier years. Gross gold and exchange reserves, which were only $77 million at the end of 1966, reached $221 million at the end of 1969, dipping to $206 million at the end of 1970. The sum of errors and omissions, net short-term private capital, private and commercial arrears and net credit from commercial banks (Table 1-4), rose from a net debit of $11 million a year during 1963–66 to a net yearly credit of $34 million in 1967–70.

The 1967–70 averages for exchange rates for both imports and minor exports surpassed those of earlier subphases (Table 1-3). Furthermore, their rise was gradual, some calculations[16] to the contrary notwithstanding. The Colombian inflation during those years dropped to about the normal levels of 1950–54 and 1959–62 and was not much ahead of the inflation registered in industrial centers during the same years.

THE PASTRANA BORRERO PRESIDENCY.

This administration, inaugurated in August 1970, maintained the gradual import liberalization trend and the promotion of minor exports, which also benefited from the 1973–74 boom in world commodity markets. By the end of this administration's term, however, a transition into Phase V had not occurred, and only about half of imports were on the free list.

Available data show that from 1970 to 1974 Colombia enjoyed the highest GDP growth rates of any comparable four-year postwar period. Both minor and coffee exports boomed and, as will be discussed in Chapter 8, foreign-exchange limitations to growth appeared to be a thing of the past. Other economic problems, however, became more severe. Partly because of influences emanating from world markets, and partly because of an overheated domestic economy, inflation accelerated, particularly during 1973 and 1974. During those years the government launched a development plan heavily stressing urban construction. Since the plan was put into effect on top of an already prosperous domestic economy, it led to excess demand pressures.

A weakening of the financial position of the public sector, in spite of the prosperity, plus favorable world prices for exportable goods stimulated proposals to reduce export subsidies, which experienced several adjustments during 1970–74. On the other hand, the inflationary pressures encouraged further import liberalization. If world market conditions and coffee prices do not experience a severe deterioration, it is conceivable that the López Michelsen administration, inaugurated in August 1974, will further liberalize the trade and payments system and take the country into a Colombian-style Phase V, while adopting anti-inflationary measures, thus culminating the trends started in March 1967.

All this looks like a happy ending to our postwar summary narrative. In the last chapter of this book I will discuss in detail the achievements and limitations of the post-1967 growth path, as well as what can be expected from further liberalization. But before we get there many details need to be filled in.

NOTES

1. Alvaro López Toro, in his brilliant analysis of the internal consistency of the population censuses of 1938, 1951, and 1964, concluded that the most acceptable estimates for Colombian population growth were 2.4 per cent per year for 1938–51, and 2.9–3.0 per cent for 1951–64. See his *Análisis Demográfico de los Censos Colombianos: 1951 y 1964* (Bogotá: Ediciones Universidad de los Andes for CEDE, 1968), pp. 85–86.

2. This paragraph is based on the concluding chapter in R. Albert Berry and Miguel Urrutia, "Income Distribution in Colombia," mimeographed (New Haven: Yale Economic Growth Center, 1974).

3. See in particular R. R. Nelson, T. P. Schultz, and R. L. Slighton, *Structural Change in a Developing Economy; Colombia's Problems and Prospects* (Princeton, N.J.: Princeton University Press, 1971); and Jaroslav Vanek, *Estimating Foreign Resource Needs for Economic Development: Theory, Method and a Case Study of Colombia* (New York: McGraw-Hill, 1967).

4. See Alasdair I. MacBean, *Export Instability and Economic Development* (Cambridge: Harvard University Press, 1966). Colombia has traditionally held large coffee stocks, thus isolating the quantity of her exports from the effects of crop fluctuations. The International Coffee Agreement was also a stabilizing influence during the 1960s and early 1970s.

5. This is also true for several other Latin American countries. See Carlos F. Díaz-Alejandro, "Planning the Foreign Sector in Latin America," *American Economic Review*, May 1970, especially pp. 170–174.

6. See Lauchlin Currie, "The Exchange Constraint on Development—A Partial Solution to the Problem," *Economic Journal*, December 1971, pp. 886–904. A glance at year-to-year growth rates indicates that if alternative measures of instability were used, construction would still rank as less stable than manufacturing.

7. Three import price indices were tried: those of UNECLA (SB and DANE) for the whole period; those in IMF-IFS for the postwar period; and, linked to those of IMF-IFS, those in UA, pp. 212–213 (estimates of William Paul McGreevey). Current export values are found in the same sources. The highest t statistic (1.72) was for the coefficient of the percentage changes in the real value of exports concurrent with the change in GDP, in the regression covering 1929–68, but the absolute value of even that coefficient is very small.

8. For an elaboration of this point see Carlos F. Díaz-Alejandro, *Essays on the Economic History of the Argentine Republic* (New Haven: Yale University Press, 1970), especially pp. 79–85.

9. Basic data obtained from UA, pp. 82 and 158; UNECLA-DANE, pp. 135 and 149; and Council of Economic Advisers, *Economic Report of the President* (Washington, D.C.: U.S. Government Printing Office, 1970), Statistical Tables. The Colombian price indices are rough.

10. Cf. Henry C. Wallich, *Monetary Problems of an Export Economy* (Cambridge: Harvard University Press, 1950), especially Chap. XIV, "A Case for Exchange Control?"

11. The coffee terms of trade calculated by UNECLA (SB and DANE) show a positive coefficient of 0.4 per cent per year for the time trend, but with a t statistic of only 1.65. The terms of trade found in UA, pp. 212–213, linked with those of IMF-IFS show an annual rate of improvement of 2.1 per cent per year and a t statistic of 5.5. Both estimates were obtained by fitting semilogarithmic equations to all observations for 1925–68.

12. See Appendix B, entries for November–December 1956 and June 1957, for explanation of the certificate market.

13. Compare Colombian GDP behavior with that of Argentina, where real GDP *fell* in 6 of the 23 years between 1945 and 1967, mainly as a result of foreign-exchange crises. In 1959, for example, the absolute value of real Argentine GDP fell by nearly 6 per cent.

14. The Committee of Nine report, "Evaluación del Programa General de Desarrollo Económico y Social de Colombia" (mimeographed), was distributed by the Pan American Union. The ad hoc committee was formed by Felipe Pazos, Harvey Perloff, Raúl Sáez, Eduardo Figueroa, Jorge Méndez, and Pierre Uri. A preliminary note to the report lists Carlos F. Díaz-Alejandro as director of the technical staff of the committee; he was also the only member of that staff during most of the preparation of the report.

15. See R. Albert Berry, "Some Implications of Elitist Rule for Economic Development in Colombia," in Gustav Ranis, ed., *Government and Economic Development* (New Haven: Yale University Press, 1971), pp. 3–29.

16. Calculations are often seen in which the exchange rate "crawl" is compared only to the rise in Colombian prices, neglecting inflation in the rest of the world. This is sometimes defended on the ground that since the Colombian exchange rate is overvalued anyway, any argument for accelerating its upward "crawl" is to be welcomed and used, presumably on unsophisticated policymakers. It is doubtful whether many policymakers would swallow such a gross calculation, particularly after the world inflation of 1973–74. At any rate, that kind of tactic will not serve an educational purpose, and in the long run it could very well backfire, once it is seen that technicians have failed, after all, to be objective and neutral outliners of options open to the politician.

Chapter 2

Minor Merchandise Exports

It was seen in the previous chapter that coffee exports enjoy an effective exchange rate which is about half that applicable to minor exports. But while this situation suggests a roughly similar gap in the average domestic resource costs of the two types of activity, the long-run growth prospects of coffee exports have appeared dim throughout most of the postwar period, making the expansion of minor exports a key policy target.

The transition from heavy reliance on a low-cost staple with obvious comparative advantage but limited growth prospects to more diversified, costly, and dynamic export earnings has been long and difficult, as documented in Chapter 1. The discontinuity in average domestic resource costs between coffee and minor exports reinforced export pessimism on both demand and supply grounds. Nevertheless, it has been clear for many years that growth of Colombia's current exchange earnings would have to be faster than was likely to be achieved from coffee exports alone if her economy was to attain a sustainable GDP expansion of, say, 6 per cent per year. Import substitution, under Colombian and postwar world circumstances, was insufficient by itself to sustain such growth consistently, much less efficiently. A more diversified and prosperous outlook for current exchange earnings was also necessary in order to decrease reliance on concessional capital inflows, and create for Colombia the option of tapping world private capital markets on commercial terms.

In this chapter, I will first describe the commodity composition of minor exports and their geographical destination and other characteristics so as to draw up a rough typology of these very heterogeneous goods. Next, I will discuss policy instruments used to encourage minor exports. I will then attempt to explain why the efforts to expand and diversify Colombian exports have been successful, giving particular attention to the role played by effective exchange rate policy; in doing so, I will be building on the substantial work of others.[1] Ideally I would like to be able to account for the annual growth rate of about 10 per cent per year in recorded (or registered) minor exports between 1948–50 and 1970–72, as well as for deviations around that trend. I will explore possible differences between the economic characteristics of minor exports to LAFTA and those to the rest of the world. Finally, I will discuss the outlook for nontraditional exports, and take a preliminary look at their role in achieving Colombian development targets.

AN OVER-ALL VIEW

During 1948–50, coffee represented 75 per cent of Colombia's noncontraband merchandise exports, with crude petroleum accounting for an additional 16 per cent. As may be seen in Table 2-1, these figures were virtually unchanged from 1957 to 1959. By 1970–72, however, minor recorded exports had reached 34 per cent of the total while the coffee share had slipped to 60 per cent. The expansion in the dollar value of minor exports between 1957–59 and 1970–72 accounts for 84 per cent of the total increase in recorded exports between those two dates.

A glance at Table 2-1 indicates that the expansion of recorded minor exports has been quite irregular, particularly during the earlier years when the base was small. Changes in world prices and variations in the contraband flow could induce enormous percentage changes in the dollar value of recorded minor exports. The point emerges more clearly from the following tabulation, showing the number of years in which the year-to-year percentage changes were registered:

	Number of Years		
Year-to-Year Percentage Change in Value of Recorded Minor Exports	Whole Period	1949–60	1961–72
More than 40 per cent	3	3	0
From 20 to 40 per cent	4	0	4
From 10 to 20 per cent	8	3	5
From 0 to 10 per cent	2	0	2
From −10 to 0 per cent	2	1	1
Less than −10 per cent	5	5	0
Total	24	12	12

TABLE 2-1

Colombian Merchandise Exports, f.o.b., 1948–72
(millions of current U.S. dollars; trade returns)

	Total Recorded Merchandise Exports	Recorded Coffee Exports	Recorded Crude Petroleum Exports	Recorded "Minor" Exports	Nonrecorded Merchandise Exports
1948	306.6	225.2	45.1	36.3	n.a.
1949	335.2	242.3	58.2	34.7	n.a.
1950	393.6	306.4	64.8	22.4	n.a.
1951	483.8	359.4	73.5	50.9	n.a.
1952	483.0	379.9	71.5	31.6	n.a.
1953	605.5	492.3	76.3	36.9	n.a.
1954	669.1	550.2	75.8	43.1	2.4
1955	596.7	487.4	61.5	47.8	8.6
1956	551.7	413.1	71.2	67.4	70.6
1957	511.1	390.1	72.3	48.7	78.8
1958	460.7	354.7	65.1	40.9	66.4
1959	473.0	363.4	73.3	36.3	69.0
1960	464.6	333.5	80.0	51.1	55.0
1961	434.8	307.9	68.2	58.7	35.0
1962	463.2	331.8	60.6	70.8	35.0
1963	446.7	303.0	77.2	66.5	25.0
1964	548.1	394.2	75.0	78.9	35.0
1965	539.1	343.9	88.2	107.0	40.0
1966	507.6	328.3	70.6	108.7	42.0
1967	509.9	321.5	61.2	127.2	43.0
1968	558.3	351.4	36.3	170.6	40.0
1969	607.4	343.9	56.7	206.8	43.0
1970	735.6	466.9	58.6	210.1	63.0
1971	686.0	399.7	51.2	235.1	63.0
1972	742.9	430.4	30.8	281.7	63.0

n.a. = not available.

SOURCE: IMF-IFS, various issues, and IMF-BOPY, various issues. Note that the latter publication contains corrections for timing and valuation when coffee exports as shown in trade returns are incorporated into the balance-of-payments accounts. The timing correction arises from changes in coffee stocks held abroad by Colombian institutions. Other minor discrepancies remain between data shown in this table and those in later ones and in the text because of the timing of revisions. See text for explanation of nonrecorded merchandise exports. The 1972 data are preliminary.

While the diversification and larger base of minor exports during the 1960s and early 1970s yielded year-to-year changes less disparate in their total value, a considerable spread remained. During the more recent period one may note four major export surges, each preceded by declines or stagnation in the export level: 1960–62; 1964–65; 1967–69; and 1971–72.

The ample opportunities which Colombian geography provides for smuggling goods into the country will be noted in Chapter 3. Overvalued exchange rates, export taxes, and prohibitions, as well as export quotas on some commodities, such as coffee, and old-fashioned criminal activities, as with emeralds, have provided the incentives for smuggling goods out of the country (nonrecorded or unregistered merchandise exports). It is common knowledge that every year considerable amounts of unregistered cattle, textiles, coffee, and other goods cross the border from Colombia to Venezuela and Ecuador. Colombian emeralds find their way to European and Japanese markets in mysterious ways. Estimates of the value of such trade are naturally gross. Unusual external events, such as the Venezuelan boom of 1956–58, as well as changes in domestic policies, lead to variations in the level of smuggling, but only the rough outlines of those fluctuations have been estimated. The last column of Table 2-1 presents the most reputable of those calculations, found in the *Balance of Payments Yearbook* of the IMF and covering all commodities. According to those figures, nonregistered exports reached 14 per cent of the value of registered exports from 1956 to 1960, and declined to 8 per cent during 1969–71.

Most nonregistered exports can be classified as minor, as may be seen in the last column of Table 2-2. Thus, during 1957–59 more minor exports seem to have left Colombia unrecorded than recorded. While not too much weight should be placed on smuggling estimates, it does appear that a small part of the expansion in registered minor exports observed between 1957–59 and 1969–71 took place at the expense of smuggling. Adding up registered and unregistered minor exports, one obtains a growth rate of 8.6 per cent per year from 1957–59 to 1969–71. This rate, while not as spectacular as the rate of 14.7 per cent per year obtained for registered minor exports alone, is still remarkable. In particular, while the surge observed for registered minor exports during 1960–62 may represent to an important extent the replacement of smuggling by legal exports, post-1963 advances cannot be questioned on those grounds. The combined series for all minor exports shows an average annual growth rate of 17.4 per cent between 1963 and 1971.

TYPES OF MINOR EXPORTS

Colombian minor exports comprise a diversified group of commodities. The five largest minor export items during 1970 (cotton, bananas, live animals,

TABLE 2-2

Colombian Minor Exports, f.o.b., 1950–71
(millions of current U.S. dollars)

| | Recorded Tobacco, Sugar, Cotton, and Fresh Fruit (mainly bananas) | | | Recorded Other Minor Exports | | | |
	Non-LAFTA Countries	All Countries	LAFTA Countries	Non-LAFTA Countries	All Countries	LAFTA Countries	Nonrecorded Minor Exports
1950		10.6			12.2		n.a.
1951		10.8			40.1		n.a.
1952		10.9			20.7		n.a.
1953		14.1			22.8		n.a.
1954		15.7			27.4		2.4
1955		19.0			28.8		8.6
1956		31.7			36.9		16.0
1957	29.4		—	11.5		5.2	60.0
1958	17.5		—	18.2		4.0	55.0
1959	15.9		—	18.8		3.8	55.0
1960	28.8		—	17.9		5.6	45.0
1961	33.0		0.9	18.1		6.2	25.0
1962	38.6		0.9	24.5		6.6	25.0
1963	34.3		1.1	25.6		5.4	15.0
1964	31.1		0.4	37.1		10.2	25.0
1965	41.5		0.2	48.1		17.2	12.0
1966	36.8		0.2	44.7		25.9	13.0
1967	57.1		0.7	48.7		19.8	28.0
1968	68.0		5.6	72.0		24.7	30.0
1969	73.5		2.1	96.7		34.6	33.0
1970	72.8		1.9	90.2		45.2	53.0
1971	n.a.		n.a.	n.a.		n.a.	59.0

n.a. = not available.
SOURCE: Basic data obtained from DANE-ADCE, various issues; also UNFAO-TY, various issues; and as in Table 2-1 for nonrecorded minor exports. DANE-ADCE is published with a considerable lag; minor inconsistencies with the sources of Table 2-1 also exist.

sugar, and fuel oil) accounted for less than half of registered minor exports. During the 1960s new items were constantly added to the list, which by now includes such varied products as gold, paper and cardboard, meat, tobacco, wood, shoes, seafood, glass, oilseed cakes, chemicals, furs, cement, hides, precious stones, tires, books, fresh-cut flowers, and dog toys. It should be noted that many minor exports, including some of the largest, are hardly "nontraditional": during the nineteenth century tobacco was a major export item, and cotton was also exported during the U.S. Civil War. Foreign-run plantations grew and exported bananas since early in this century, often under dismal conditions which more than once led to bloodshed. A more precise idea of recent minor export diversification is given by the following tabulation, showing the number of SITC three-digit categories having the indicated export values in U.S. dollars:

	1960	1964	1968	1970
More than $5 mill.	3	4	6	9
Between $1 mill. and $5 mill.	6	12	22	24
Between $0.5 mill. and $1 mill.	1	9	9	12
Between $0.1 mill. and $0.5 mill.	10	20	46	47

Both tables 2-3 and 2-4 also show the diversification of minor exports, the former from 1957 through 1970, and the latter in greater detail for 1970. A look at these tables suggests that various minor exports are likely to have different domestic supply price elasticities as well as different input requirements. As indicated in tables 2-2 and 2-4, the destination of minor exports, as between LAFTA and non-LAFTA countries, fluctuates sharply from item to item. Foreign demand income elasticities will also vary as between, say, textiles and meat.

Somewhat loose but convenient and complementary classification schemes are used in tables 2-2, 2-3, and 2-4, and can be summarized as follows:

	Share in Registered Minor Exports		Average Annual Growth Rate from 1957–59 to 1968–70
	1957–59	1968–70	
Bananas, cotton, sugar, tobacco	50.6%	38.1%	11.8%
Manufactured goods[2]	34.2	41.0	17.1
Miscellaneous minor exports	15.2	20.9	18.6
Total	100.0	100.0	15.2
Non-LAFTA	89.5	80.6	14.1
LAFTA	10.5	19.4	21.8
Total	100.0	100.0	15.2

Four important primary products, which made up half of minor exports during the late 1950s, still accounted for nearly 40 per cent of those exports in 1968–70. In spite of their primary-product label, their dollar value grew at an impressive annual rate. Since both manufactured goods and the miscellaneous category are far from homogenous in their economic characteristics, regardless of what classification is followed, a closer look at each of the three subgroups is in order.

Bananas, Cotton, Sugar, and Tobacco (BCST).

It is sometimes asserted that before a developing country can expand its exports and diversify away from its traditional staple, it must go through a

TABLE 2-3

Registered Minor Colombian Merchandise Exports, f.o.b., 1957–70
(millions of current U.S. dollars)

SITC Number and Category	1957	1958	1959	1960	1961	1962	1963	1964	1965	1966	1967	1968	1969	1970
0 Food and live animals excl. coffee	26.9	16.1	15.5	15.4	21.1	20.9	22.4	18.6	40.1	41.3	45.3	53.5	63.1	70.4
051 Fresh fruits and nuts (bananas)	26.2	15.5	13.9	13.7	14.1	10.7	13.3	12.4	18.6	20.0	25.0	24.7	19.9	18.2
061 Sugar and honey	0.3	0	0	0	5.2	7.4	5.5	3.3	7.8	9.1	12.9	15.9	15.6	14.8
Other	0.4	0.6	1.6	1.7	1.8	2.8	3.6	2.9	13.7	12.2	7.4	12.9	27.6	37.4
1 Beverages and tobacco	2.9	2.0	2.0	2.4	4.1	5.7	7.3	9.5	7.2	5.6	4.4	4.9	7.3	7.2
12.1 Tobacco, unmfrd.	2.9	2.0	2.0	2.4	4.0	5.7	7.2	9.4	7.2	5.6	4.4	4.9	7.3	7.2
Other	0	2.0	0	0	0.1	0	0.1	0.1	0	0	0	0	0	0
2 Crude materials, inedible, excl. fuels	3.2	2.6	2.8	15.8	13.9	19.2	13.9	13.2	15.7	8.4	21.6	38.7	45.9	46.8
26.3 Cotton	0	0	0	12.7	10.6	15.8	9.5	6.4	8.1	2.3	15.5	28.1	32.8	34.5
Other	3.2	2.6	2.8	3.1	3.3	3.4	4.4	6.8	7.6	6.1	6.1	10.6	13.1	12.3
3 Mineral fuels, lubricants, etc., excl. crude petroleum	5.0	10.1	8.9	7.8	6.0	7.4	4.6	7.9	7.9	9.7	13.5	14.4	20.3	14.6
4 Animal and veg. oils and fats	0	0	0	0	0	0.1	0	0	0	0	0	0	0	0
5 Chemicals	0.8	1.0	1.0	1.3	1.4	2.7	2.4	4.4	6.1	6.6	4.7	8.6	10.0	8.7
6 Mfrd. goods classified by material	4.0	3.9	4.4	3.4	6.3	10.0	11.3	19.6	24.1	30.2	31.4	40.9	49.1	42.2
7 Machinery and transport equip.	0.8	0.5	1.0	2.1	2.0	1.1	1.7	1.9	2.0	3.6	3.4	4.2	5.1	5.6
8 Misc. mfrd. articles	0.5	0.3	0.3	0.2	0.4	0.5	0.8	1.8	2.6	2.2	1.8	4.6	5.5	6.3
9 Commodities and transactions, n.e.s.	1.9	3.2	2.6	3.9	3.2	3.1	2.1	1.9	1.0	0	0.1	0.6	0.6	8.4
Total	46.0	39.6	38.5	52.3	58.2	70.6	66.3	78.8	107.0	107.6	126.3	170.3	206.9	210.1
Summary of main groups														
Fruits, sugar, tobacco, cotton	29.4	17.5	15.9	28.8	33.9	39.6	35.5	31.5	41.7	37.0	57.8	73.6	75.6	74.7
Mfrd. goods (3, 5, 6, 7, and 8)	11.1	15.8	15.6	14.8	16.1	21.7	20.8	35.6	42.7	52.3	54.8	72.7	90.6	77.4
Misc. minor	5.5	6.3	7.0	8.7	8.2	9.3	10.0	11.7	22.6	18.3	13.7	24.0	40.7	58.1

SOURCE: Basic data obtained from DANE-ADCE, various issues, and UN-YOITS, various issues.

TABLE 2-4

LAFTA Share of Colombian Minor Exports by SITC Categories, 1970

| | | Registered Minor Exports | |
	SITC Number and Category	Millions of U.S. Dollars	Per Cent Shipped to LAFTA
001	Live animals	$17.41	90.0%
011	Fresh meat	4.72	5.3
031	Fresh fish	4.83	0
051	Fresh fruits and nuts (mainly bananas)	18.21	0.5
061	Sugar and honey	14.78	0
081	Animal products	6.25	34.8
(0-other)	Other food and live animals	4.23	55.8
121	Tobacco, unmanufactured	7.17	0.3
(1-other)	Other beverages and tobacco	0.05	6.1
263	Cotton	34.55	5.1
266	Synthetic fibers	3.75	92.8
(2-other)	Other crude materials, inedible, excluding fuels	8.53	6.7
(3-other)	Other mineral fuels, lubricants, etc., excluding crude petroleum	14.58	12.7
4	Animal and vegetable oils and fats	0.04	0
513	Inorganic chemical products	2.43	61.4
514	Other inorganic chemicals	0.60	93.9
541	Medical and pharmaceutical products	2.68	75.8
581	Plastics, cellulose, resins	1.02	69.5
(5-other)	Other chemicals	1.96	44.8
61	Leather, skins, and their manufactures	5.67	2.9
62	Rubber manufactures, n.e.s.	1.29	82.6
63	Wood and cork manufactures	1.95	0.8
64	Paper and manufactured paper products	1.37	56.3
651	Threads and spun fibers	4.18	8.3
652	Cotton textiles	7.51	8.6
(65-other)	Other textile yarn and fabrics	1.02	24.5
661	Cement and construction materials	3.55	40.8
665	Manufactures of glass	3.16	13.1
667	Pearls and precious stones	3.55	0.5
(66-other)	Other nonmetallic and mineral manufactures, n.e.s.	1.49	29.6
67	Iron and steel	0.42	72.0
68	Nonferrous metals	4.42	3.8
69	Manufactures of metals, n.e.s.	2.58	55.5
7	Machinery and transport equipment	5.58	58.9
841	Clothing	1.10	11.2
851	Shoes	0.74	0.3
892	Printing	2.23	58.5
(8-other)	Other miscellaneous manufactured articles	2.20	45.8
9	Commodities and transactions, n.e.s.	8.37	0.1
	Total	210.14	22.4

TABLE 2-4 (*concluded*)

SITC Number and Category	Registered Minor Exports	
	Millions of U.S. Dollars	Per Cent Shipped to LAFTA
Summary of main groups		
Fruits, sugar, tobacco, cotton	74.71	2.5
Manufactured goods (3-other, 5, 6, 7, and 8)	77.26	26.8
Miscellaneous minor	58.18	42.1

Source: DANE-ADCE (1970).

process of import-substituting industrialization. Clearly, industrialization was not a precondition for expanding Colombian BCST exports from annual levels of $11 million during 1950–52 to $21 million during 1957–59 and $75 million during 1968–70. The expansion of BCST exports between the last two dates accounted for 35 per cent of the total increase in registered minor exports. Cotton alone was responsible for 21 per cent of that expansion, with sugar providing another 10 per cent. Import substitution in bananas, sugar, or tobacco was not a preliminary step to exporting; for cotton, however, the postwar story is different, as will be seen below.

Comparative advantage for these four commodities is rooted in the availability of Colombian natural resources, working within a certain range of labor and transport costs. By themselves, of course, these factors do not explain the level of BCST exports actually achieved during the postwar period nor their growth rate.

The relatively standardized nature of the items in the BCST group makes it possible to develop not only dollar-value time series but also both export quantity and unit-value series. These figures, presented in Table 2-5, show that the rapid growth in the dollar value of BCST exports between 1957–59 and 1968–70 was based on an expansion in their physical volume (averaging 15.5 per cent per year), with unit dollar prices declining between those two dates. It can also be seen that during the same interval, domestic output of these crops grew at a significantly lower rate than the quantity of exports (8.3 per cent vs. 15.5 per cent).

The behavior of the BCST export unit value series is interesting. One may note, first of all, its instability, which for 1957–70 has been about as great as that for coffee, although the BCST index comprises four different commodities. The average year-to-year change in coffee prices, disregarding signs, was 8.8 per cent; in the BCST unit value index, it was 8.7 per cent. During the difficult years of 1958 and 1959 both coffee and BCST prices plunged, and the crisis in the second half of 1966 was aggravated by the simultaneous deteriora-

TABLE 2-5

Value, Quantity, Price, and Production Indices for Bananas, Cotton, Sugar, and Tobacco (BCST), 1950–70

(averages for 1957–69 = 100)

	Exports			Physical Quantity of Domestic Production
	Dollar Value	Quantity	Unit Value	
1950	26.6	n.a.	n.a.	35.7
1951	27.1	n.a.	n.a.	38.4
1952	27.4	n.a.	n.a.	39.5
1953	35.4	n.a.	n.a.	51.5
1954	39.4	n.a.	n.a.	59.7
1955	47.7	n.a.	n.a.	60.2
1956	79.6	n.a.	n.a.	61.6
1957	73.7	40.8	180.6	54.7
1958	43.9	37.0	118.8	57.8
1959	39.9	42.8	93.3	81.7
1960	72.3	75.0	96.5	87.4
1961	85.2	90.6	94.1	90.8
1962	91.1	88.2	103.2	90.4
1963	88.8	83.3	106.6	91.4
1964	79.1	73.7	107.3	84.7
1965	104.7	101.4	103.3	95.3
1966	92.9	109.7	84.6	115.8
1967	145.2	161.2	90.1	132.9
1968	185.1	202.6	91.3	160.2
1969	189.9	193.8	98.0	156.9
1970	187.7	193.8	96.8	147.3

n.a. = not available.

SOURCE: Export quantity and value data for each of the commodities obtained from DANE-ADCE, various issues. Domestic output for each of the commodities obtained from the national accounts. The composite index for the whole group was obtained by using the following weights, based on the percentage share of each of the commodities in their total export value (in dollars) during 1957–69: bananas (fruit), 44.04; cotton, 27.40; sugar, 16.02; and tobacco, 12.54. The same weights were used to obtain the export and domestic production quantity indices. The export unit-value index was obtained using the export value and quantity indices. The method of calculating the export quantities does not take account of possible quality changes in the four products. The banana index includes a small quantity of other fruits.

Notes to Table 2-5 (*concluded*)
    It should be noted that the contributions of each of the four crops to the *increase* in BCST exports between 1957–59 and 1967–69 were quite different from their participation in total exports during 1957–69. Their percentage contributions to that increment were as follows: bananas (fruit), 9.8; cotton, 53.0; sugar, 30.6; and tobacco, 6.6.

tion of coffee and BCST prices, the former slight and the latter severe. On the whole, however, and fortunately for Colombia, the correlation between changes in dollar coffee prices and those in the BCST export unit value index is far from perfect ($R = +0.43$) through 1970. It may be too much to expect that diversification will take place into commodities whose prices are negatively correlated. Colombia has at least moved into other primary products which do not systematically follow the gyrations of coffee markets.

For BCST, exports represent an important outlet for domestic production; yet they account for a very small share in total world BCST exports. The following tabulation shows these relations in about 1965–69:[3]

	Exports as Per Cent of Domestic Production	Colombian Exports as Per Cent of World Exports
Bananas	90.1	6.2
Cotton	31.3	0.8
Sugar	22.5	0.8
Tobacco	26.9	1.2

The share of production exported every year has fluctuated considerably, particularly for cotton and sugar. As supplying the local market receives first priority, exports bear the brunt of poor crops (which have triggered export prohibitions in some cases) and become the key outlet for bountiful ones. In the case of bananas output has been particularly vulnerable to pests and hurricanes, but the other three crops also show fluctuations associated with primary production.

The small shares which Colombian BCST exports have in world markets do not necessarily imply very high price elasticities in the foreign demand for these goods. For one thing, bananas, cotton, sugar, and tobacco are hardly homogeneous products in world markets. Colombian tobacco is far from a perfect substitute for the Cuban leaf, for example. Secondly, "the world market" is a fragmented one, and exports to country A may not be substituted for by exports to country B. The clearest example of this was the pre-1974

TABLE 2-6

Cotton in Postwar Colombia, 1948–52 to 1966–69
(annual averages in thousands of metric tons)

	Production	Imports	Exports	Apparent Domestic Consumption
1948–52	8	17	0	25
1953–55	25	8	0	33
1958–59	50	9	0	59
1960–61	73	1	20	54
1962–65	71	4	18	57
1966–69	109	2	35	76

SOURCE: UNFAO-PY and UNFAO-TY, various issues. Data for 1956–57 not available.

sugar market, in which Colombia was subjected to export quotas imposed by the United States as well as by the International Sugar Agreement and also encountered discriminatory barriers in European and other countries. It should also be noted that the Colombian market shares, though small, have been tending to grow, and that part of such expansion was due to unique events (the embargo against Cuba, for example). Nevertheless, while foreign demand for BCST may not be perfectly price-elastic, the small Colombian market shares do provide support for the view that during the period under study foreign demand for Colombian exports has been rather price-elastic and that at least for the next few years, given the likely increases in Colombian output, there is little ground for "elasticity pessimism" regarding BCST exports. In circumstances under which a given commodity bumps one year against foreign-imposed (demand) quotas and the next year is subject to export prohibitions and supply quotas, it is difficult to be more precise about the shape of the idealized foreign demand schedule.

One may add that almost the whole of BCST exports are to countries outside the LAFTA preferential trading bloc, as shown in Table 2-2, in sharp contrast to the other registered minor exports. Therefore, the foreign exchange they earn is in an important sense more valuable than that earned from exports to LAFTA, under the reasonable assumptions that "reciprocity" will be more narrowly enforced with LAFTA, and that such commerce will involve some trade diversion.

Another characteristic of the BCST group is that, besides being subject to influences emanating from foreign trade policy, it has benefited from special agricultural policies, which regulate its internal prices and provide subsidized credit. The case of cotton is perhaps the most dramatic example of the payoff to such ad hoc, crop-specific programs. As shown in Table 2-6, during the postwar years Colombia passed from being a net importer to a net exporter of that commodity within a short period of time. During the 1950s cotton growers (mainly large-scale growers, it may be noted) received generous tax concessions as well as credit and price support from an institute designed exclusively to promote that crop. Such policies have continued, raising not only output but also yields. (While Colombia became an important cotton exporter during the 1960s, competing exports from some traditional sources, such as Mexico, stagnated.) Sugar and bananas have also benefited greatly from special government credit programs.

The production of BCST crops is overwhelmingly in Colombian hands. Foreign ownership in the production of bananas existed until a few years ago; now foreign participation is limited to marketing. In cotton, sugar, and tobacco both production and marketing, as in the case of coffee, are largely Colombian. The expansion of BCST exports, therefore, can hardly be credited to any special foreign presence in the production or sale of these commodities.

The BCST crops are grown at several points well spread out within the country: sugar comes mainly from the Cauca Valley and bananas from the Gulf of Urabá, while cotton is increasingly grown on the Atlantic coast.

Manufactured Exports.

Colombian manufactured exports have gone from an annual average of $10 million during 1957–59 to $80 million during 1968–70. That expansion accounted for 43 per cent of the total growth in registered minor exports between these dates. By 1968 the share of all Colombian exports in SITC categories 5, 6, 7, and 8 was larger than the corresponding figure for New Zealand.

As shown in Table 2-4, it would be a mistake to assume that all these exports are made up of labor-intensive commodities: the list includes not only cotton textiles, shoes, and near handicrafts, but also fuel oil, chemicals, and cement. As will be seen below, some aspects of Colombian export promotion policy may in fact encourage the latter type more than the former. The variety and heterogeneity of manufactured exports highlighted in Table 2-4 also helps explain the difficulty of obtaining export quantity and unit value indices, as was done in the case of BCST. For the years shown, characterized by a relatively stable world dollar price level, such a lack of quantity indices does not represent a serious problem. For more recent years, for which disaggregated data are not yet available, the problem seems more severe, and it is to be hoped that Colombian statistical authorities will develop quantity and price indices for the chief types of minor exports.

A rough analytical classification of all manufactured exports could be as follows:

1. Those which involve some slight processing of primary products. These are mostly included under SITC categories 0, 1, and 2; so they are excluded from our definition of manufactures. Examples are refined sugar and oilseed cakes.
2. Capital-intensive commodities, sold sporadically in competitive world markets. These are exports designed to use up planned or unplanned excess capacity. They are sold at marginal cost ("dumped") by plants whose output is, over the long run, expected to go mainly (say, 95 per cent and above) to the local market. Examples are exports of some chemicals, cement, glass, and petroleum products.
3. Capital-intensive commodities, whose plants have been designed to sell a good share of their output (say 5 to 30 per cent) within the LAFTA area, taking advantage of tariff preferences. This category is expected to gain in importance. Examples are petrochemicals and automobile parts.
4. Labor-intensive commodities, or parts of final products, sold at world prices.

This classification, of course, could be further refined, especially with the help of product-cycle concepts. Sporadic dumping of capital-intensive exports within LAFTA as well as in world markets can occur, as reported for some petrochemical exports to Mexico. Labor-intensive commodities may be sold from plants totally or partially devoted to the export market (the former are still rare). Neither the line between "labor-intensive" and other goods or processes nor that between manufactures and primary products is a sharp one. To give one example combining both ambiguities: about half the value of exports of cotton textiles ("manufactures") is made up of raw cotton ("primary product"), and it is not clear whether cotton spinning and weaving are more or less labor-intensive than the growing of cotton. Finally, some exports of manufactures are close complements of primary-product exports; for example, cardboard exported as banana boxes. Others, although capital-intensive, may exploit locational advantages, for example, cement exports from the Colombian Atlantic coast. It is not possible, at this stage, to classify Colombian manufactured exports according to the categories outlined above. But the discussion at least should alert us to the possibility of spontaneous or policy-induced "Leontief paradoxes."

Colombian manufactured exports represent a small fraction of both domestic manufactured production and world trade in manufactured goods. With few exceptions, local plants seldom have planned to export, as a regular business, more than 10 per cent of their output. Some enterprises are cautiously moving into higher ranges (textiles, for example), and there are a handful of small plants which ship 100 per cent of their production abroad (e.g., some leather-processing near handicrafts and clothing plants located in the Barranquilla bonded free-trade facilities). There are few manufactures for which Colombian exports have more than a tiny fraction of world trade. Nevertheless, in textiles Colombia faces U.S. and European import quotas, and in cement Colombian exports have some influence within the Caribbean and Gulf of Mexico markets. On the whole, it appears that Colombia has just begun to tap foreign market possibilities for her manufactures, both inside and outside the LAFTA region. Elasticity pessimism seems even less justified for manufactures than for BCST exports.

As shown in Table 2-4, LAFTA members take the larger share of Colombian exports such as synthetic fibers, rubber tires, pharmaceuticals, machinery and transport equipment, and plastics, which appear to be capital- or import-intensive, or both (the reason for the latter will be seen below). On the other hand, cotton textiles and leather and wood manufactures are primarily sold to the rest of the world. In a later section of this chapter, I will further explore systematic differences between LAFTA and non-LAFTA exports.

While the exact degree of direct foreign investment in Colombian manufactured exports is not known, the sample data presented in Chapter 6 indicate that during 1970 companies that were at least 50 per cent foreign owned represented no less than 27 per cent of all Colombian manufactured exports. It is doubtful whether the exact percentage went above 35. Two Colombian-owned corporations (COLTEJER and FABRICATO) dominate textile exports, and it appears that most firms exporting leather products and clothing are also Colombian owned. Foreign participation looms larger in chemicals, glass, rubber tires, and paper. As of 1972, foreign-owned assembly-type operations hooked into multinational businesses ("export platforms") were rare, and their exports from bonded free-trade zones were also modest. On the whole, the expansion of Colombian manufactured exports appears to owe little so far to the specific talents of export-oriented foreign investors.

As in the case of BCST crops, manufactured exports come from several points within Colombia. The geographical advantages of the Atlantic coast cities of Cartagena and Barranquilla, however, may make them dominant exporting centers if exporting continues to grow in importance in the planning of new industrial plants.

Miscellaneous Minor Exports.

Besides manufactured and BCST exports there is a residual category made up mainly of primary products. It contains some items, such as flowers, live animals, meat, and lumber, that have remarkable growth potential because of a combination of favorable world markets and a fairly elastic domestic supply. In some cases, as with meat and cattle on the hoof, border trade (or nonrecorded exports) has been important for many years. The diversified Colombian geography seems capable of generating a generous supply of a wide variety of these miscellaneous exports, from live tropical fish to less exotic beans and shrimp, for which the Colombian share in world markets remains small. Comparing 1957–59 with 1968–70, the miscellaneous category accounts for 22 per cent of the increase in all minor exports. This type of export appears to be mostly Colombian owned, but other generalizations are difficult. Flowers, for example, are quite labor-intensive, but beef cattle require much land and relatively little labor.

A CLOSER LOOK AT THE CUSTOMERS
FOR COLOMBIAN EXPORTS

Besides the appearance of LAFTA and of its subregion, the Andean Common Market, there have been other significant changes during the 1960s and early 1970s in the importance of the different customers for Colombian exports. The United States share in all recorded Colombian exports dropped from 70 per cent during 1957–58 to 40 per cent during 1967–69 and to 35 per cent during 1970–72. That for the (unenlarged) European Common Market rose from 13 to 24 per cent between 1957–58 and 1967–69, and then dipped to 22 per cent during 1970–72. The absolute average annual dollar value of Colombian exports to the United States, in fact, declined by a remarkable one-third between 1957–58 and 1967–69. The LAFTA share in all recorded exports, in spite of sharp increases from 1 per cent to 7 per cent and then to 9 per cent, remained modest. By 1970–72 the Andean group alone accounted for 7 per cent of all Colombian exports.

The increased geographical diversification of Colombian exports has not come about only as a result of greater product diversification. It may be seen in Table 2-7 that a marked diversification in markets for coffee occurred between 1957–58 and 1967–69, with the United States losing almost half of its still dominant share. A similar trend has been registered for BCST exports, with the European Common Market losing a large chunk of its leading share. In spite of large increases in their absolute level, the geographical spread in non-BCST minor exports changed surprisingly little between the two periods shown. Both the U.S. and LAFTA shares rose, but not by much. European and Japanese markets for these nontraditional exports have remained on the whole flabby relative to the purchases of more traditional primary products (coffee and BCST).

These trends emerge more clearly in Table 2-8, which focuses on geographical shares of the net increments of annual exports between 1957–58 and

TABLE 2-7

Geographical Distribution of Colombian Exports, 1957–58 and 1967–69

(percentages of total recorded exports in each commodity category)

	1967–69 Exports				1957–58 Exports			
	Coffee	Oil	BCST	Non-BCST Minor	Coffee	Oil	BCST	Non-BCST Minor
United States	44.4	54.9	17.2	35.4	81.1	40.7	8.7	31.4
Canada	1.3	0	0.6	3.1	1.8	0	0	0.5
United Kingdom	0.7	9.6	15.4	1.5	0.2	6.0	0	13.9
Japan	1.5	0	3.9	1.6	0.2	0	0	0.1
European Common Market	27.9	1.4	43.6	9.0	11.3	4.3	75.0	7.1
Other industrial Western European	6.9	0	4.8	3.7	3.4	0.2	14.4	0.2
Other nonsocialist European	10.5	2.6	5.1	1.1	1.6	0	0	0.1
Andean Common Market	0	8.5	2.7	16.7	0	0.2	0	13.9
Other LAFTA	1.1	0	1.4	10.0	0	1.0	0	9.9
Central American Common Market	0	0	0	4.2	0	0	0.1	6.1
Other Western Hemisphere	0	23.0	0.7	12.5	0	47.7	0	16.9
Socialist	5.5	0	3.2	0.1	0.3	0	0.1	0
Others	0.2	0	1.5	1.3	0.2	0	1.7	0

BCST = bananas, cotton, sugar, and tobacco.

SOURCE: DANE-ADCE, various issues.

TABLE 2-8

Geographical Distribution of the Increment in the Average Annual Dollar Value of Colombian Exports Between 1957–58 and 1967–69

(percentages of total increment in each commodity category)

	All Registered Exports	All Registered Minor Exports	BCST	Non-BCST Registered Minor Exports
United States	−155.4	31.0	21.6	36.3
Canada	1.8	2.7	0.9	3.7
United Kingdom	15.9	7.5	23.4	−1.6
Japan	11.7	3.4	5.8	2.0
European Common Market	96.9	16.0	27.5	9.4
Other industrial Western European	19.3	2.9	−0.1	4.6
Other nonsocialist European	49.2	3.6	7.7	1.3
Andean Common Market	27.5	12.5	4.0	17.4
Other LAFTA	16.4	7.1	2.2	10.0
Central American Common Market	4.1	2.4	−0.1	3.8
Other Western Hemisphere	−17.4	7.6	1.1	11.4
Socialist	27.7	1.8	4.7	0.2
Others	2.4	1.5.	1.4	1.6

BCST = bananas, coffee, sugar, and tobacco.
SOURCE: Basic data as in Table 2-7.

1967–69. Besides the changes already noted for all exports, the growing importance of the markets in "Other nonsocialist Europe" (with Spain as the key country) and in socialist countries is worth noting. In both cases the major export was coffee, sold under bilateral arrangements that were steadily but mildly criticized by the IMF and others. These arrangements together with the LAFTA and Andean pacts were the major Colombian departures from multilateral rules of the game for trade. The bilateral pacts, of course, limited the convertibility of export proceeds. By 1971 bilateral payments agreements had dwindled to those with the Democratic Republic of Germany, Hungary, Poland, Spain, Rumania, Bulgaria, and Yugoslavia. In 1958 there had been bilateral agreements also with Denmark, Ecuador, Finland, France, and Czechoslovakia.

The concentration of the expansion of non-BCST minor exports within the Americas emerges clearly from Table 2-8. The share of that increase going to the sheltered LAFTA zone was 27 per cent. The Caribbean and Central American areas, where Colombia has to meet competition from the rest of the world without the shelter of preferential treatment, accounted for an additional 15 per cent. The United States and Canada picked up another 40 per cent of the increase in non-BCST minor exports, leaving only about 17 per cent of the increment for the rest of the world. In contrast with this pattern, the Americas absorbed only 30 per cent of the expansion of BCST exports.

POLICY VARIABLES INFLUENCING MINOR EXPORTS

We can now turn to an examination of the most important variables manipulated by Colombian authorities in their search for larger minor exports. They include the exchange rate, export subsidies and taxes, drawbacks on import taxes, membership in preferential trade agreements, subsidized credits, and other subsidized facilities.

The Effective Exchange Rate.

Before the reforms of March 1967, "the effective exchange rate applied to minor exports" was often a blurry concept, subject to frequent changes. A quantification attempt, which becomes more robust as more recent years are approached, is presented in Table 2-9. It involves, first, the nominal exchange rate given for most merchandise exports except coffee and petroleum. Frequently during the 1950s and early 1960s this rate was *not* applicable to exports of gold, bananas, raw hides, precious stones, and a few other goods, or to manufactured exports having more than a given percentage of imported inputs. The rate was allowed to float freely during some periods, as during 1959, when it coincided with the free rate applicable to most capital account transactions. At other times, it was pegged at a level different from that applicable to coffee and imports, as during 1963. Since June 1968 it has corresponded to the basic certificate exchange rate, which with minor exceptions, such as petroleum, applies to nearly all current and capital account transactions.

The more notable features of the fiscal system as it affects new exporters are summarized in the second column of Table 2-9. The emergency measures taken after the overthrow of General Rojas Pinilla in 1957 included export taxes: 15 per cent during the third quarter of 1957 and 2 per cent subsequently through the first quarter of 1961 for most minor exports. These taxes were justified as part of the austerity package aimed at working off short-term foreign debts accumulated under the previous government.

Starting effectively in June 1961, it was assumed on the basis of Law 81 of December 22, 1960, that export profits were as much as 40 per cent of gross exports, and presumed export profits were allowed to be excluded from taxable profits. Not included in the benefits of this law, besides coffee and

TABLE 2-9

Exchange Rate Applied to Most Registered Minor Colombian Exports, 1949–72

		Basic Rate (pesos per U.S. dol.)	Subsidies Via Tax System (per cent[a])	Wholesale Price Index: Colombian Deflated by U.S. (1963 = 100)	PPP-EER Applied to Most Minor Exports (1963 prices)
1949		3.02	—	34.9	8.65
1950		3.12	—	38.0	8.20
1951		2.53	—	36.7	6.89
1952		2.92	—	37.1	7.86
1953	I	3.55	—	38.7	9.17
	II	3.41	—	39.8	8.57
	III	3.48	—	40.9	8.52
	IV	3.43	—	40.9	8.39
1954	I	3.53	—	41.9	8.42
	II	3.46	—	43.6	7.93
	III	3.45	—	43.0	8.02
	IV	3.50	—	41.9	8.35
1955	I	3.50	—	43.0	8.14
	II	3.85	—	43.0	8.95
	III	4.05	—	43.6	9.29
	IV	4.04	—	43.6	9.26
1956	I	4.28	—	44.7	9.58
	II	4.67	—	45.8	10.19
	III	4.82	—	46.9	10.28
	IV	6.05	—	48.5	12.49
1957	I	6.34	—	49.0	12.94
	II	6.23	—	54.1	11.52
	III	4.95	− 15	57.6	7.31
	IV	5.23	− 2	58.6	8.76
1958	I	5.92	− 2	60.0	9.67
	II	6.10	− 2	63.0	9.49
	III	6.10	− 2	64.0	9.34
	IV	6.10	− 2	66.0	9.06
1959	I	7.42	− 2	66.3	10.96
	II	8.00	− 2	69.3	11.31
	III	7.74	− 2	70.3	10.80
	IV	6.93	− 2	71.0	9.56
1960	I	6.81	− 2	71.0	9.39
	II	6.82	− 2	72.0	9.28
	III	6.92	− 2	72.0	9.42

TABLE 2-9 (*continued*)

	Basic Rate (pesos per U.S. dol.)	Subsidies Via Tax System (per cent[a])	Wholesale Price Index: Colombian Deflated by U.S. (1963 = 100)	PPP-EER Applied to Most Minor Exports (1963 prices)
IV	7.12	−2	73.0	9.56
1961 I	7.55	−2	74.3	9.97
II	8.23	—	78.0	10.55
III	8.63	14	78.0	12.62
IV	8.77	14	78.0	12.82
1962 I	8.80	14	78.0	12.86
II	8.91	14	79.0	12.86
III	8.61	14	79.0	12.43
IV	10.22	14	80.0	14.56
1963 I	10.09	14	90.0	12.78
II	9.99	14	101.0	11.28
III	9.99	14	103.0	11.06
IV	9.99	14	107.0	10.64
1964 I	9.99	14	112.0	10.17
II	9.98	14	119.0	9.56
III	9.98	14	119.0	9.56
IV	11.74	14	119.0	11.24
1965 I	13.57	14	118.8	13.02
II	16.63	14	122.6	15.47
III	13.50	14	124.3	12.38
IV	13.50	14	132.0	11.66
1966 I	13.50	14	136.2	11.30
II	13.50	14	142.9	10.77
III	13.50	14	142.5	10.80
IV	13.50	14	145.3	10.59
1967 I	13.50	14	147.5	10.43
II	14.02	18	150.1	11.02
III	14.86	18	151.7	11.56
IV	15.54	18	153.5	11.95
1968 I	15.84	18	153.8	12.15
II	16.14	18	157.3	12.11
III	16.39	18	157.0	12.32
IV	16.73	18	156.7	12.60
1969 I	16.96	18	157.1	12.74
II	17.19	18	160.0	12.68
III	17.45	18	160.9	12.80

TABLE 2-9 (*concluded*)

		Basic Rate (pesos per U.S. dol.)	Subsidies Via Tax System (per cent[a])	Wholesale Price Index: Colombian Deflated by U.S. (1963 = 100)	PPP-EER Applied to Most Minor Exports (1963 prices)
	IV	17.69	18	163.7	12.75
1970	I	18.00	18	162.8	13.04
	II	18.30	18	167.1	12.92
	III	18.56	18	166.7	13.14
	IV	18.92	19	169.3	13.30
1971	I	19.29	19	171.7	13.37
	II	19.69	19	175.7	13.34
	III	20.14	19	178.5	13.43
	IV	20.64	19	182.8	13.44
1972	I	21.16	20	183.8	13.81
	II	21.66	20	188.7	13.78
	III	22.10	20	192.4	13.78
	IV	22.54	20	198.1	13.66

SOURCE: Basic rates applied to most minor exports were obtained from IMF-IFS and IMF-AROER, various issues. It should be noted that, especially during the 1950s, minor exports were seldom treated as a homogeneous category. Export taxes (see note a, below) were also obtained from IMF-AROER.

Subsidies via the tax system are estimates of the average impact of an allowance for income tax deductions for exporters, effective from the third quarter of 1961 through the first quarter of 1967, plus the tax-exempt CAT granted to minor exporters from the second quarter of 1967 through 1972. Both subsidies affected companies differently depending on their particular tax situation and bracket; an average tax rate of 30–35 per cent can be assumed in computing the net subsidy. On the other hand, the CAT is a negotiable instrument which when first introduced could be used in lieu of cash to pay taxes up to one year from issue. The redemption date was reduced to nine months in October 1970. Late in 1971, the redemption date for CATs was further reduced from nine to three months for manufactured products and from nine to six months for all other eligible exports. Thus, the exact present value of CATs has fluctuated with these changes in redemption dates as well as with fluctuations in interest rates. Discounts of 18–20 per cent can be assumed. Depending on their own specific circumstances, companies could choose to hold or sell their CATs. The net subsidy shown in the table, therefore, represents a rough average.

Wholesale prices for Colombia and the United States obtained from IMF-IFS.

a. Minus sign signifies export tax.

petroleum, were bananas, precious metals, and hides. If a marginal income tax of around 35 per cent is assumed for exporting corporations, the *average* (taxable-equivalent) subsidy amounts to about 14 per cent. Note that the bigger the corporation and, presumably, the higher its marginal tax rate, the larger the subsidy. Firms making little or no profit could not benefit from this measure.

Articles 166 through 171 of Law 444 of March 22, 1967, replaced the fiscal incentive of Law 81 with the neater device of tax certificates given to exporters of goods other than coffee, petroleum and its by-products, and raw cattle hides. These certificates (CATs) amounted to 15 per cent of the f.o.b. value of exports and could be used to pay income, sales, and import taxes. Originally, they could not be used for these purposes at face value until one year after they were issued, but the owner could sell them freely to others, at the discount indicated by short-term interest rates. Redemption dates for CATs were lowered in 1970 and 1971. CATs were tax exempt. While under previous tax exemption an exporter had to have a given level of profits from other activities before he could benefit from the system, CATs can be readily converted into cash by any exporter, regardless of his tax status. On balance, the tax-exempt status of CATs more than offsets their discount, yielding an average taxable-equivalent subsidy of around 18 to 20 per cent.[4]

Once account is taken of differential price trends in Colombia vis-à-vis the rest of the world, the purchasing-power-parity-adjusted effective exchange rate (PPP-EER) applied to most minor exports can be estimated. The calculations shown in Table 2-9 simply compare Colombian and U.S. wholesale prices, a method which, although rough, provides a fairly accurate picture of the major trends in the real effective exchange rate for the period shown. Given the growing Colombian trade diversification and the post-1971 international monetary order, future calculations of this sort should take into account Colombian exchange rates and differential price movements vis-à-vis several of her major trade partners.[5]

Five features of the computed PPP-EER for minor exports may be briefly considered: average annual levels, year-to-year changes, a more refined instability index, and its differences compared with both the PPP nominal import rate and the PPP-EER for coffee. It may be seen in the first column of Table 2-10 that recent net exchange rates for minor exports exceed those dominant during the 1950s. The upward trend, however, was far from steady until recent years, as can be seen in the second and third columns. The instability measure presented in the latter column uses the average of the absolute value of quarter-to-quarter percentage changes for the four consecutive quarters of a given year. Thus, this column shows that during 1954 the quarter-to-quarter changes in the exchange rate, whether positive or negative, averaged 2.9 per

TABLE 2-10

Effective Purchasing-Power-Parity Exchange Rate (PPP-EER) for Minor Exports, 1953–72

	Annual Levels (pesos per U.S. dol.)	Year-to-Year Changes (per cent)	Index of Instability (per cent)	PPP-EER for Minor Exports	
				Ratio to Aver. PPP Nominal Rate for Imports	Ratio to Coffee PPP-EER
1953	8.66	10.2	.n.a.	1.39	1.74
1954	8.18	−5.5	2.86	1.39	1.73
1955	8.91	8.9	4.15	1.54	1.80
1956	10.64	19.4	8.05	1.97	1.99
1957	10.13	−4.8	17.74	1.41	1.68
1958	9.39	−7.3	4.21	0.84	1.53
1959	10.66	13.5	10.04	1.08	1.97
1960	9.41	−11.7	1.49	1.03	1.62
1961	11.49	22.1	7.83	1.32	1.86
1962	13.18	14.7	5.20	1.52	2.02
1963	11.44	−13.2	7.43	1.27	1.84
1964	10.13	−11.5	7.00	1.32	1.84
1965	13.13	29.6	15.10	1.66	2.52
1966	10.87	−17.2	2.50	1.19	2.20
1967	11.24	3.4	3.31	1.20	2.12
1968	12.30	9.4	1.50	1.19	2.10
1969	12.74	3.6	0.73	1.19	2.13
1970	13.10	2.8	1.53	1.19	2.17
1971	13.40	2.3	0.38	1.18	2.15
1972	13.76	2.7	0.98	1.19	2.29

n.a. = not available.

SOURCE: Basic data obtained from the last column of Table 2-9 and from the sources listed there. See text for explanation of the third column. The purchasing-power-parity average nominal import exchange rate is taken from Table 4-8. The effective purchasing-power-parity coffee exchange rate was obtained as for Table 1-3.

cent, while during 1957 that average rose to a remarkable 17.7 per cent. Besides 1957, other particularly unstable years were 1959 and 1965. One of the key advantages of the crawling peg emerges clearly from this index after 1967.

The fourth column of Table 2-10 presents ratios of the annual minor export rate to the average nominal merchandise import rate, also expressed in 1963 prices. The latter excludes the incidence of duties, controls, and prior deposits on the effective cost of importing; it is simply a purchasing-power-parity exchange rate, and as such conceptually different from the more complicated effective rate for minor exports to which it is compared. For example, the gap shown for 1968–72 arises mainly from the inclusion of the effective value of the CAT in the export rate. Nevertheless, the data in the fourth column highlight one striking fact: in the years following exchange reform in Colombia, such as 1958, 1963, and 1966, (a) *increases* occurred in the purchasing-power-parity nominal import rate and (b) *declines* occurred in the effective rate applied to minor exports; there was, therefore, (c) a tendency toward unification of those two rates. In other words, the goal of exchange rate unification was pursued at the expense of incentives for minor exports. With the exception of the peculiar circumstances of 1958, however, the effective minor export rate remained above the nominal rate for imports.

Finally, the last column of Table 2-10 shows the politically sensitive and economically revealing gap between the effective rate for minor exports and that for coffee. Since 1966, this gap has remained quite steady, with the coffee rate running at about half the minor export rate in spite of variations in the dollar coffee price. The relative stickiness of this relationship has turned the politically powerful coffee growers into champions of the crawling peg.

The Vallejo Plan.

Since around 1956, and at first motivated by a desire to use excess industrial capacity, the import content of certain exports, mainly manufactured goods, has been exempted (ex ante) from import duties, prior deposits, consular fees, and the need to obtain prior import licenses, subject to some stringent conditions. These now include the signing of an ad hoc contract with the government, clearly specifying the export goods; submission of proof that the imports are being financed according to Law 444; a deposit with customs of a guarantee (from a bank or an insurance company) amounting to twice the corresponding import duties; a guarantee that those imports which have not been used and are on the prohibited list will be re-exported; and a commitment to carry a special set of accounting books for these contracts. Not surprisingly, the major (but not exclusive) users of this "Plan Vallejo," as it has been known in Colombia since 1959, have been large manufacturing firms. More general drawback (ex post) systems are also allowed in principle by Law 444 and its predecessors but have not been implemented in practice, with the exception of the "Plan Vallejo Jr." or reposition provision, which since 1964 has allowed exporters who had used imported inputs and paid duties on them to import the same quantity and quality of merchandise free of duties, prior deposits, and the requirement of obtaining a prior license.

It may be seen in Table 2-11 that a vigorous implementation of the Vallejo Plan started in about 1962, after the system was reformed in 1959. From 1967

TABLE 2-11

Exports and Imports Under the Vallejo Plan, 1960–71
(millions of current U.S. dollars)

	Imports	Exports	Imports as Per Cent of Exports
1960	0.10	0.06 ⎫	
1961	0.20	0.18 ⎬	43
1962	0.17	0.84 ⎭	
1963	2.22	5.80	38
1964	5.08	12.87	39
1965	9.83	26.19	38
1966	12.06	41.69	29
1967	16.97	40.79	42
1968	17.86	51.95	34
1969	13.65	62.80	22
1970	24.70	58.10	43
1971	26.00	64.90	40

SOURCE: INCOMEX, "Análisis Sobre el Desarrollo de los Sistemas Especiales de Importación-Exportación," mimeographed (Bogotá: Banco de la República, 1971). Imports include both raw materials and machinery.

through 1970, Vallejo Plan exports have accounted for about 30 per cent of all minor exports and a dominant share of manufactured exports.

The import content (which includes machinery as well as raw materials) of these exports is substantial, and exceeds the average import content of all Colombian industry, estimated at about 13 per cent.[6] The alert reader will have noted that the joint impact of the CAT plus the Vallejo Plan can have not only a significant incentive effect, far exceeding the sum of the impacts of each scheme in isolation, but also one biased in favor of import-intensive exports. Take a simple example of a product with an import content of 40 per cent. The effective protection for exports of that product, excluding transaction costs involved in using the Vallejo Plan are:

Assumed world sales price	$100
Plus effective CAT (about 18 per cent)	118
Minus world purchases ($40); equals value added at domestic prices	78
Value added at world prices	60
Effective protection	30 per cent

This effective protection of 30 per cent may be compared with that which would result if neither the CAT nor the Vallejo Plan existed and if the average domestic price for imported inputs were raised by import restrictions to 30 per cent above the world market price. In that case, effective protection would be *minus* 20 per cent, or a swing of fifty percentage points. Clearly, activities with lower import components will receive lower effective protection for their exports and their swing will be less, ceteris paribus.

Whether the effective protection applicable to manufactured exports is higher or lower than the rates that can be calculated for the share of the output sold in the domestic market will depend on the corresponding domestic prices for output and inputs (both reflecting import restrictions without exemptions).

Table 2-12 contains some (partial) estimates of the differential incentives given for a sample of 105 manufactured products, depending on whether they were sold in Colombia or were exported and on whether the several export incentive schemes are taken into account. On the import side, however, only tariffs are included, on the assumption that they equal the difference between domestic and foreign prices. This is, of course, not true for many products, either because the tariff contains "water" or because of import controls. So the table serves primarily to illustrate (very rough) orders of magnitude for the differences among columns for the same product, rather than differences in treatment among products in the same column. In the third column, account is taken of the effective CAT and the Vallejo Plan.

It may be seen that while the export promotion schemes did not equalize the tariff-intended effective protection between exports and domestic sales, they narrowed the gap relative to a situation without export promotion schemes. Indeed, in the sample of 105 products, there were 18 for which the figures in the third column were higher than those in the first. The data in the table again show that the combined effect of a CAT based on sales value plus exemption of duties on imported inputs was quite powerful, in many cases clearly offsetting the negative effect of overvaluation on the peso prices of exports relative to nontradable goods, even when the former prices remain unfavorable compared with those of import-competing goods.[7]

Although the combined effect of the CAT plus the Vallejo Plan did discriminate among activities, the spread of the figures in the third column is smaller than that of the first. This indicates that variations in tariffs on outputs (or on finished products) were greater than those on inputs.

LAFTA and the Andean Group.

Depending on one's viewpoint, these associations can be regarded as part of the Colombian export-promotion package or as extensions of import-

TABLE 2-12

Effective Protection Yielded by Tariffs and Export Promotion Schemes, About 1970, for 105 Products

(per cent; figures in parentheses show number of products included in each category)

		For Export	
	For Sale in Colombia	Without Promotion Schemes	With Promotion Schemes
Foodstuffs, tobacco, and beverages (8)	198	−91	43
Textiles (5)	267	−34	43
Clothing (7)	387	−52	40
Wood and wood products (6)	120	−71	38
Paper and paper products (7)	133	−67	47
Printing and publishing (3)	79	−7	27
Leather and leather products (6)	203	−149	58
Rubber and rubber products (2)	59	−36	47
Chemicals and petrochemicals (14)	49	−27	37
Stone, earth, and clay products (7)	97	−9	25
Metals and metal products (19)	101	−39	40
Nonelectrical tools and machinery (6)	33	−17	27
Electrical products and machinery (4)	57	−52	52
Transport equipment (6)	59	−30	38
Others (5)	149	−48	42
Total (105)	130	−48	39

SOURCE: Data summarized from unpublished calculations of Gonzalo Giraldo, Planning Department, Colombia. The sample of 105 manufactured products was selected as representative of actual or potential exports within the Andean Common Market, of which Colombia is a member. In the calculation of effective protection, only tariffs and export promotion schemes were taken into account (see text). Input coefficients actually observed in Colombia were used; imports of capital goods were excluded. An effective CAT of 20 per cent was assumed, a figure which may be regarded as somewhat high for 1970. Special regimes exempting some imports from duties were disregarded for this calculation.

substitution efforts. It is not yet clear whether trade creation or trade diversion will predominate in the Colombian dealings with these preferential trade associations, but exports to LAFTA appear to differ, on balance, from those to the rest of the world.

For exports to LAFTA, the incentive effects of the CAT plus the Vallejo

Plan can reach high levels, in some cases possibly detrimental to the Colombian economy. This can be shown by going back to the simple example presented earlier. Suppose, in addition to the assumptions already made, that some Colombian exports are sold to LAFTA countries at prices 50 per cent above world prices. The calculation of effective protection inclusive of LAFTA margins would now be as follows:

Assumed LAFTA price	$150
Plus effective CAT (18 per cent)	177
Minus world purchases; equals value added at	
Colombian prices	137
Value added at world prices	60
Effective protection on exports to LAFTA	128 per cent

In other words, if LAFTA protective margins are similar to those Colombia applies vis-à-vis the rest of the (non-LAFTA) world, Colombian producers may actually prefer to sell to LAFTA rather than to the domestic market, as the CAT-Vallejo Plan benefits could easily outweigh transport costs.

It should be emphasized at this point that not all Vallejo Plan exports go to LAFTA (and that not all Vallejo Plan exports involve manufactured goods). From 1967 through 1969, in fact, only 23 per cent of Vallejo Plan exports went to LAFTA, amounting to less than 8 per cent of all registered minor exports. Manufactured exports to LAFTA are sometimes sold under conditions of dumping, bringing their export prices closer to those prevailing in nonpreferential world markets; the benefits to Colombia of this kind of sale, however, are not always clear.

PROEXPO.

Law 444 of 1967 created other export-promotion schemes, centered around a fund (PROEXPO) generously financed by a 1½ per cent tax on the c.i.f. value of all imports. The law (articles 181–202) gave that fund broad powers and great flexibility to engage in export promotion. PROEXPO provides local producers with information on foreign markets and technical advice on transport, packing, quality control, etc., as well as on the production of exportable goods. In a country where "shortage of working capital" is a permanent entrepreneurial complaint, it channels credit under liberal terms to exporting firms; and under special circumstances it can provide equity capital. It also insures against political and other noncommercial export risks, and has helped to prepare a four-year export plan. By means of imaginative domestic advertising, including billboards proclaiming that "Exporting is the best business in Colombia," it tries to develop an "export mentality."[8]

Abroad, PROEXPO also advertises and holds fairs, even sending a Navy ship with Colombian goods around the Caribbean. During 1970, its credit activities amounted to 409 million Colombian pesos plus 6.8 million U.S. dollars.

It is difficult to measure the effect of something like PROEXPO on nontraditional Colombian exports. Some of its activities, in particular its credit operations, are enthusiastically praised by entrepreneurs otherwise starved for cheap working capital. Others, such as its advertising and fairs, have a less clear net value and can easily degenerate into boondoggles. Even less clear and less readily quantified is the value of such an institution in affecting private expectations regarding the firmness of a government's commitment to support export activities.

The PROEXPO credit program is one example of how Colombian authorities have used domestic distortions to give greater leverage to export-promoting schemes; if Colombian capital markets were perfect, there would be little power in that program. Similarly, the potency of the Vallejo Plan would disappear if all non-exchange-rate import restrictions were eliminated. Note that these measures do not always serve simply to offset the harmful effects of other policies on exporting; for some firms they may offer a net gain relative to an idealized pure neoclassical situation.

Other Export-Promotion Policy Instruments.

Especially since 1967, the many instruments of the Colombian government have been increasingly tilted in favor of exporters of products other than coffee or oil. Credit, besides that from PROEXPO or aimed at specific exportable crops, is channeled preferentially, under the more or less explicit tutelage of central-bank authorities, toward exporters. That preference affects not only short-term but also long-term credit provided by several special development funds. The encouragement given to exporters has also stimulated the granting of *foreign* credit to them. Entrepreneurs are notified both formally and informally that the fate of their requests regarding import licenses, release from price controls, or of any other request having to do with any field where public-sector action is important—and there are few where that action is not—will very much depend on their export record. The medals and banners regularly presented by the Colombian President to distinguished exporters, in other words, are not simply moral incentives, for they give recipients some muscle when dealing with the numerous public agencies capable of making the life of businessmen either easy or miserable and profitable or unprofitable.

Finally, there are other export-promoting ideas that are just beginning to be exploited in Colombia to an important degree. One is the creation of areas in the country equipped with adequate export and overhead facilities to which imports can be brought free of duties and import restrictions, to be used exclusively by exporting firms located there. In 1973 there were two such free zones (*zonas francas*): one in Barranquilla, intended to compete with similar facilities located in Panama, and a more recently built one near Cali (Palmaseca). Others are being considered. Trading houses, particularly useful for marketing exports from small- and medium-scale producers, were rare until a few years ago, but recently several private ones have sprung up. Some international companies, such as Volkswagen, have set up separate organizations to promote exports, not all related to their usual line of business.

THE SUPPLY RESPONSE OF COLOMBIAN MINOR EXPORTS

The export promotion package just described appears to have succeeded in generating a rising dollar value of Colombian minor exports, particularly since 1967. Part of that upward trend may be due to increases in export dollar prices, which, however, to judge from the scanty data available, do not seem to have reached large and sustained proportions until 1972–74. On the whole and for the period under study, it is reasonable to suppose that the observed time series for the value of minor exports trace out mainly quantity movements along, or shifts in, the Colombian supply curve for exports. While world demand for these exports fluctuated about a reasonably steady average price throughout the period under study, there were undoubtedly few products for which world demand in any one year was not close to being perfectly price elastic in the range relevant for Colombia. Nevertheless, in spite of these convenient generalizations, serious problems remain in the estimation of the supply schedule for minor exports.

There are, first of all, the difficulties arising from the heterogeneity of these exports and the lack of quantity indices. It has also been noted that in some years several commodities received special, sui generis treatment, such as bananas, gold, and emeralds. Another set of problems arises from the proliferation of export-promotion policies adopted by Colombia, many difficult to quantify, and from their collinearity.

Related problems arise in the handling of trends during the 1960s and early 1970s which are said to have encouraged the growth of minor exports, such as the rapid growth of world trade and, more relevantly, the creation of LAFTA and the Andean group. Access to a preferential trading arrangement makes it possible for a participating country to sell exports to its partners at prices higher than those in the world market. In exchange, of course, it must buy *their* exports at higher-than-world-market prices. As a result, assessment of the LAFTA and Andean arrangements also is hindered by the previously mentioned lack of quantity indices for most minor exports.

Disaggregation by product and customer might seem to provide a partial answer to these complications. However, it also introduces other problems. Any subcategory of Colombian minor exports is likely to be quite thin during most of the period under study, and thus subject to apparently erratic behavior as a result of particular events, independent of general policy variables. Temporary excess capacity in three or four important plants, for example, could give manufactured exports a boost, while a poor crop could send the quantity of some exports way down.

Whatever the exchange rate and export incentives may be, it can normally be expected that as a country's productive capacity expands, its supply curve for exports will steadily shift to the right. There is thus a case, not based on the expansion of world demand, for including a trend term in regressions intended to explain export supply response. But this procedure, although it yields high R^2s, often results in ambiguous coefficients, because of the strong upward trend of minor exports and of key policy variables such as the effective exchange rate.

The model implicit in supply-response calculations to be shown below, i.e., a perfectly elastic world demand interacting with a supply of exports which in turn reflects the difference between the domestic supply of and demand for exportable goods, involves some conceptualization strain when applied to commodities such as sugar, meat, and cotton. These goods and others are subject among other things to domestic regulations of various sorts (including occasional export quotas). As a result, the quantities of these commodities available for export are determined by other factors in addition to their price and their domestic elasticities of demand and supply.

Because of problems of collinearity and serial correlation,[9] it was decided to estimate supply-response equations, focusing on (a) independent variables mainly related to the effective purchasing-power-parity exchange rate, to see how far it was possible to carry the analysis with just these variables and (b) annual percentage changes of the relevant variables. The impact of changes in the own dollar price of exportables and the influence of several export-promotion programs discussed above were left out. On the other hand, a variable related to exchange-rate instability, usually excluded from supply-response analyses, was introduced, and some exploration of the complicated dynamic path of supply response was carried out.

Regression Results.

The most up-to-date and best results of the approach outlined above are presented in tables 2-13 and 2-14. In the following discussion, I will first highlight the results most favorable to the hypothesis that "the exchange rate matters." This will be followed by an examination of failures in the hypothe-

TABLE 2-13

Regressions for Annual Percentage Changes in Minor Exports, Based on Annual Data for 1955–70 or 1955–72

(t ratios in parentheses)

		Independent Variables					
Regression Number	Constant	Change in the Exchange Rate	Instability of Exchange Rate	Lagged Change in BCST Output	R^2	F Statistic	DW
Total Dollar Value of Recorded Minor Exports, 1955–72							
(1)	19.92	0.81	−1.85		0.36	4.20	2.04
	(3.34)	(2.50)	(2.16)				
(2)	14.40	0.87	−1.48	0.53	0.47	4.18	2.01
	(6.44)	(2.84)	(1.78)	(1.73)			
Dollar Value of BCST, 1955–70							
(3)	−9.25	1.13	0.70	1.91	0.61	6.23	2.74
	(0.74)	(2.54)	(0.49)	(3.63)			
Dollar Value of Non-BCST Recorded Minor Exports, 1955–70							
(4)	25.48	0.59	2.37		0.25	2.19	1.73
	(2.82)	(1.38)	(1.93)				

BCST = bananas, coffee, sugar, and tobacco.

R^2 = coefficient of multiple determination.

DW = Durbin-Watson statistic.

NOTE: For method, see text. The first two regressions have 18 observations, the last two only 16, owing to lack of up-to-date customs data. Basic data obtained from earlier tables in this chapter. Except for the instability index, all values are expressed as year-to-year percentage changes.

sis, including those not shown in the tables, as well as of other remaining problems of interpretation.

THE IMPORTANCE OF THE EXCHANGE RATE

In the regressions based on annual data (Table 2-13), the dependent variables shown include the year-to-year percentage changes in the dollar value of all minor exports and in the value of BCST and non-BCST exports. Because of differences in the availability of data, the regressions cover 1955–72 for all minor exports and 1955–70 for BCST and non-BCST exports. The independent variables are the year-to-year changes in the effective purchasing-power-parity exchange rate for minor exports; the index of instability of the rate; and the lagged year-to-year percentage change in the domestic output of BCST crops. The simple average values for these variables stated in terms of annual percentage changes, except for the instability index, are as follows:

Recorded minor exports (1955–72):	12.7
BCST exports (1955–70):	14.4
Non-BCST minor exports (1955–70):	13.3
Effective exchange rate (1955–72):	3.7
Instability index (1955–72):	5.5
Domestic BCST output, lagged (1955–72):	6.2

The first three regressions in Table 2-13 show clearly significant coefficients for changes in the effective exchange rate, implying supply elasticities between 0.81 and 1.13. These results are similar to those obtained by other researchers (see footnote 1 in this chapter). Two of the equations also indicate clearly that exchange instability is quite harmful to the expansion of minor exports, thus supporting a widespread hunch. In the first regression, for example, the coefficient for instability tells us that a reduction of the average quarterly fluctuation in the effective exchange rate from, say, 6.0 to 4.0 will, ceteris paribus, raise the growth trend of minor exports by 3.7 percentage points. The same equation tells us that to achieve a similar result by just changing the effective exchange rate, it would be necessary to carry out a net effective devaluation of 4.6 per cent *every year*.

The links between export growth, the exchange rate, and its instability literally implied by regression 1, and others, may be clarified by the following example. Suppose the effective exchange rate has been held steady at 10 pesos per U.S. dollar, but that it is then decided to carry it to an *average* of 11 pesos in "Year Two" and to 12 pesos in "Year Three," after which it will again be held steady. The transition takes place entirely in Year Two, when for each of its quarters the exchange rate can be taken as 10.0, 10.6, 11.4 and 12.0 pesos, respectively. Thus, for that year the instability index will average

4.7 per cent, while for all others it will be zero. Under these circumstances, growth rate in minor exports predicted by regression 1 will be: Year One, 19.9 per cent; Year Two, 19.3 per cent; Year Three, 28.0 per cent; and Year Four, 19.9 per cent.

In other words, during Year Two the positive effect of the net devaluation will be more than offset by the negative instability effect; in Year Three there will be no instability to drag down the positive effects of the net devaluation, but by Year Four growth will be back to a long-term trend unaffected by the exchange rate. This is surely but a crude attempt to capture the dynamics of response to net devaluation, but for Colombia it does reflect an important experience, even if it leaves out such matters as thresholds, expectations, and considerations of the exchange-rate level.

Fluctuations in the domestic output of BCST crops (in the short run caused to a large extent by weather), entered with a one-year lag in the regressions of Table 2-13, clearly influence changes in BCST exports, and this with an elasticity near 2.0. Such a value is compatible with the priority given by authorities to the domestic consumption of these commodities and the marginal role assigned to exports.

Although the R^2s in Table 2-13 are not as large as those in regressions using untransformed variables coupled with time trends, serial correlation and collinearity problems plaguing those other versions of supply response seem to have been avoided in my case.

The result that "the exchange rate matters," obtained from annual data, is confirmed by Table 2-14, showing regressions based on quarterly data, but in which, as before, the variables include annual percentage changes in all minor exports and in the effective exchange rate. It has not been possible to disaggregate quarterly minor exports. For exports and the exchange rate, therefore, the percentage change between this year's first quarter and last year's first quarter, and so on, were used. This approach avoids seasonality considerations. The index of instability is defined as before: for a given quarterly observation the index refers to the average fluctuation in the exchange rate during that quarter and the previous three quarters. The average values for 1955I through 1972IV for the variables used in Table 2-14 are 19.5 for recorded minor exports, 4.3 for the effective exchange rate, and 5.6 for the instability index.

The standard deviations of these annual changes based on quarterly data are of course higher than those derived from annual data. For example, the standard deviation of the average percentage change in minor exports is 42.1 using quarterly data and only 19.5 using annual data. Extreme values, caused by exogenous circumstances, affect averages of quarterly data much more than those for annual data.

The supply elasticities estimated in Table 2-14 are close to those obtained

TABLE 2-14

Regressions for Changes in Minor Exports, Based on Quarterly Data for
1955–72

(*t* ratios in parentheses)

Independent Variables	Dependent Variable: Annual Changes in All Recorded Minor Exports		
	1955I Through 1972IV	1955I Through 1963IV	1964I Through 1972IV
Constant	23.32	33.76	19.95
	(3.28)	(2.72)	(2.10)
Changes in the exchange rate	0.95	0.68	1.04
	(3.59)	(2.02)	(2.07)
Instability of exchange rate	−1.42	−2.92	−0.10
	(1.51)	(2.11)	(0.06)
R^2	0.19	0.31	0.13
F statistic	7.98	7.51	2.37
DW	1.60	1.19	1.96
No. of observations	72	36	36

NOTE: For method, see text. Quarterly data on minor exports obtained from IMF-IFS.

in annual regressions and are all significant. The instability index again performs reasonably well, although better for the earlier years. Identical regressions covering 1954I through 1971II give even better results for R^2 and *t*. After 1968, the independent variables show little movement, while export data, particularly the quarterly figures, maintain considerable variability (some of which looks spurious).

Tests were made of the hypothesis that the change in minor exports depends not only on changes in the exchange rate and its instability but also on the *level* of the exchange rate; the results were insignificant in all cases. Another experiment involved using the percentage change in the exchange rate squared, but keeping its original sign, to examine the proposition that large changes in the effective exchange rate cannot be expected to yield correspondingly large changes in minor exports, either because of adjustment lags or for other reasons. Most coefficients in this experiment were insignificant. The best regression covered 1963I through 1971III; as expected, this procedure increased the coefficient for the change in the exchange rate to 1.71

(with a t ratio of 2.8), and resulted in a negative sign for the squared term, which had a coefficient of -0.017 and a t ratio of 1.6. R^2 and the Durbin-Watson statistic rose (slightly) to 0.31 and 1.50, respectively; and the stability coefficient remained insignificant. The 1963–71 regression can be interpreted as yielding an upper estimate for the supply elasticity of minor exports with respect to the exchange rate. Finally, a dummy variable was also introduced in regressions of the type presented in Table 2-14, having a value of 1 whenever the exchange rate change was negative, and zero otherwise. This test of possible asymmetric responses to positive and negative exchange-rate movements yielded no evidence for asymmetry.

Direct experimentation with lagged values for exchange rates, still using quarterly data, yielded clearly positive results in only one case. For the period 1954I–1962IV, the coefficient for changes in the exchange rate lagged one full year was 0.78, with a t statistic of 3.0. The coefficient of the unlagged exchange-rate change *increased* to 0.99, with a t statistic of 3.9. For the instability index the coefficient was -4.01 and the t statistic was 4.2. R^2 rose to 0.57, and the Durbin-Watson statistic, to 1.50. Note that the sum of the two exchange-rate coefficients gives a long-term elasticity practically identical to that obtained for 1963–71 when the squared exchange-rate change was included in that regression.[10]

IMPORTANCE OF OTHER POLICIES

The evidence discussed so far is consistent with the hypothesis that exchange-rate policy, including its stability, considerably influenced minor exports. It does not, however, support the presumption that it is the only policy which has mattered. Note how in all but one of the regressions in tables 2-13 and 2-14 the constant terms are large and significant. The results of regression 1 in Table 2-13, for example, indicate that a perfectly stable effective purchasing-power-parity exchange rate for minor exports, at a level similar to that observed during the period under study, would be consistent with a growth in those exports of about 20 per cent per year, far exceeding growth in the rest of the Colombian economy. With the instability observed, on the average, from 1955 through 1972, the upward trend would still be about 10 per cent per year. An upward creep of 3.7 per cent per year in the real effective exchange rate, always according to the same regression, brings the rate of expansion in minor exports to about the 13 per cent actually observed. Note that given the annual averages for 1955–72, a supply elasticity of about 3.4, or more,[11] would be needed for the changes in the effective exchange rate alone to explain all of the increase in minor exports.

What lies behind the powerful constant terms? First of all, they could be picking up inflationary trends in the world economy, but this cannot account for very much and would be limited to non-BCST exports (BCST dollar prices have declined on average during 1957–70). The major answer must rely on other direct and indirect export-promotion schemes discussed earlier. Note how the constant term drops in regressions 2 and 3 in Table 2-13 when the lagged change in domestic production of BCST is brought in; these latter changes, as discussed earlier, have been heavily influenced in the long run by credit and other promotional policies of the public sector (and in the short run, of course, by weather).

Unfortunately, the evidence regarding the influence of exchange-rate policy on minor exports is less robust than it appears at first sight. Even in tables 2-13 and 2-14 disaggregation into BCST and non-BCST exports and the use of subperiods decrease the t statistics for some coefficients. Non-BCST minor exports, for example, appear less sensitive to exchange-rate changes, but more sensitive to instability, than BCST exports. It is not obvious why this should be so, a priori. Furthermore, regressions in which the BCST export quantity index (presented earlier in this chapter) was used as the dependent variable yielded insignificant coefficients for exchange-rate variables. Other regressions (not shown) in which the dependent variables (1958–69 only) were changes in dollar values of non-BCST exports to LAFTA and non-LAFTA countries separately, as well as changes in manufactured exports only, yielded insignificant coefficients for all variables except the constant terms.

Other independent variables, for which yearly data were used, also yielded insignificant coefficients. These included changes in domestic industrial output (to test for the influence of *generalized* cyclical excess capacity on non-BCST and manufactured exports);[12] concurrent (i.e., unlagged) changes in the domestic production of BCST; and all lagged variables except BCST output.

Aggregating unregistered with registered minor exports and using annual changes in their combined total as the dependent variable also worsens the results, and yields insignificant coefficients for the independent variables. Together with the insignificant results obtained with most lagged variables, this failure generates some suspicion that at least part of the apparent exchange-rate elasticity of registered minor exports may arise from substitution effects induced by the contrast of the legal exchange rate with the black-market rate, between smuggling and registration, and between one year and another or one quarter and another, according to John Sheahan's results. Especially before 1967, for example, the timing of exports of storable BCST crops could have been influenced by the exchange rate without that implying much for the long-run expansion of those exports.

It can be argued with some force that the exchange rate used in the regressions is more applicable to some minor exports than others. It is not just a matter of neglecting ad hoc exchange regulations for some products; it is also that for minor exports going to LAFTA, account should be taken not only of the U.S. wholesale price index, but of price levels and exchange rates in Latin American countries as well. Nevertheless, it remains disturbing that the disaggregated results are so much poorer than those for all registered minor exports lumped together.

What to make of this bundle of results? In spite of the shortcomings noted, the hypothesis that exchange-rate policy has been a major influence on the evolution of Colombian minor exports has more evidence to back it up than its extreme opposite. But it is not possible, given the information available, to credit different policy variables with exact shares of the increase in those exports. The untangling of the impact of different policies on export promotion may only be possible, in fact, using cross-sectional data for several countries. Even then, important interaction effects among export-promotion policies in a given country as well as the degree of credibility of these policies among entrepreneurs may be impossible to quantify. For example, by how much does commitment to a crawling peg enhance the credibility of export incentives? Are there discontinuities (or floors and ceilings) for the effects of some variables, depending on the value of others? Will PROEXPO efforts be apparent only if the real net exchange rate is above a certain minimum? And will further increases above that minimum bring fewer additional exports than, say, expanding the benefits of the Vallejo Plan? Will subsidies to selected industries generate foreign exchange at lower domestic resource costs than a more devalued exchange rate? Or avoid generating quasi rents? Alas, neither a priori reasoning nor empirical work appears capable at this point of yielding convincing answers to these questions, at least for Colombia, whose experience with substantial minor exports is, after all, relatively short. Throughout economic history many export booms have shown Schumpeterian patterns difficult to explain fully using solely concepts such as the price elasticity of export supply. The Colombian minor export boom, particularly after 1967, falls into that category.

LAFTA VS. NON-LAFTA MINOR EXPORTS: SOME
ECONOMIC CHARACTERISTICS

It was seen earlier that one of the most dynamic components of Colombian minor exports was that destined to LAFTA countries, including the Andean group. On the face of it, preferential tariff treatment abroad must be combined with domestic promotion policies to explain the above-average growth rate of exports to LAFTA. It is of some interest to explore whether there are systematic differences between the economic characteristics of LAFTA and non-LAFTA exports.

Even without the existence of preferential trade arrangements differences would be expected between Colombian exports to the rest of Latin America and those shipped to, say, the United States and the European Common Market. Whatever the positive theory of trade adopted, whether Heckscher-Ohlin, Linder, product cycle, or almost any other, differences between the predicted commodity composition of those trade flows will emerge. But a first task is to see whether, in fact, the difference is significant.

LAFTA Share and Capital-Labor Ratios.

It was suggested earlier in this chapter that the more capital-intensive a given export item of Colombian manufacture is, the larger will be the LAFTA share in its geographical destination. Colombian capital-labor ratios are not

TABLE 2-15

Regressions Explaining LAFTA Share of Three-Digit SITC Minor Export Items as a Function of the Capital-Labor Ratio

(t statistics in parentheses)

	Constant	Logarithm of Capital-Labor Ratio	R^2	F Statistic	No. of Observations
1968					
All export items	−48.47	9.81	0.06	5.90	100
		(2.43)			
Export items over $100,000	−59.37	10.22	0.09	6.56	65
		(2.56)			
1969					
All export items	−96.39	15.22	0.12	13.53	104
		(3.68)			
Export items over $100,000	−128.25	18.07	0.20	15.24	62
		(3.90)			
1970					
All export items	−96.27	15.89	0.13	14.43	97
		(3.80)			
Export items over $100,000	−129.49	18.83	0.25	20.32	64
		(4.51)			

SOURCE: See text. The means for the LAFTA shares were as follows:

1968	
All export items	40.8%
Export items over $100,000	33.5
1969	
All export items	42.5
Export items over $100,000	36.1
1970	
All export items	48.7
Export items over $100,000	41.1

available to test this proposition in the necessary detail, so the test can be carried out only if it is assumed that the ranking of activities according to capital-labor ratios is the same in Colombia as in the United States. Furthermore, the test will only refer to direct capital-labor ratios.

Using 1965 capital-labor ratios computed by Gary C. Hufbauer for the United States[13] and LAFTA shares in matching three-digit SITC Colombian exports, primarily of manufactured goods, for 1968, 1969, and 1970, the results presented in Table 2-15 are obtained. While capital intensity is only one of the many variables determining whether a given item is exported to LAFTA or elsewhere, the strong *t* ratios confirm that there is a significant link between LAFTA shares and capital intensity. It is noteworthy that in Table 2-15 the more recent the year, the stronger is the result.

LAFTA Share and Import Intensity.

Using unpublished data from Planeación, Larry Senger has tried to explain the share of minor export items going to LAFTA, covering both manufactured and nonmanufactured goods, as a function of imports per worker and value added per worker in the sectors generating those exports. Only the direct import, value-added, and labor requirements of the sector were considered. For every year from 1961 through 1968, the coefficient for the logarithm of imports per worker is positive and highly significant, with *t* statistics between 4.5 and 8.8. Contrary to my earlier results, the coefficients for the logarithm of value added per worker are negative, but with erratic *t* statistics depending on the year; for 1965, for example, the *t* statistic is -1.3, but for 1968 it is -2.1. The R^2s range from 0.16 to 0.32, with the number of observations ranging from 104 to 239.[14]

Interpretation of the Results.

The evidence indicating that Colombian minor exports to LAFTA are more capital- or import-intensive than those shipped elsewhere is fairly strong. But the difference in capital intensity could be expected even without the existence of preferential trading arrangements, at least following some trade theories, as the Colombian factor endowment is closer to that of the rest of Latin America than to those of North America and Europe, where most of her non-LAFTA exports go.

Comparing the unit values for LAFTA exports with those for non-LAFTA exports for three-digit SITC minor exports, one obtains the expected result that the former are higher than the latter, on average, for 1968 and 1970. However, the standard deviation is very high, casting doubt on the significance of these averages. The ratio of LAFTA unit values to non-LAFTA ones for 1968 is 1.87, with a standard deviation of 3.56, and is for 100 SITC three-digit items. The comparable figures for 1970 are 1.33 and 1.16, for 112 items.

When the ratios of LAFTA to non-LAFTA unit values are correlated with the Hufbauer capital-labor ratios used above, very poor results are obtained for every year, whether all items are used or only those values above $100,000. One cannot, therefore, establish a link between high capital-labor ratios and trade diversion by this route. No firm link appears either between the ratios of LAFTA to non-LAFTA unit values and the LAFTA share for each export item.

While the basic explanation of the higher capital intensity of exports to LAFTA remains moot, their higher import intensity would not be expected on a priori grounds, and the most plausible explanation for it rests on the powerful combination of incentives formed by LAFTA preferential margins, the CAT, and the Vallejo Plan.

LAFTA and the Andean group, particularly the latter, seek broad objectives which may even justify some sacrifices in economic efficiency narrowly defined. These preferential arrangements provide Colombia, inter alia, with at least some insurance against a sudden collapse in world trade, such as that of the 1930s. Nevertheless, possible efficiency costs in this area should be monitored and minimized by close examination of the nature of LAFTA trade and by a re-examination of export-promotion schemes.

OUTLOOK FOR MINOR EXPORTS

Whatever its defects, the policy package put together in March 1967 has been consistent with an acceleration in the growth of minor exports. The effects of the greater stability and the higher level of the effective exchange rate, as well as other export-promoting features of Law 444, appear to be still filtering through the economy, strengthening the new "export mentality" and triggering fresh learning effects, as the timid imitate those already successful in exporting. If these policies are maintained, including the upward creep in the effective exchange rate, and if the world economy does not suffer a dramatic change in trend, a growth rate in minor exports averaging about 15 per cent can be expected during the next ten years in spite of the expanding base. The diversified list of minor exports should continue to expand; mining projects for nickel, gas, and coal may provide important new entries. It may be added, on the optimistic side, that we have only discussed *merchandise* exports; Colombia has hardly begun to explore her potential in the export of services, of which tourism is an obvious example. Service exports, it may be noted, do not receive CATs.

The recent growth of minor exports has witnessed the simultaneous

strengthening of a lobby favoring the continuation of export-promotion policies, still not as potent as the lobbies of coffee growers and import-competing
industries, but growing in distinctiveness and power. That lobby also puts
pressure on public officials to remove barriers to exporting involving social
overhead facilities, such as harbors, and regulated services, such as transport.

Some may find it strange that no further dismantling of the import control
apparatus has been given as a precondition for future minor export expansion.
Such dismantling could, of course, serve as an additional impetus, together
with other policy changes, but Colombian experience, as well as that of other
countries, shows that it is not a sine qua non for export growth. In fact, the
achievement of the 15 per cent target will allow continuation of the gradual
relaxation of import controls, which has been going on since 1967. This
"virtuous circle" of export expansion–import liberalization–more export
growth is the opposite of the vicious circle of export contraction–import
controls–fewer export incentives which dominated many Latin American
economies for about thirty years after the crisis of 1929. In the triggering of
the virtuous circle, export expansion, and not import liberalization, is given
pride of place; launching a massive import liberalization program without a
secure export front can lead to serious setbacks for the whole liberalization
effort, as the 1965–66 Colombian experience shows. Indeed, in retrospect
such experiments, putting the cart before the horse, appear as risky "chicken
games" designed to force the hand of those policymakers reluctant to devalue.
The events of November 1966 showed the limitations of that tactic.

Nor is the creation of firms that are wholly devoted to exporting a
necessary condition for rapid export growth; a gradual increase in the
exported share of many firms from 5 to 10 per cent and then to 20 per cent can
give impressive boosts to exchange earnings, and even a constantly rotating
group of sporadic exporters can achieve meaningful results.

The last chapter contains detailed speculation on the probable role of
minor exports in furthering Colombia's development. Here it will be sufficient
to observe that since the long-term prospects for coffee exports as well as for
concessional capital inflows are mediocre, the availability of machinery and
equipment required for achieving an average growth rate of between 6 and 7
per cent per year during the next ten years will very much depend on
achieving a growth in minor exports of about 15 per cent per year to buyers
who are either efficient suppliers of capital goods or of freely convertible
foreign exchange. Colombian prospects for placing her debt in world capital
markets at commercial terms also depend on the outlook for her current-
account earnings.

Under a relaxed balance-of-payments position, continuing expansionary
fiscal and monetary policies could be instituted. The result would be to
mobilize domestic productive resources which in the past too often remained

idle or underutilized because of stop-go macroeconomic management induced by balance-of-payments crises, even when the domestic activities thus penalized were not heavy users of foreign exchange.

What will this scenario imply for the problem of underemployment and the related issue of a skewed income distribution? The achievement of annual growth rates of 15 per cent for minor exports and 7 per cent for GDP will not automatically result in a lower rate of unemployment or a better income distribution in ten years' time. Remember first that the greater availability of foreign exchange will allow an expansion of machinery and equipment imports. How this enlarged flow is spread out and allocated can make the difference between having more capital-intensive activities, perhaps labor-displacing, or having a large number of new labor-absorbing units. Unless import liberalization and other public policies are formulated that specifically avoid giving incentives to the first type of development, faster growth could conceivably lead to more unemployment or underemployment, particularly in rural areas.

Several minor exports, particularly those going to LAFTA, seem to be quite capital-intensive, and also frequently import-intensive. Their rapid expansion will have little impact on the demand for unskilled labor; indeed, some purely import-substituting activities and most home goods (nontradables) are likely to be less capital-intensive. A gradual "fine-tuning" of export incentive schemes could help correct such a situation by changing the incentive structure without necessarily modifying its average level. Steps in this direction could include, for example, the imposition of a uniform tariff on Vallejo Plan imports, compensated for by an increase in the CAT flat rate or in the upward crawl of the exchange rate. Smaller firms and those whose exports have a higher domestic value-added content will benefit; both are likely to be relatively labor-intensive and involve domestic entrepreneurs to a larger degree. The spread in the effective protection generated by export incentives would also be narrowed.[15] The application of these reforms should, of course, be carried out with extreme care, so that healthy export growth will not be cut off in the process of discarding distorted policies. If nothing else, the imperfect state of knowledge regarding the exact impact on minor exports of each of the various promotion policies makes such caution very advisable.

Even with refined and improved export-promotion and import-allocation policies it is unlikely that the twin targets of 15 and 7 per cent growth for minor exports and GDP will improve Colombian income distribution by very much. By 1973 minor exports had reached between 5 and 6 per cent of GDP; their direct and indirect domestic value added was probably between 4 and 5 per cent of GDP. If such value added also grows by 15 per cent per year during the next ten years, and GDP grows at 7 per cent, by the end of that time direct and indirect value added in minor exporting activities will have reached between 8 and 10 per cent of GDP. So even if all the additional exports were labor-intensive, their net impact on the aggregate demand for unskilled labor would remain, at least for the next ten years, modest. Note also that further expansion of primary-product exports, such as meat, cotton, and sugar, can hardly be counted upon to improve land tenure conditions. In fact, the need to promote exports has already been used as an argument against land reform, particularly in the Cauca Valley and along the Atlantic coast. The relatively high share of coffee output produced in small- and medium-sized farms is not a feature duplicated in most new rural exports.

The major contribution of faster export growth and of a foreign trade sector free of the periodic crises so prevalent before 1967 may very well turn out to be that it gives policymakers the opportunity, which they may or may not grasp, to turn their attention away from the basically unnecessary and superficial balance-of-payments hysterics and toward more important and difficult problems, such as raising the welfare of the poorest half of the population within a reasonably short period of time. That task will require policy measures beyond the manipulation of exchange rates, CATs, tariffs, and such.

NOTES

1. The list of those seduced by the hope of explaining the irregular surge of Colombian minor exports is impressive. It includes John Sheahan and Sara Clark, "The Response of Colombian Exports to Variations in Effective Exchange Rates," Research Memorandum 11, mimeographed (Williamstown, Mass.: Williams College Center for Development Economics, June 1967); Antonio Urdinola and Richard Mallon, "Policies to Promote Colombian Exports of Manufactures," Economic Development Reports 75, mimeographed (paper presented at the Harvard Development Advisory Service Conference, Sorrento, Italy, September 1967); José Diego Teigeiro and R. Anthony Elson, "The Export Promotion System and the Growth of Minor Exports in Colombia," IMF *Staff Papers,* July 1973, pp. 419–470; Alberto R. Musalem, "Las Exportaciones Colombianas, 1956–1969," mimeographed (Universidad de los Andes, May 1970); Richard R. Nelson, T. Paul Schultz, and Robert L. Slighton, *Structural Change in a Developing Economy: Colombia's Problems and Prospects* (Princeton, N.J.: Princeton University Press, 1971), especially pp. 210–213; Jonathan W. Eaton, "Effective Devaluation as an Export Incentive in Less Developed Countries" (B.A. thesis, Harvard University, March 1972), Chap. 6.

2. Many definitions have been put forth for manufactured exports; the one used here simply includes SITC categories 3 (except crude petroleum), 5, 6, 7, and 8. This omits synthetic fibers (SITC 266) while including minerals and ores with little refinement.

3. Data obtained from UNFAO-PY and UNFAO-TY, various issues.

4. Richard C. Porter, "The Birth of a Bill Market," Discussion Paper 11, mimeographed (Center for Research on Economic Development, University of Michigan, August 1970), has analyzed in detail the relationships between the marginal tax and discount rates of a given firm and the extent of the export stimulus offered by CAT and its predecessor subsidy scheme. He shows that both CAT and the exemption scheme yield larger export incentives to firms with higher marginal tax rates and lower discount rates (typically larger firms). However, he argues that

relative to the previous tax exemption, the CAT system increased the export stimulus for firms with marginal tax rates *below* 37.5 per cent and reduced it for firms with higher tax rates.

5. As an illustration, it may be noted that the Colombian PPP-EER for minor exports computed with respect to the German mark rose by 78 per cent between 1960 and 1972, while the equivalent rate with respect to the U.S. dollar rose by only 46 per cent. Indices for both effective rates (1960 = 100) were as follows:

	Based on U.S. Dollar	Based on German Mark		Based on U.S. Dollar	Based on German Mark
1955–59	106	107	1965–69	128	133
1960–64	118	123	1970–72	143	164

6. As noted by my colleague Benjamin I. Cohen, the expansion of import-intensive export activities may soon call for the computation of data for net rather than gross exports, at least for some types of exports, particularly in countries that have gone deeply into export-oriented assembly-type activities with heavy use of imported parts. Part of the addition in import requirements associated with export booms may show up under the service account as trips abroad, and these are likely to multiply, for such reasons (legitimate or spurious) as attendance at fairs, contacts with customers, and searches for new outlets.

7. It can be shown that in a locally monopolized industry selling both at home and abroad, but at different prices, a lowering of import duties can lead to a contraction of exports and an expansion of domestic sales. This apparently paradoxical result, however, is unlikely to have much practical relevance over the long run. The basic argument is developed in an unpublished paper of Gonzalo Giraldo of the Colombian Planning Department. It is similar to the analysis showing that the imposition of a minimum wage can expand employment under conditions of labor monopsony.

8. The advertising is similar to that sponsored sporadically by the Bureau of International Commerce, U.S. Department of Commerce. See, for example, the ad "It took a Texan to cool the Japanese," *Wall Street Journal*, January 26, 1972, p. 11.

9. In earlier work, Durbin-Watson statistics in supply-response regressions were very low. See also Eaton's thesis, mentioned in footnote 1, above.

10. Regressions using untransformed quarterly data, but in logarithmic form and with explicit trend variables, yielded elasticities near 1.0. When trend terms were excluded the elasticities rose to about 2.7 for the whole period. The instability index also performed well in these regressions, and the R^2s were, of course, much higher with trend (around 0.85). The Durbin-Watson statistics, however, were always below 1.0, often less than 0.5. Dummies indicated the presence of significant seasonal factors, particularly a positive factor in the second quarter. As in the work of John Sheahan, referred to in footnote 1, above, the regression coefficients for the lagged exchange rate were insignificant or had the wrong sign.

11. But in ten years' time the increase in minor exports growing at 12.7 per cent per year will be 230.6 per cent. The corresponding figure for an exchange rate growing at 3.7 per cent will be 43.8 per cent. Consequently, while for the annual rates the ratio (elasticity) is 3.4, for the ten-year span it is 5.3.

12. For example, during the difficult year of 1967 industrial output rose by only 3.6 per cent, compared with an average rise of 5.7 per cent for the previous two years. Pure manufactured exports, however, rose by only 4.8 per cent in dollar value during that year, in contrast with an average rise of 21.2 per cent during the previous two years. It is possible that more disaggregated indices of excess capacity would yield better results.

13. See Gary C. Hufbauer, "The Impact of National Characteristics and Technology on the Commodity Composition of Trade in Manufactured Goods," in Raymond Vernon, ed., *The*

Technology Factor in International Trade, Universities–National Bureau Conference 22 (New York: NBER, 1970), pp. 145–231, particularly Table A-2. But see also the comments of Jagdish N. Bhagwati in the same volume, pp. 273–274.

14. See Larry Senger, "General Characteristics, Factor Intensities and Destinations of Minor Colombian Exports" (Senior Essay, Yale University, March 1974), Table VIIIa.

15. These and similar suggestions have been put forth and elaborated by the staff of the Colombian National Planning Department, at least since 1970.

Çhapter 3

Determination and Composition of Merchandise Imports and Their Link to Capital Formation

In this chapter and the three that follow, the focus will be on merchandise imports, with some attention given to service imports. The first steps will be to explore the possibility of measuring an "import function" for the postwar Colombian economy, to examine how imports have been allocated into different categories, and to analyze the crucial link between imports and capital formation. Finally, an over-all look will be taken at the different policy instruments used to repress and manipulate the demand for imports, and at the arguments given for relying on several of these instruments.

In chapters 4, 5, and 6 these instruments will be examined in detail, including tariffs, prior import deposits, the exchange rate, and administrative import controls, emphasizing actual practice during 1970 and 1971, with retrospective looks at the postwar evolution of the different mechanisms for containing imports.

AN AGGREGATE IMPORT FUNCTION

The import function to be estimated is somewhat unusual. Time series for merchandise imports entering Colombia legally cannot be assumed to result solely from the interplay of the ex ante domestic demand for imports, itself the difference between the domestic supply of and demand for importables, and a perfectly price-elastic foreign supply of imports. During most of the period under study, the institutional mechanism of import control explicitly aimed at

80

regulating import permits so that actual imports would be in line with foreign-exchange availability. Such actual and expected availability influenced the amount of import permits granted and, as was seen in Chapter 1, payment crises were blamed on departures from "prudence."

It would seem better, therefore, to seek the implicit average rules of prudence econometrically rather than follow the usual path of making observed imports a function of income and relative prices. Indeed, that usual path is open to serious conceptual criticisms where imports are regulated, as in Colombia. It can be argued that imports in such a case should be considered the independent variable, with income and relative prices both becoming dependent variables.

In what follows, an attempt is made to explain observed annual and quarterly imports as a function of variables which Colombian policymakers typically regarded as proxies for actual and expected foreign-exchange availability, i.e., the level of reserves, expected merchandise exports, and aid.

Why reserves? If the authorities had in mind a desired level of reserves, and always forecasted foreign-exchange earnings exactly, imports would fluctuate with the latter, but would show no correlation with the former. It may be supposed, however, that forecasting is far from perfect, and that unexpected increases or decreases in reserves will be followed by relaxation or tightening of controls, which will be reflected in the level of imports with some lag. The hypothesis is that imports in a given year or quarter will be influenced by the difference between actual and desired central-bank reserves during *previous* years or quarters.

In the regressions that follow, gross central-bank reserves will be used. Earlier experiments showed that gross, rather than net, reserves gave the best fits. This may be due to data problems involved in accurately defining net reserves, but it could reflect a certain type of liquidity preference of central bankers. Desired (gross) reserves were defined in a straightforward and unsophisticated way. Using either occasional public declarations of the government or the actual average ratio of gross reserves to imports for the whole period under study, one obtains an estimate for the desired level of gross reserves amounting to about one-fourth of annual imports, or three months' worth of imports. This relationship has been applied below to actual annual or quarterly imports to calculate desired reserves for each time period. In the annual regressions, only the imports of the previous year were used to calculate desired reserves. If, for example, the average of imports during the previous two years had been used for the calculation a less variable series would have been obtained for desired reserves. No extensive experimentation was carried out on this point either for annual or quarterly regressions, but the assumption of a relatively short memory for exchange-control authorities, going back only about a year, appears to work as well as longer alternatives.

Note that from the time an import license is granted for a commodity to the time the commodity enters Colombia—at which point it is included in our time series—an average of four or five months is said to elapse. Imports of a given time period can then be made to depend on lagged (actual and desired) reserves, avoiding most problems of interdependence, particularly in quarterly regressions.[1]

There are several possible ways of handling expected (nonaid) foreign-exchange earnings, the bulk of which, and probably its most volatile major part, comes from merchandise exports. One way is to use lagged *changes* in reserves as a proxy for these expectations. That approach was tried, yielding on the whole poor results. Another (not tried) would be to rely on lagged changes in coffee prices. In what follows, it was simply assumed that for a given time period, the ex ante guesses of the authorities on average came close to actual, realized merchandise exports. Since there is a lag between the granting and using of import licenses, it should be clear that a given quarter's actual exports can have little direct (Keynesian or monetary) effect on realized imports of that quarter. Therefore, the simultaneous use of imports and exports of the same quarter in a regression need not give rise to identification problems. For the annual observations it is not so easy to dismiss the possibility that exports will influence imports via income or money multipliers; for that case it is necessary to rely primarily on a priori knowledge of how import controls operate and of the chronic (but variable) presence of excess demand for imports.

The inclusion of aid as an independent variable explaining imports in a foreign-exchange–constrained economy seems natural. As the aid variable is based on disbursements, which are in fact typically measured by documentation regarding import flows, the regressions can be viewed as measuring the impact of the other two independent variables on the level of non-aid-financed imports. It was, however, difficult accurately to measure quarterly, as contrasted with annual, aid flows. Repayments of principal were subtracted from gross disbursements to yield net aid used in the regressions. Other capital inflows were excluded from the explanation of imports because it was difficult to separate them for the whole period into those which, like aid, could be considered autonomous and those induced by changes in the import level, and which may be regarded as accommodating, rather than explaining, import fluctuations.

As in the case of minor exports, the over-all conceptual scheme used for measuring aggregate functions has some weaknesses when applied to parts of the import bill. During the period under study there have been, after all, some imports placed under free lists, requiring no prior licenses from control authorities. Recently, imports from Andean countries have been exempted

TABLE 3-1

Recorded Merchandise Imports by Geographical Source, 1957–58 to 1970–72
(per cent of total)

	1957–58	1959–62	1963–66	1967–69	1970–72
United States	59.6	55.2	49.0	47.2	42.3
Canada	2.8	2.9	2.7	2.4	3.0
United Kingdom	4.4	5.6	5.4	5.2	4.6
Japan	1.0	2.8	3.4	4.1	7.2
European Common Market	18.8	18.8	18.1	15.1	18.1
Other industrial Western European	5.8	5.7	5.0	4.7	5.2
Other nonsocialist European	0.7	1.8	4.3	7.3	5.9
Andean Common Market	1.8	1.2	2.3	2.8	4.8
Other LAFTA	0.8	1.0	4.7	6.0	5.3
Central American Common Market	0.3	0.3	0.1	—	0.1
Other Western Hemisphere	2.6	3.2	2.8	1.9	0.9
Socialist	0.5	0.8	1.7	2.6	1.8
Other	0.8	0.7	0.7	0.7	0.8
Total	100.0	100.0	100.0	100.0	100.0

SOURCE: For 1957–69, DANE-ADCE, various issues; for 1970–72, IMF-DOT, various issues.

from quantitative controls. Presumably, these imports are influenced by traditional independent variables, such as relative prices and real incomes. Nevertheless, it remains true that the total import bill was under the control of import authorities who in fact regulated the flow of licenses partly in response to the behavior of unregulated imports. Indeed, the existence and size of a free list was one of the instruments used to control the total import flow.

It is likely that the geographical sources of Colombian imports have been influenced from time to time by the policy instruments used to repress import demand and by the inflow of tied aid, but it is doubtful that such influences have been particularly strong or lasting. More to the point of this chapter, changes in the geographical pattern of imports suggest little about either the past or the future levels of the import bill. Variations in such patterns, shown in Table 3-1, reflect primarily trends regarding the relative competitiveness of industrialized nations, as well as Colombian preferential trade arrangements with other Latin American countries, all of which had led to a fairly diversified import bill in the early 1970s.

TABLE 3-2

Basic Data Used in Annual Import Regressions, 1950–72
(millions of current U.S. dollars)

Year	Merchandise Imports, c.i.f.	Average Gross Reserves in Current Year	Actual Minus Desired Reserves in Previous Year	Net Aid	Merchandise Exports	Actual Imports as Per Cent of Imports Estimated by Eq. 3-1
1950	364.7	122.2	29.6	−4	393.6	95.5
1951	419.0	111.8	31.0	5	483.8	88.7
1952	415.4	140.8	7.0	46	483.0	83.1
1953	546.7	183.4	36.9	22	605.5	90.7
1954	671.8	223.0	46.7	21	669.1	101.1
1955	669.3	157.6	55.0	20	596.7	110.7
1956	657.2	126.0	−9.7	20	551.7	125.8
1957	482.6	165.8	−38.3	9	511.1	105.8
1958	399.9	133.4	45.1	6	460.7	86.5
1959	415.6	186.0	33.4	−3	473.0	91.1
1960	518.6	195.0	82.1	12	464.6	104.5
1961	557.1	142.8	65.3	77	434.8	105.5
1962	540.3	122.2	3.5	80	463.2	104.7
1963	506.0	92.6	−12.9	104	446.7	98.0
1964	586.3	99.8	−33.9	85	548.1	102.4
1965	453.5	82.2	−46.8	79	539.1	82.5
1966	674.3	64.0	−31.2	98	507.6	122.1
1967	496.9	77.6	−104.6	93	509.9	99.1
1968	643.3	115.2	−46.6	131	558.3	103.4
1969	686.0	183.2	−45.6	155	607.4	99.1
1970	754.6	247.0	11.7	160	735.6	88.9
1971	857.5	182.2	58.3	114	686.0	109.1
1972	836.5	238.0	−32.2	181	742.9	98.5

Notes to Table 3-2

SOURCE: Data on imports, exports, and reserves from IMF-IFS. Average gross reserves in current year is the mean of reserves in March, June, September, and December of the current year plus December of the previous year. Actual minus desired reserves are described in the text. Net aid refers to disbursements, as registered in IMF-BOPY, covering long-term loans received by central and local governments as well as those received by the private nonmonetary sector from the IADB, IBRD, IFC, and U.S. government *minus* amortizations of those loans. Data on loans for 1950–55 involved rough estimates of some components.

Regression Results.

Table 3-2 contains data used in the annual regressions and additional data on how the independent variables for reserves and aid were constructed. Using those data, the following result is obtained, where the figures in parentheses are t statistics.

$$M_t = 17.11 + 0.89X_t + 0.65GR_{t-1} + 1.06A_t \qquad (3\text{-}1)$$
$$(0.19) \quad (4.88) \quad (1.81) \qquad (3.05)$$

$$R^2 = 0.80; \; F \text{ statistic} = 25.82; \; DW = 1.93; \text{ observations} = 23$$

where

M_t = merchandise imports in year t

X_t = merchandise exports in year t

GR_{t-1} = actual minus desired reserves in previous year

A_t = net aid in year t

DW = Durban-Watson statistic.

The fit of equation 3-1 is good; from the last column of Table 3-2 it may be seen that it is particularly good for the years since 1966 taken as a whole, during which actual imports averaged 99.7 per cent of predicted imports, and absolute deviations around that mean were relatively small. Nevertheless, adding 1971 and 1972 to the regression lowers the t statistics for the GR_{t-1} coefficient; a regression covering just 1950–70 yields a t statistic of 2.20 for that coefficient. If equation 3-1 is taken as embodying the average rule of thumb followed by prudent import control authorities, its residuals should be of interest and would be subject to runs reflecting persistent departures from prudence. For example, the 1955–56 excesses stand out clearly, and are followed by the 1958 austerity. Similarly, the swing from extreme tightness to liberalization during 1965–66 is also reflected in the residuals. A more perceptive look at these subphases, however, will be obtained from quarterly data.

The coefficients for exports and net aid are not significantly different from 1.0 while the constant term is insignificant, all of which one would expect a priori, given the relative unimportance of service imports. The coefficient for the difference between actual and desired reserves has the expected sign and is significant at the 5 per cent level; it implies that 65 per cent of the excess (or shortfall) in gross reserves during the preceding year is spent on (or withheld from) imports during the current year. Experiments introducing further lags in the GR variable were unsuccessful.[2]

Reliable quarterly data start in 1957; Table 3-3 contains the series used in the following regression:

$$M_t = 62.72 + 0.33X_t + 0.19GR_{t-1} + 1.87A_t \qquad (3-2)$$
$$ (4.48) \quad\; (2.71) \quad\; (2.93) \qquad (6.42)$$

$$R^2 = 0.65; F \text{ statistic} = 37.87; DW = 0.67; \text{observations} = 64$$

The subscript t now refers to a given quarter; GR_{t-1} refers to actual minus desired reserves throughout the previous four quarters. The regression fit is again good; the Durbin-Watson statistic indicates, not surprisingly, the presence of runs above and below the prudent norm.

Regression 3-2, taken literally, suggests that a given quarter's imports are made up of some minimum amount, given by the constant term of about $63 million (contrasted with average quarterly imports of $147 million), plus one-third of that quarter's current exports, plus a multiple of the aid inflow, all adjusted by previous deviations between actual and desired reserves. As the GR_{t-1} variables in equations 3-1 and 3-2 cover a similar time span, while the dependent variable does not, the coefficient for GR_{t-1} in equation 3-2 should be multiplied by four, yielding 0.76, before comparing it to the 0.65 coefficient obtained in 3-1.

The coefficient for net aid in equation 3-2 is higher than the expected 1.0; similar results were also obtained using gross aid. It should be noted that the quarterly aid figures are rough estimates. Nevertheless, an aid coefficient significantly higher than 1.0 may be picking up the effect of aid "leverage" on import liberalization, an avowed policy goal of aid-providers during the period under study. It could also reflect a perverse de facto positive correlation of aid disbursements with good times (compare the figures for 1965 and 1967 with those for earlier and later years).

Experiments introducing seasonal dummy variables, as well as actual minus desired reserves further lagged, yielded insignificant results, but no systematic effort was made to calculate the best reserve lag structure.

The last column of Table 3-3 presents actual imports as percentages of those predicted by equation 3-2. Quarterly import series naturally reflect brief unusual events more clearly than do annual data. Some are interesting for our study, e.g., a temporary closing of the office issuing import permits, as during late in 1962, but other, less relevant events, are also reflected, such as harbor

TABLE 3-3

Basic Data Used in Quarterly Import Regressions, 1957–72
(millions of current U.S. dollars)

Year and Quarter	Merchandise Imports, c.i.f.	Average Actual Minus Desired Gross Reserves in Previous Four Quarters	Net Aid	Merchandise Exports	Actual Imports as Per Cent of Imports Estimated by Eq. 3-2
1957 I	91.5	−38.9	2.3	140.0	86.1
II	98.2	1.8	2.3	117.4	92.3
III	138.9	41.3	2.3	138.2	114.9
IV	148.0	56.4	2.3	124.1	124.3
1958 I	120.9	55.4	1.5	105.7	108.7
II	99.4	24.5	1.5	93.1	98.3
III	89.3	−1.3	1.5	134.3	81.2
IV	90.4	12.4	1.5	119.7	83.9
1959 I	86.3	30.5	−0.8	99.9	86.1
II	107.3	55.4	−0.8	116.0	97.2
III	116.9	74.4	−0.8	139.9	95.9
IV	104.9	78.5	−0.8	117.2	91.1
1960 I	124.3	88.7	3.0	111.3	101.7
II	129.6	86.7	3.0	97.5	110.5
III	134.7	83.6	3.0	122.4	107.8
IV	128.6	77.9	3.0	133.4	100.8
1961 I	124.5	60.7	19.3	101.0	86.5
II	147.9	46.2	19.3	113.4	101.7
III	138.0	20.8	19.3	112.5	98.4
IV	146.7	8.8	19.3	106.5	107.9
1962 I	145.9	−3.3	20.0	99.3	110.0
II	141.6	−15.1	20.0	109.4	105.9
III	147.3	−7.3	20.0	146.8	99.8
IV	105.5	−13.9	20.0	107.8	79.1
1963 I	93.4	−17.3	26.0	87.2	68.1
II	136.6	−11.2	26.0	111.3	93.4
III	139.3	−18.5	26.0	141.5	90.0
IV	136.6	−24.7	26.0	106.1	96.2
1964 I	143.4	−32.0	21.3	127.8	103.1
II	147.6	−40.5	21.3	131.7	106.4
III	156.4	−44.0	21.3	140.1	111.0
IV	138.9	−47.3	21.3	148.5	97.1
1965 I	110.4	−43.6	19.8	119.8	84.2
II	126.9	−41.3	19.8	138.2	92.1
III	111.0	−48.9	19.8	141.6	80.8
IV	105.2	−43.1	19.8	138.2	76.6

TABLE 3-3 (*concluded*)

Year and Quarter	Merchandise Imports, c.i.f.	Average Actual Minus Desired Gross Reserves in Previous Four Quarters	Net Aid	Merchandise Exports	Actual Imports as Per Cent of Imports Estimated by Eq. 3-2
1966 I	140.4	−36.6	24.5	123.8	98.3
II	168.0	−55.4	24.5	140.7	116.0
III	193.4	−67.9	24.5	131.6	138.7
IV	172.4	−91.0	24.5	110.3	134.7
1967 I	149.3	−112.6	23.3	114.1	121.5
II	111.1	−105.8	23.3	129.0	86.0
III	118.1	−85.3	23.3	129.9	88.6
IV	118.5	−61.5	23.3	136.8	84.5
1968 I	157.4	−46.5	32.8	128.4	99.7
II	167.0	−52.0	32.8	140.1	103.9
III	162.7	−55.0	32.8	144.0	100.8
IV	156.2	−50.7	32.8	145.7	96.0
1969 I	133.8	−37.6	38.8	131.5	77.8
II	168.5	−6.7	38.8	168.2	88.7
III	203.1	5.0	38.8	150.6	108.9
IV	180.6	8.4	38.8	157.1	95.4
1970 I	161.8	14.3	40.0	210.4	76.9
II	176.9	34.3	40.0	202.2	83.7
III	209.7	60.9	40.0	175.1	101.1
IV	206.3	75.0	40.0	139.0	104.1
1971 I	228.3	64.8	28.5	161.6	125.3
II	232.2	22.0	28.5	186.0	127.5
III	216.8	−20.6	28.5	166.8	129.3
IV	205.2	−43.9	28.5	171.6	124.5
1972 I	220.0	−44.4	45.2	156.5	115.2
II	190.0	−36.6	45.2	122.0	105.0
III	207.4	−13.8	45.2	225.5	94.4
IV	219.1	10.6	45.2	238.9	95.7

SOURCE: Same as for Table 3-2. Figures in second column computed using end-of-quarter data for four quarters preceding current quarter. Yearly net aid figures were allocated to quarters in four equal parts.

and shipping strikes. Noteworthy runs in actual imports are those of 1958III–1959I (austerity), and the remarkable swings from austerity (1965I–1965IV) to excess (1966II–1967I) and back to austerity (1967II–1967IV).[3] Throughout 1971 and 1972, regression 3-2 underestimates actual imports; it may be conjectured that easier access to world private capital markets, buttressed by a favorable exchange earnings outlook, is changing the Colombian import rules that have applied throughout the postwar period.

UNREGISTERED MERCHANDISE IMPORTS

Given the long Colombian coasts on both the Pacific and Atlantic and its frontiers with Venezuela, Brazil, Peru, Ecuador, and Panama, which add up to more than nine thousand kilometers (more than fifty-six hundred miles) of sea and land borders, coupled with a rigorous import control system, one may wonder whether some merchandise imports escape official registration, control, and taxes.[4]

It is obvious that some smuggling does take place. During August 1971 smuggled foreign cigarettes were openly sold in Bogotá's main avenues, and I was pleasantly startled to find Cuban cigars available in a Cartagena restaurant. Businessmen often tell of sending an employee to Miami to bring back, well hidden in his suitcase, small but critical parts and pieces, which they feel

TABLE 3-4

Ratio of Registered Colombian Imports (c.i.f.) to Exports to Colombia Registered by Other Countries, 1958–69

	World	United States, United Kingdom, and Canada	European Common Market	Other Countries
1958	1.07	1.24	1.09	0.63
1959	1.13	1.16	1.03	1.12
1960	1.13	1.17	1.08	1.02
1961	1.11	1.11	1.08	1.18
1962	1.18	1.20	1.18	1.09
1963	1.03	1.00	1.06	1.08
1964	1.11	1.09	1.11	1.14
1965	1.08	1.07	1.07	1.11
1966	1.07	1.06	1.11	1.05
1967	1.12	1.06	1.18	1.23
1968	1.02	1.01	1.06	1.00
1969	1.03	1.02	1.04	1.04
Averages	1.09	1.10	1.09	1.06

SOURCE: Basic data from IMF-DOT, various issues. The corresponding ratios for the group formed by the United States, the United Kingdom, and Canada during 1948–57 were as follows:

Year	Ratio	Year	Ratio	Year	Ratio
1948	1.17	1951	1.17	1955	1.23
1949	1.09	1952	1.16	1956	1.25
1950	1.09	1953	1.13	1957	1.16
		1954	1.16		

would be unduly delayed or excessively taxed under the import control mechanism. Some cities on the Venezuelan and Ecuadoran borders are well-known centers of two-way unregistered trade. But the extent of such commerce is, of course, difficult to ascertain. Yet for the purpose of this chapter, it is necessary to try to establish at least whether or not unregistered imports invalidate the results obtained by manipulating registered import data.

A first approach will be to compare Colombian official import data with what trade partners claim they have exported to Colombia. This is done, for three broad geographical categories, in Table 3-4. As Colombia reports imports c.i.f., and most countries register their exports f.o.b., a gap of roughly 10 per cent is to be expected between the two sets of figures; and, on average, the gap between the figures for 1958 through 1969 are close to that. There are, however, considerable year-to-year fluctuations and a downward trend if U.S., U.K., and Canadian figures for 1948–57 are compared to those for 1958–

TABLE 3-5

Unregistered Merchandise Imports, c.i.f., 1957–72
(millions of U.S. dollars)

	Border Trade (Imports)	Ships Purchased by Great-Colombian Fleet	Other, Incl. Parcel Post	Border Trade as Per Cent of Recorded Imports
1957	20	5	0	4
1958	20	6	0	5
1959	20	2	0	5
1960	20	3	0	4
1961	20	3	0	4
1962	51	0	0	10
1963	40	0	0	8
1964	50	7	0	9
1965	30	7	−11[a]	7
1966	25	19	0	4
1967	28	4	1	6
1968	33	0	10	5
1969	37	0	10	5
1970	43	0	13	5
1971	39	29	18	4
1972	35	33	17	5

SOURCE: IMF-BOPY, various issues.

a. Refers to military grants, which by international convention are omitted from the balance of payments.

69. A good deal of the year-to-year variation appears to simply reflect statistical difficulties, but some of it can be linked to events in the Colombian payments system. For example, unusual gaps between Colombian and U.S.-U.K.-Canadian data in 1955–56 and 1962 suggest that overinvoicing was used as a means of speculating against an overvalued peso.[5]

Most smuggled merchandise will appear in the official trade figures of neither the importing nor the exporting country, or if they appear in the latter data they will not be allocated correctly among importing countries (i.e., much merchandise apparently sent to Panama and Venezuela may end up in Colombia; note that both Panama and Venezuela have followed relatively liberal import policies). The importance of this trade has prompted "guesstimates" of its value, one of which is presented in Table 3-5. The figures in the second and third columns reflect minor statistical adjustments to import data as reported to the IMF by Colombia; the first column represents an attempt to estimate import smuggling. The "border trade" is estimated to have fluctuated between 4 and 10 per cent of registered imports. Not surprisingly, the high point was reached during troubled 1962, while the estimates for liberal 1966 are much lower. One may speculate that most, but not all, border trade imports involve consumer goods (liquor, cigarettes, radios, watches, and even pornographic materials). But given the orders of magnitude involved it appears that neither the results to be shown in Table 3-7 nor those of earlier regressions would be much changed by inclusion of border trade.

THE ALLOCATION OF OBSERVED MERCHANDISE IMPORTS INTO DIFFERENT CATEGORIES

Since we have derived an over-all import function, it is natural to analyze how that import capacity was distributed among commodity types. Several ways of classifying imports are possible. In this section three subdivisions are used, based on annual data: consumer goods, raw materials and intermediate goods, and capital goods. These data are shown in Table 3-6.

The allocation of imports among these categories will, of course, be influenced by long- and short-term forces. Among the former, import-substituting industrialization looms large, but from the viewpoint of this study, it will be of greater interest to explore hypotheses regarding whether (and how) import control authorities modify import structure on the basis of import capacity.

It is part of the conventional wisdom that during difficult times import control authorities squeeze capital goods first, while trying to maintain the flow of raw materials and intermediate goods. If so, the share of capital goods

TABLE 3-6

**Allocation of Registered Merchandise Imports Among Major Use Categories,
1951–72**

(per cent of total imports, c.i.f.; underlying data in U.S. dollars at current prices)

Year	Consumer Goods Plus Residual Category	Raw Materials and Intermediate Goods	Capital Goods Incl. Construction Materials
1951	13.1	53.6	33.4
1952	11.9	50.8	37.3
1953	16.0	45.7	38.3
1954	18.4	44.6	37.0
1955	14.9	44.8	40.3
1956	9.6	50.0	40.4
1957	9.6	57.6	32.8
1958	8.3	58.7	33.0
1959	7.5	55.7	36.8
1960	7.8	48.8	43.4
1961	10.1	42.4	47.4
1962	9.5	47.8	42.8
1963	8.3	50.5	41.3
1964	8.9	45.9	45.1
1965	8.3	47.4	44.3
1966	8.4	56.8	34.7
1967	9.9	46.0	44.1
1968	9.8	46.4	43.9
1969	11.5	46.0	42.5
1970	12.1	43.7	44.2
1971	11.9	44.8	43.3
1972	13.4	47.6	39.0

SOURCE: BdlR-IAGJD, various issues. Data for 1971 and 1972 refer to import registrations with INCOMEX. Because of the delay in processing customs data, even the BdlR used those INCOMEX data in its annual report for 1972.

in the import bill should be positively related to the level of imports, while that for raw materials and intermediate goods should show an inverse relationship. The latter expectation is confirmed by the results given in Table 3-7, but the former does not emerge as statistically significant, although the sign is the expected one. There is little doubt that the severe import restrictions of 1957–58 were particularly harsh on machinery and equipment imports. However, the regressions for the whole period warn us against generalizing from that experience and from assuming that more liberal import policies will necessar-

TABLE 3-7

Regressions for Shares in the Import Bill of Major Use Categories, 1951–72
(*t* statistics in parentheses)

	Consumer Goods	Raw Materials and Intermediate Goods	Capital Goods
Constant	−53.81	128.54	25.56
	(3.82)	(4.69)	(0.96)
Logarithm of dollar	10.85	−12.66	1.76
import value	(4.71)	(2.83)	(0.41)
Time trend	−0.49	0.43	0.06
	(3.90)	(1.76)	(0.24)
Net aid as per cent	0.13	−0.39	0.26
of all imports	(1.50)	(2.23)	(1.52)
R^2	0.60	0.46	0.37
F statistic	9.11	5.05	3.53
DW	1.63	2.11	1.61
No. of observations	22	22	22

R^2 = coefficient of multiple determination.
DW = Durbin-Watson statistic.
SOURCE: See text. Basic data obtained as in earlier tables of this chapter. The following simple correlation coefficients are of interest:

	Net Aid as Per Cent of All Imports	Log of Dollar Import Value
Share of consumer goods	−0.14	0.39
Share of raw materials and intermediate goods	−0.45	−0.55
Share of capital goods	0.60	0.35
Logarithm of dollar import value	0.43	—

ily lead to a bigger *share* for capital goods imports. Observe how in 1966 that share fell as imports rose dramatically. A positive link between the share of consumer goods and import levels, however, can be established with confidence for the whole period.

In countries with weak machinery and equipment industries, aid flows, designed partly to promote investment, can be expected to influence the share of capital goods in total imports. Such influence need not be dollar for dollar; for example, food aid that supports a shift of agricultural workers to construction projects can contribute to capital formation even though it has no direct impact on imports of capital goods. But typically, a link can be expected; this is indeed the case for Colombia, as shown in Table 3-7. Indeed, the most significant coefficient in the regression explaining the share of capital goods in the import bill is that for net aid.

The trend for the share of consumer goods in all imports is clearly downward, matched by a rising trend for raw materials and intermediate goods.

IMPORTS AND CAPITAL FORMATION

In Chapter 1, I noted the clear and strong link that has existed in Colombia between foreign trade and capital formation, contrasting it with the weaker (short-term) correlation between changes in GDP or manufacturing output and trade conditions.[6] The link between foreign trade and capital formation does not involve subtle and mysterious relationships between exports (or terms of trade) and propensities to save. The matter is much simpler. During 1950–54 imported commodities accounted for 94 per cent of Colombian gross investment in machinery and equipment; by 1971–72 that share was still a remarkable 68 per cent in spite of rapid growth in the local output of machinery and equipment. During the period under study Colombian investment other than construction could hardly be realized, at least during a longish medium term, without a matching capacity to import. Coffee and, later, aid and minor exports were the basis of nonconstruction capital formation. Note that nothing in the argument assures us that the flow of imported capital goods will be assigned wisely or used fully; therefore, even in the long run no rigid link need exist between growth and the capacity to import. Indeed, it can be argued that periods of import bonanza may lead to a careless allocation of investment, while austerity strengthens the hand of cost-benefit analysts. But without substantial import capacity, even heroic ex ante savings decisions are likely to be frustrated before ever becoming tangible in ex post nonconstruction investments.

The capital formation–import link is documented in Table 3-8, where imports and a time trend appear as the independent variables. The link emerges quite clearly from these regressions; one can discount part of the excellence of the fit on grounds of national accounting methodology without losing the main conclusion.

The elasticity of real gross investment in machinery and equipment with respect to merchandise imports is not significantly different from 1.0; that for all investment emerges as slightly below 1.0. Even investment in construction shows some significant elasticity with respect to imports, although its trend

TABLE 3-8

Links Between Capital Formation and Imports:
Regression Results, 1950–72
(*t* statistics in parentheses; all variables except trend are in logarithms)

	Building and Construction	Machinery and Equipment	All Gross Fixed Domestic Capital Formation	Imports of Capital Goods (national accounts)
Constant	5.24	0.64	3.64	−0.02
	(8.95)	(0.88)	(8.67)	(0.02)
All recorded merchandise imports	0.32	1.12	0.72	1.22
	(3.31)	(9.33)	(10.34)	(9.46)
Time trend	0.041	−0.002	0.020	−0.020
	(12.09)	(0.37)	(8.06)	(4.36)
R^2	0.95	0.87	0.96	0.82
F statistic	174.50	69.51	233.43	47.05
DW	1.24	2.11	2.60	2.13
No. of observations	23	23	23	23

R^2 = coefficient of multiple determination.
DW = Durbin-Watson statistic.
SOURCE: Time series on gross investment and imports of capital goods in constant 1958 Colombian pesos from BdlR-CN, including unpublished estimates. Current-dollar value of merchandise imports from IMF-IFS. All gross fixed domestic capital formation is the sum of building and construction plus machinery and equipment.

variable, as expected, shows a heftier *t* statistic than that for machinery and equipment. The Durbin-Watson statistics for the construction regressions also suggest that important independent variables have been left out in the explanation of that type of investment, a fact we know from Chapter 1.

As import quantity indices are available only with a long lag, the regressions shown in Table 3-8 were estimated using current-dollar values for recorded imports. The trend coefficients, therefore, particularly the coefficient for machinery and equipment, reflect two offsetting forces: a positive one arising from the fast growth in local production of capital goods, and a negative one arising from the upward creep in dollar prices paid by Colombia for imports, which may be estimated at about 2 per cent per year during the period under study.

In the last column of Table 3-8, the time series for imports of capital goods used in the BdlR national accounts is compared with total imports. Here, in apparent contrast to the results presented earlier (Table 3-7), the elasticity of capital goods imports with respect to import levels is greater than 1.0, but the level of significance of this result is not sufficiently high to change my earlier conclusion of proportionality, excluding trend and aid flows.

The fits obtained in Table 3-8 could be further improved by making investment depend not on total imports, but only on imports of capital goods. Such refinement, however, seems unnecessary and even inelegant given the proportionality conclusion and the national accounts methodology. Finally, it may be noted that the rapid growth observed for the whole period in the domestic production of machinery and equipment suggests that in the future the link between imports and capital formation will be less tight than in the past.

POLICY INSTRUMENTS USED TO REPRESS IMPORTS

The import function estimated earlier in this chapter emphasized the power of authorities to limit imports according to foreign-exchange availabilities. The mechanisms used specifically to contain imports have been mainly four: the tariff, prior import deposits, the exchange rate applicable to imports, and import licensing. Other more general policy variables, such as credit, have also been manipulated for the purpose of containing imports, often at the expense of growth. The focus of the next three chapters will be on just the four specific mechanisms listed, leaving the discussion of interactions between trade and macroeconomic policies for chapters 7 and 8.

Since the Great Depression, the typical assumption of Colombian policymakers has been that the imports demanded by the public would exceed the foreign exchange available to finance them. At the exchange rates, tariffs, and other import charges which prevailed during most of the period, this was indeed the case; so available foreign exchange ended up being rationed also by the system of exchange and import licensing. The burden carried by each of the rationing mechanisms, as the authorities struggled to bring the demand for imports into line with exchange availabilities, changed from year to year, and there has been a constantly fluctuating mix of those four instruments since World War II. In retrospect, the authorities appear to have had a vague desire to avoid having any single instrument bear an excessive burden in the task of repressing imports. In other words, when pressures on the licensing authorities became great, i.e., when delays and rejections of import and exchange license requests rose above some tolerable level, there was a tendency to devalue the import exchange rate, or to raise tariffs and surcharges, or to increase prior import deposits. On the other hand, if the exchange rate was considered adequate, surges in import demand tended to be met by tighter licensing procedures, higher duties, or higher prior import deposits.

Much of this balancing among instruments was done "by ear," and in different ways according to the types of imports. As a result, it is difficult to trace historically the import-repressing weight carried by each policy in a given year. It is clear, however, that the ultimate weapon, not always brought into play at the opportune time, was import and exchange licensing, based, in turn, on actual and expected exchange availability. It is also clear that in practically all years under study (1950–72), the import and exchange controls had a certain bite, in the sense that the exchange rate, tariffs, and import deposits left an ex ante demand for imports higher than what the authorities thought could be financed.

The reasons given in Colombia for relying on a variety of import-repressing mechanisms rather than just one (e.g., the exchange rate, perhaps coupled with a uniform across-the-board tariff) are several. The most interesting relate to the instability of the world coffee market and to the consequent burden of adjustment expected to fall on Colombia. Assume that Colombia is a price taker in the international coffee market and that there is just one flexible exchange rate. Without a licensing mechanism, and with domestic full employment policies, a sudden and unexpected drop in world coffee prices will lead to a devaluation, while an increase will lead to an appreciation of the exchange rate. It has been argued by many influential Colombians that even in the medium run, price elasticities are such that without the licensing mechanism, the exchange rate must fluctuate as much as world coffee prices.[7] The shifting of resources in and out of the import-competing and export sectors would have unfavorable effects on welfare, while asymmetrical reactions to devaluation and appreciation, it is further argued, would also impart an inflationary bias to the economy. Exchange-rate instability reflecting the instability in world coffee prices would tend to destroy the "moneyness" of the Colombian peso.

The holding of much larger Colombian foreign-exchange reserves would be an alternative to a totally flexible exchange rate, but it has been argued that import and exchange licensing coupled with a moderate reserve level is a cheaper and safer way of tackling the instability problem. The possibility that either domestic or foreign speculators would take up the whole burden of offsetting gyrations in coffee prices or exchange rates is not taken very seriously (with good reason).

Note that in this argument import and exchange licensing are closely interlinked, a lesson painfully learned during 1956–58. Granting import licenses freely and holding back later on permits to buy foreign exchange obviously lead to a piling up of commercial arrears and to the transformation of private debts to suppliers into national foreign debt as the external credit of the country is damaged by payment delays and pressure is exerted by foreign creditors on Colombian authorities. There are, of course, other reasons for maintaining exchange controls, particularly regulating the capital account of the balance of payments and, also, some service items in the current account, particularly profit and royalty remittances. Furthermore, there is in Colombia, as elsewhere, skepticism regarding the effectiveness of prices in regulating quantities demanded; in particular, the long duration of import controls and ill-fated brief liberalization attempts have generated the myth of an irrepressible import and exchange demand that cannot be curbed except by the imposition of extravagant prices.

NOTES

1. The definition of desired reserves makes one of the independent variables, actual minus desired reserves, partly a function of the lagged dependent variable. In the determination of desired reserves the import level is best viewed as a proxy for the expected level of payments imbalances.

2. The (economic) expectation was that proper specification of the lags would yield coefficients for the GR variables adding up closer to 1.0, but that expectation could not be realized econometrically.

3. Given a priori knowledge regarding import licensing during these runs, a case could be made for introducing different dummy variables for these periods, thereby improving the regression results. But little of substance would be gained by such a procedure.

4. The Colombian islands of San Andrés, off the coast of Nicaragua in the Caribbean, have free-port privileges. Heavy tourist traffic between these islands and the Colombian mainland adds to the smuggling possibilities. The existence of the free port of Leticia plus the export zones mentioned in Chapter 2 adds to the worries of those charged with controlling inward smuggling.

5. Thus, some of the departures from prudence detected in the first part of this chapter should be interpreted broadly, to include excesses in the licensing of imports, capital exports, or both.

6. In a correlation of year-to-year percentage changes in real GDP ($\widehat{GDP}$) and manufacturing output ($\widehat{MA}$) with those for the dollar value of merchandise imports ($\widehat{M}$), during the same year (t), and the year before ($t - 1$), the following results were obtained for the period from 1951 through 1972:

$$(\widehat{GDP})_t = 4.74 + 0.04\hat{M}_t + 0.01\hat{M}_{-1}$$
$$\quad\quad (14.39) \quad (2.70) \quad\quad (0.65)$$

$$R^2 = 0.28$$

$$(\widehat{MA})_t = 6.30 + 0.04\hat{M}_t + 0.001\hat{M}_{-1}$$
$$\quad\quad (15.22) \quad (2.13) \quad\quad (0.06)$$

$$R^2 = 0.20$$

If the value of imports in year t relative to import levels during $t - 1$, $t - 2$, and $t - 3$ is used as the independent variable, similarly weak results are obtained. Both types of regression show that while there *is* a significant link between import and output growth, the constant terms account for most of the GDP and manufacturing year-to-year growth. See also the interesting article by Alberto Corchuelo R. and Luis Bernardo Florez E., "El Sector Externo y las Fluctuaciones de Corto Plazo de la Economía," in DANE-BME, November 1971, pp. 9–21.

7. Consider the following Colombian-like situation before and after a 20 per cent drop in world coffee prices, assuming no change in the quantity of coffee exports:

	Before	After
Coffee exports	$400	$320
Other exports	150	180
Imports	550	500

To bring about the increase in other exports and the contraction of imports, assuming a supply price elasticity of 1.0 for other exports and of about -0.45 in the price elasticity of import demand, a 20 per cent devaluation in the noncoffee exchange rate would be required, assuming no increase in the prices of home goods. These arguments assume that stabilizing speculation is limited in both the coffee and the foreign-exchange markets.

Chapter 4

Tariffs, Prior Deposits, and the Import Exchange Rate

In this chapter and the next two, I will go into some detail on the mechanics of the different import-restraining policy instruments. Emphasis will be placed on how they operated in about 1971, with retrospective glances whenever data warrant them. These chapters will be largely descriptive, leaving a good share of the discussion on the effects of these policy instruments on resource allocation, growth, income distribution, employment, and national autonomy for Chapter 8. Both economically and bureaucratically, the several import-repressing mechanisms overlap and interact; so it will not be either possible or desirable to discuss each mechanism in isolation from all the others, i.e., to omit all references to, say, import controls when discussing tariffs.

THE TARIFF

The universal debate between protectionists and free traders took Colombian root quite early in the nineteenth century and, as elsewhere, has never been resolved.[1] Historically, transport costs from the Colombian coasts to its central highlands, where a large share of the population lives, have been high, providing a significant but declining natural protection for some areas of the country. On the other hand, because of these high transport costs, enterprises located in regions near the Atlantic coast or the banks of the Magdalena river found it more convenient to import manufactures from Europe or North America than to buy them from the struggling craftsmen and infant industries of the highlands.[2]

100

It has been argued conventionally that the primary function of the Colombian tariff during the 1920s was to provide the central government with revenue.[3] A completely new tariff schedule was adopted in 1931, using the balance of payments as a partial justification. For a *sample* of nontraditional industries, David Chu has found that although Colombian nominal tariffs rose between 1927 and 1936, the median level of effective protection fell slightly, from 19 to 17 per cent in ad valorem equivalents. The ranking of industries according to the level of effective protection also changed little between those two dates, but perhaps enough to stimulate some leading industrial sectors. The average of nominal tariff rates for all imports was 23 per cent in 1927, 25 per cent in 1936, and 15 per cent in 1945. As prices rose during the Second World War, the 1931 tariff modifications, based on specific taxes, became less effective, and multiple exchange rates were introduced in part as an alternative to tariffs.

Major revisions of the tariff schedule took place again in 1951 and in 1959; both of them were protectionist in intent.[4] Average nominal duties, in ad valorem equivalents, for items not on the prohibited list were 17 per cent in the 1951 tariff and 48 per cent in the 1959 tariff. The tariff increase was greater for manufactured consumer goods, rising from 18 to 53 per cent in ad valorem equivalents, than for intermediate inputs into industry, which rose from 22 to 40 per cent. The tariff at both dates included specific as well as ad valorem duties; as late as 1962, 30 per cent of the value of assessed tariffs came from specific duties.[5]

In December 1964 a new tariff schedule was decreed, adopting the Brussels nomenclature (BNM) and containing only ad valorem duties. However, since that date, and acting under special powers, the government introduced a bewildering number of changes in the tariff, particularly during the import liberalization episode of 1965–66 and again in 1968–71. The duty rates on many items have been changed several times between 1964 and 1971, under special laws by which Congress granted the Executive, or the latter assumed, the power to carry out such changes without detailed congressional approval, but for limited periods of time. Merely between January 1965 and December 1966, it is estimated that nearly one thousand tariffs were changed (mostly increases); there were also temporary surcharges, for three or four years, on many consumer goods and even on intermediate and capital goods aimed at smoothing the liberalization process. The power of the Executive to carry out such changes without congressional approval expired in 1971, but the government quickly requested from Congress a new general law allowing frequent (although limited) rate changes. The process of selecting which duties were to be changed, and by how much, has remained somewhat of a mystery even to close observers of the committee on tariff policy, which has been responsible for tariff modifications.

TABLE 4-1

Import Duties Collected as Percentages of Peso Value of Merchandise Imports and of Central Government Tax Revenues, 1943–72

Year	Ratios of Duties to Imports	Ratios of Duties to Central Govt. Tax Revenues	Year	Ratios of Duties to Imports	Ratios of Duties to Central Govt. Tax Revenues
1943	14.8%	26.1%	1958	7.6%	13.5%
1944	14.9	24.4	1959	13.6	22.4
1945	14.7	29.2	1960	16.6	29.2
1946	12.2	27.2	1961	15.1	28.2
1947	10.3	26.1	1962	14.1	26.9
1948	10.0	20.8	1963	12.6	19.2
1949	8.3	13.5	1964	12.7	16.7
1950	12.7	21.2	1965	15.0	15.9
1951	21.8	36.8	1966	22.5	31.9
1952	18.9	32.1	1967	15.1	15.2
1953	18.3	35.7	1968	13.1	15.9
1954	20.0	36.9	1969	14.1	15.5
1955	16.1	25.8	1970	17.3	19.0
1956	13.4	20.6	1971	15.4	16.5
1957	9.4	17.7	1972	14.6	15.9

SOURCE: Basic data from DANE-AGDE, various issues, and BdlR-RdBdlR, various issues.

During 1973 and early 1974 a large number of duties were reduced, partly to offset increases in the world price level and partly to fight smuggling. About 2,500 tariff items were changed. Colombia has also been following the tariff reduction timetable of the Andean Common Market, applicable to trade among the members and calling for annual cuts in segments of ten percentage points from a base no higher than 100 per cent, starting on December 31, 1971.

A first attempt at quantification of the impact of the tariff is presented in Table 4-1, showing the de facto "average tariff" (first column) and the share of central government tax revenues accounted for by duties collected over the years from 1943 through 1972. The most striking feature of the data in this table is the repeated pattern of gradual declines followed by abrupt increases in both percentages without any obvious over-all trend for the whole period. The abrupt increases (in 1951, 1959–60, and 1965–66) coincide with tariff reforms. The unusually high tariff revenues in 1966 are also partly accounted for by increased imports of automobiles, which even at rates lower than those of earlier years yielded substantial sums.

The course of the average tariff (duties collected as a percentage of import values) from 1951 through 1972 can be quite well explained statistically as a function not only of years elapsed since the last major tariff reform but also of the level and composition of imports. The best results of attempts at explanation are presented in Table 4-2. It can be argued that after adjustment is made for years elapsed since the last major tariff reform as indicated by the always significant dummy, remaining increases in the average tariff reflect import liberalization. Thus, there is a significant and positive link between the average tariff and the level of imports whether measured in absolute or in relative terms. Significant links also exist with the share of consumer goods in the import bill (positive, because these goods are taxed at above-average rates) and with that of capital goods (negative, because these goods are taxed below the average). No such links were found with the share for raw materials and intermediate products. These conclusions are also supported by a regression (not shown) of the average tariffs as a function of the shares of consumer, intermediate, and capital goods in the import bill, without a constant term. The respective average tariffs estimated for each of those groups according to this regression are 72, 10, and 7 per cent; but only the coefficient for the share of consumer goods has a t statistic larger than 2.0.

It may be thought that the gradual erosion in tariff revenues following reforms may be due to the presence of specific duties within a worldwide inflationary setting. The pattern, however, has been present even following the 1965 conversion of all duties into ad valorem rates. A more plausible and general explanation for the power of the dummy in Table 4-2 is the tendency for tariff reform to involve, for fiscal reasons, an increase in the rates charged to intermediate and capital goods, plus those on a few luxury consumer durables, as well as a tightening of loopholes and abolition of ad hoc exemptions. On balance, these measures, which are favored by the Treasury, lower the effective protective rates for most existing industries, since in most cases direct competitors are kept out by prohibitions and the licensing mechanism. As a result, shortly after its inception the reform faces a relentless gnawing by special interests, who seek lower input rates and exemptions, until that process goes so far as to arouse fresh demands for tariff reforms.

Table 4-3 shows estimates based on a sample of products for the extent of exemptions from import duties shortly after the tariff reform of December 1964. In the key categories "other intermediate goods" and "other capital goods," making up nearly 60 per cent of all sampled imports, the gradual expansion of exemptions can be seen. Besides the Vallejo Plan, discussed in Chapter 2, other total or partial exemptions include those relating to imports from Andean and other LAFTA sources, those for "basic industries" (e.g., sulphur, pig iron, coal, chemical pulp, fishing, etc.), imports for the public sector, imports financed with AID credits, plus other ad hoc exemptions.

TABLE 4-2

Regressions for Import Duties Collected as Percentages of Peso Value of Merchandise Imports, 1951–72

(t statistics in parentheses)

	(1)	(2)	(3)	(4)
Constant	−27.81	−42.64	5.39	11.37
	(2.15)	(3.42)	(2.60)	(3.51)
Dummy for tariff reform	−1.37	−1.57	−0.78	−0.73
	(6.58)	(7.48)	(4.65)	(4.99)
Logarithm of dollar value	6.76	11.82		
of imports	(3.10)	(5.42)	—	—
Relative import level	—	—	0.10	0.12
			(4.34)	(7.84)
Share of consumer goods	0.45	—	0.14	—
in imports	(2.91)		(0.86)	
Share of capital goods in	—	−0.29	—	−0.17
imports		(2.85)		(2.29)
R^2	0.77	0.77	0.83	0.86
F statistic	20.50	20.14	29.33	37.80
DW	2.06	1.51	1.48	1.42
No. of observations	22	22	22	22

R^2 = coefficient of multiple determination.
DW = Durbin-Watson statistic.
SOURCE: Basic data as in tables 3-2, 3-4, and 4-1. The dummies for tariff reform are as follows:

1951 = 0	1959 = 0.5	1966 = 1
1952 = 1	1960 = 1.5	1967 = 2
1953 = 2	1961 = 2.5	1968 = 3
1954 = 3	1962 = 3.5	1969 = 4
1955 = 4	1963 = 4.5	1970 = 5
1956 = 5	1964 = 5.5	1971 = 6
1957 = 6	1965 = 0	1972 = 7
1958 = 7		

Relative import level refers to total imports of a given year divided by the average imports during the previous three years, with the result multiplied by 100.

TABLE 4-3

Duties Collected, Dutiable Imports, and All Imports, by Use Categories, 1965–67

Category	Duties Collected as Per Cent of Dutiable Imports in Each Category			Dutiable Imports as Per Cent of All Imports in Each Category			Aver. Share of Each Category in All Sample Imports, 1965–67
	1965	1966	1967	1965	1966	1967	
Automobiles	228	51	85	71	71	71	2.2
Other consumer goods	28	28	24	81	84	70	3.4
Foodstuffs	20	10	17	99	9	22	4.2
Other raw materials	14	15	17	100	100	100	4.1
Intermediate goods for agriculture	3	13	6	99	100	100	2.0
Other intermediate goods	17	25	24	93	93	88	34.0
Transportation equipment	23	42	27	90	85	74	6.0
Capital goods for agriculture	3	8	5	80	82	78	3.1
Other capital goods	17	13	16	61	57	48	24.8
Unclassified	20	49	12	62	87	63	16.2
Total sample	19	28	22	79	79	70	100.0

SOURCE: Unpublished estimates of DANE and Contraloría (Colombian Office of the Comptroller), based on a sample of different types of imports. Average duties for all imports in this table, therefore, need not coincide with those in Table 4-1.

These are not always automatic; many require applications that are subject to review and approval. By 1967, 30 per cent of all imports were exempted from duties; more than half of nonagricultural capital goods imports were tariff-free. A rough estimate places exempted imports at 33 per cent of the total in 1969.

Other tariff loopholes arise from the practice of levying different rates for the same product, depending on its final use. For example, a much lower duty will be levied on an automobile which allegedly is to be used as a taxi ("public service") than an identical car imported for private use. That is why one finds cars painted as taxis which do not seem to stop for any customer. That practice also lends itself to the setting up of special tariff subcategories benefiting powerful interests; the knowledgeable can tell why input X bears a tariff of only 10 per cent if used in producing product Y, while bearing one of 50 per cent "for other industries." Clearly, the tariff is not a purely independent variable in the Colombian socioeconomic system.

It will be seen in Chapter 5 that the import control authority can grant "global licenses" covering several items making up a factory or a productive unit. When such a license is obtained, the importer will pay a single tariff rate on the value of the whole group of commodities. The duty will be the one for the "key machine" in the productive unit. As the importer has the option of seeking a global license or a sequence of ordinary ones, often the global license is requested when the "key machine" carries a low duty and the peripheral items higher ones. The committee supervising tariff policy can also grant a low ad hoc tariff rate to some global licenses.

To obtain a more detailed and yet manageable view of the Colombian tariff structure as it stood in about 1971–73, the rates for a sample of 125 important products, first chosen for 1962 by Santiago Macario,[6] have been analyzed. This will allow us, inter. alia, to examine net changes occurring between 1962 and 1973. The regime to which each of the products was subjected in the import control mechanism, i.e., whether it was placed on the free, prior license, or prohibited list, was noted. These three lists will be examined in the next chapter; the free list covers commodities for which no prior license was needed, while the prohibited list includes those for which the import ban was absolute, *unless* they were imported under the Vallejo Plan or for other very restricted purposes. The import duties listed for the prohibited category are thus not totally unimportant, as the deposit which Vallejo Plan users must make with the government as guarantee that those imports will be used exclusively for exporting is related to the size of the duties for the "prohibited" items. Finally, the 1971 prior import deposit for each product was also recorded. This information is summarized in Table 4-4; note that since it is based on rates and information read off the tariff books, it refers to nonexempt items.

Consider first the tariff as it stood in 1971. On the whole, the rates look quite "reasonable," particularly for items not on the prohibited list. There are few extravagantly high duties. As shown in Chapter 2, however, the tariff schedule *by itself* is capable of generating very high ERPs which fluctuate a good deal among activities. It may be seen in Table 4-4 that duties on industrial raw materials, capital goods, and semimanufactured products were substantially lower than those for processed foodstuffs and all kinds of consumer goods. The average duties for industrial raw materials and capital goods on the prior license list are 16–26 per cent, a level which at best is unlikely to exceed by very much the degree of overvaluation of the peso.

The simple mean of the duties in 1971 for the 367 items that make up Chapter 84 of the Colombian tariff (nonelectrical machinery) is 27 per cent, which is similar to that for capital goods in the sample. The corresponding figure for the 161 items of Chapter 85 (electrical machinery) is somewhat higher, 38 per cent, but this chapter includes many consumer goods.

Francisco Thoumi has called attention to another feature of the tariff—

TABLE 4-4

**Colombian Duties and Other Restrictions on Selected
Nonexempt Imports from Non-LAFTA Sources,
1962, 1971, and 1973**
(standard deviations in parentheses)

Import	Ad Valorem Duties (Per Cent)			Ad Valorem Prior Import Deposits (Per Cent)		Number of Items in Group Subject to Each Regime		
	1973	1971	1962	1973	1971	1973	1971	1962
Unprocessed foodstuffs	53	53	185	67	96	13	13	13
	(29)	(29)	(217)	(44)	(54)			
Prohibited	69	64	272	100	130	7	8	8
Prior license	34	35	23	29	40	6	5	4
Free list	—	—	145	—	—	0	0	1
Industrial materials	18	19	35	53	72	10	10	10
	(12)	(16)	(32)	(50)	(59)			
Prohibited	44	44	72	100	130	1	1	3
Prior license	15	16	20	48	66	9	9	3
Free list	—	—	19	—	—	0	0	4
Capital goods	31	26	19	27	32	27	27	27
	(21)	(16)	(15)	(30)	(36)			
Prohibited	—	—	30	—	—	0	0	1
Prior license	33	26	26	30	35	23	24	12
Free list	23	25	12	8	7	4	3	14
Semimfd. products (incl. processed fuels), other than products of traditional industries	27	27	27	50	67	32	32	32
	(17)	(16)	(37)	(41)	(51)			
Prohibited	29	29	200	100	130	2	2	1
Prior license	26	27	23	45	63	26	25	14
Free list	28	27	19	58	58	4	5	17
Processed foodstuffs	90	91	341	95	116	14	14	14
	(53)	(51)	(326)	(19)	(28)			
Prohibited	102	100	426	100	120	9	9	10
Prior license	69	74	90	86	110	5	5	3
Free list	—	—	250	—	—	0	0	1
Durable consumer goods	74	80	108	90	97	11	11	11
	(40)	(26)	(31)	(30)	(39)			
Prohibited	—	84	114	—	100	0	1	4
Prior license	74	79	93	90	96	11	10	6
Free list	—	—	175	—	—	0	0	1

TABLE 4-4 (*concluded*)

Import	Ad Valorem Duties (Per Cent)			Ad Valorem Prior Import Deposits (Per Cent)		Number of Items in Group Subject to Each Regime		
	1973	1971	1962	1973	1971	1973	1971	1962
Other consumer goods (incl. semimfd. products of traditional	87	87	163	80	99	17	17	17
industries)	(66)	(66)	(145)	(36)	(47)			
Prohibited	142	142	247	100	130	6	6	10
Prior license	62	62	44	75	90	10	10	4
Free list	—	—	45	1	1	1	1	3
Total	49	49	104	60	75	124	124	124
	(44)	(44)	(174)	(43)	(52)			
Prohibited	94	91	265	100	126	25	27	37
	(62)	(58)	(247)	(0)	(11)			
Prior license	40	39	39	52	64	90	88	46
	(31)	(31)	(32)	(42)	(50)			
Free list	23	24	31	29	35	9	9	41
	(17)	(16)	(50)	(41)	(55)			

SOURCE: Data for 1962, as well as the classification scheme and product list, were obtained from Santiago Macario, "Protectionism and Industrialization in Latin America," *Economic Bulletin for Latin America*, March 1964, pp. 61–101. Data for 1971 (September) were obtained from República de Colombia, *Arancel de Aduanas* (Bogotá: Alfonso Valderrama A., 1971). Data for 1973 (March) were obtained from ibid. (Bogotá: Gustavo Ibarra Merlano, 1973).

All figures shown are simple arithmetic averages. When an item (say, forklifts) had been subdivided into more than two classes, each with its own duty or prior deposit, sometimes determined not by the *nature* of the product but by its *final use,* a simple average of all the classes was taken. (In several cases there were large differences among the duties averaged.) When a given item had been subdivided into just two classes, only the duty applied to the class judged most common was recorded. In cases of subdivision, the predominant import regime was recorded. In all cases of doubt, the more liberal regime was used.

Import duties include the standard ad valorem rates plus consular fees and across-the-board surcharges. During 1971, the fees and surcharges amounted to 4 per cent ad valorem: consular fees were 1 per cent ad valorem, and the surcharges for financing PROEXPO and the Coffee Fund were 1½ per cent each.

Promotion laws exempt many imports from all duties, but this is not taken account of in the table.

which frequently makes it more protectionist than it appears at first sight, and always more distortive—involving the treatment of used goods, particularly used durable consumer goods. Many second-hand goods are valued when imported as if they were new, on the feeble grounds that otherwise valuation would be difficult to ascertain exactly, thus allegedly opening the door to all sorts of "irregularities." The tariff legislation explicitly states, for example, that used automobiles are to be valued at the prices they had when they came fresh from the factory. When these regulations are applied to capital goods not produced in Colombia, they tend to reduce the effective protection given to their users, while discouraging a more efficient use of the nation's available foreign exchange (and probably of its labor force also).

There appear to be at least two conflicting considerations in establishing interactions between tariffs and import controls. On the one hand "essentials" tend to be treated more leniently by both instruments, while "luxuries" are penalized by both, as evidenced by the mostly redundant high duties on items on the prohibited list. On the other hand, some attempts have been made, particularly during 1965–66, to raise tariffs on items on the free list, consciously coordinating the use of both tariffs and import controls. While that coordination is assured on paper, the facts are that tariffs and import control regimes are each set by a different bureaucratic organization. As a result, except during periods of major policy changes, when high-ranking authorities are very conscious of this issue, each policy variable is handled without much regard to how the other is being manipulated.

As a member of the Andean Common Market, Colombia has agreed to bring its tariff schedule in line with the Andean *Minimum* Common External Tariff (AMCET) by 1975 and to adopt the Andean Common External Tariff (ACET) by 1980. The AMCET, agreed upon by the member countries in December 1970, is in fact fairly close to the Colombian tariff schedule, but with a lower average tariff and less spread.[7] It is far from clear, however, what the final ACET will look like.

The net changes in the tariff between 1962 and 1971–73, according to Table 4-4, may be summarized as follows: a lowering of average rates, mainly by the reduction of very high rates for items on the prohibited list, and a narrowing of the spread of duties, not only by the elimination of extravagantly high ones but also by the increase of very low ones. This may be seen more clearly in Table 4-5: by 1971–73, duties had on average fallen on those items which in 1962 had duties of 40 per cent or more; at the same time, duties were on the whole higher on those items which in 1962 had duties of less than 40 per cent. These changes are more dramatic among goods which in 1962 had duties above 99 per cent and below 20 per cent. By 1973, of the 124 sampled items, 71 per cent had duties within the range from 20 per cent to 70 per cent; in 1962, that percentage was only 42 per cent. This information is complemented by the data in Table 4-6, which shows that the most arithmetically significant tariff cuts occurred among items that were on the prohibited list both in 1962 and 1971, and that there were less extensive cuts in the items transferred from the 1962 prohibited list to the 1971 prior license list. Duties were raised on the few items which were on the free list both in 1962 and 1971.

The trend between 1962 and 1971–73, then, has been toward a rationalization of the tariff and a diminution of its distorting effects. The changes of the

TABLE 4-5

Average Ad Valorem Duties of Selected Imported Products in 1962, 1971, and 1973, Grouped by Their 1962 Duties

	Average Duties for Group of Same Products			Number of Products in Each Group		
Level of 1962 Duties	1962	1971	1973	1962	1971	1973
100% and higher	276%	87%	87%	38	16	14
70% to 99%	81	54	49	9	7	8
40% to 69%	48	38	38	13	30	32
20% to 39%	27	26	30	30	41	48
Zero to 19%	6	15	15	34	30	22

SOURCES AND METHOD: Same as Table 4-4.

last decade, furthermore, leave Colombia with a tariff schedule which would require relatively few changes if import controls were abolished, particularly if ad hoc tariff exemptions were also eliminated.[8]

It should be added that the Colombian sales tax also contained protectionist elements, as its rates bore more heavily on imports than on domestic production for a (small) number of commodities, such as alcoholic beverages, canned goods, and clothing. The Musgrave Report recommended abolishing the use of the sales tax as a supplementary instrument of protection as well as instituting a better coordination of tariffs with luxury taxation, but as with most of the other recommendations in the report Congress had failed to act as of 1971.[9] Indeed, during December 1970 Congress levied a heavy sales-consumption tax on foreign cigarettes, which led to a drying up of registered imports of these goods and a dramatic increase in contraband traffic in them, which became a subject of scandalized public discussion during August and September 1971.[10]

Another institutional fact of some interest concerns the frequent complaints of law-abiding importers regarding the actual management of some customs offices, which allegedly impose not only normal tariff burdens on some, but also costly delays and petty nuisances, while freeing luckier or less scrupulous importers from their taxes. Even with the best will confusion can arise over product specification, but it is not unusual for an importer to face a hostile stance from customs officials. Furthermore, warehouses and other facilities in major ports are said to be in poor shape, inducing losses.[11] These circumstances, of course, are also widespread in other countries, and are hardly unique Colombian features.

A detailed FEDESARROLLO study[12] of tariffs as they stood on December 1972 and June 1974 on the whole confirms the results described above. The average nominal tariff rates, including the charges implicit in prior

TABLE 4-6

Changes in Regime and Average Duty Between 1962 and 1971 for Selected Imported Products

Regime in 1962	Regime in 1971	Number of Products	Average Ad Valorem Duty	
			1962	1972
Free list	Free list	5	6%	19%
Free list	Prior license	35	33	33
Free list	Prohibited	1	88	24
Prior license	Free list	4	42	30
Prior license	Prior license	42	38	37
Prior license	Prohibited	0	—	—
Prohibited	Free list	0	—	—
Prohibited	Prior license	11	116	65
Prohibited	Prohibited	26	328	93
All products		124	104	49

SOURCES AND METHOD: Same as Table 4-4.

deposits, are lower than those shown in Table 4-4 (35 per cent for 1972 and 29 per cent for 1974). But the same pattern is observed in duties classified according to import regimes; for 1972, for example, the averages of nominal duties for items on the prohibited, prior license, and free lists were, respectively, 60 per cent, 39 per cent, and 12 per cent. Weighting methods did not change results significantly.

The average effective rate of protection generated just by these nominal rates (including the opportunity costs of prior deposits) were calculated, using the Corden method, at 34 per cent in 1972 and 35 per cent in 1974. But a large dispersion of effective rates of protection was also found, a dispersion that apparently increased between 1972 and 1974. Sectoral rankings according to effective and nominal rates of protection are *not* significantly different at the 5 per cent confidence level; rankings with and without the tariff implicit in prior deposits are also similar. No significant links could be found between rankings according to protection and economic characteristics of various sectors, such as labor intensity.

PRIOR IMPORT DEPOSITS

Prior import deposits were initiated in 1951 and set at a modest 10 per cent of the desired import value. Thus, during most of the period under study, before an importer could even apply for an import license, he had to deposit a stipulated amount, expressed as a percentage of the import value, with the Banco de la República, and the money had to remain on deposit, earning no interest and eroded by inflation, until after the specific merchandise had cleared Colombian customs. During 1971–72 the advance deposit was calculated on the f.o.b. value of imports, at the average exchange rate for the previous month. The time elapsing between deposit of the money and its return has varied from period to period. During 1958 the lag began to be deliberately stretched, with a decree stating that deposits would not be returned to the importer until sixty days after the goods had reached a Colombian port. By 1963, import deposits were immobilized for an average of ten months. The lag was about six or eight months during 1964, with free-list imports typically involving shorter deposit periods than those approved under the prior license regime. By 1966 the corresponding figure was estimated at nine months. Around 1971, the lag averaged roughly seven or eight months.

Beginning in 1964, additional advance deposits have also been required for obtaining the foreign exchange needed to pay for the imports once they cleared customs. The advance payments deposits in about 1971 were equivalent to 95 per cent of the import value and had to be placed with the Banco de la República at least twenty days prior to the issuance of the exchange license needed to obtain the foreign currency.

Prior deposits were originally introduced as one more mechanism to repress imports, but their increased use during the balance-of-payments troubles of the second half of the 1950s, particularly since mid-1957, turned them into a critical tool of monetary policy. By 1960, as may be seen in Table 4-7, the stock of import deposits reached 24 per cent of the import flow for that year, and 16 per cent of the stock of total domestic credit (or 22 per cent of the money supply). At least since that time, prior deposits became a widely disliked institution, by both businessmen and policymakers. Only the weakness of more orthodox monetary tools, such as reserve requirements and rediscounting, arising from the power of commercial banks and some other private groups, such as the Coffee Federation, vis-à-vis the central bank, induced the survival of prior deposits. Nevertheless, the importance of prior deposits has, on the whole, been declining since 1960, although that trend has not been smooth. During prosperous 1973, prior import deposit rates were sharply reduced and almost eliminated. Advance deposits for buying foreign exchange, however, were increased.

As tools of monetary policy, prior import deposits and advanced deposits for buying foreign exchange are clumsy and inflexible and can lead to serious conflict between the goals of import liberalization and monetary stability. For example, the reductions in prior deposit rates adopted beginning in October 1965, as part of the import liberalization program, resulted, with a lag, in an unwanted increase in the money supply, particularly after June 1966, in spite of the import surge. Fears of undesirable monetary repercussions still keep

TABLE 4-7

Prior Import Deposits as Percentages of Merchandise Imports and Domestic Credit, 1950–72

	Deposits as Percentages of Imports, c.i.f.	Deposits as Percentages of Domestic Credit		Deposits as Percentages of Imports, c.i.f.	Deposits as Percentages of Domestic Credit
1950	5.3	4.1	1962	22.0	11.1
1951	4.6	4.3	1963	21.2	11.1
1952	3.4	2.9	1964	20.7	10.6
1953	3.4	3.3	1965	25.8	9.3
1954	4.3	4.1	1966	14.6	8.8
1955	7.4	5.5	1967	14.0	5.8
1956	10.1	5.7	1968	12.8	6.7
1957	11.0	5.9	1969	13.2	7.0
1958	17.7	10.2	1970	13.5	6.1
1959	22.6	12.9	1971	11.0	5.3
1960	23.9	16.0	1972	9.4	4.1
1961	20.0	12.6			

SOURCE: Data for prior import deposits and for domestic credit refer to average stocks during the year. The former were obtained from Alberto Roque Musalem, *Dinero, Inflación y Balanza de Pagos: La Experiencia de Colombia en la Post-Guerra* (Bogotá: Talleres Gráficos del Banco de la República, 1971), p. 153; and from BdlR-RdBdlR, various issues. Peso values for imports and total domestic credit obtained from IMF-IFS. Advance deposits for exchange needed to pay for imports are not included in any of the preceding figures. Measured as average stocks during the year, those deposits amounted in 1968 to 39.5 per cent of prior import deposits; 1969, 33.0; 1970, 28.7; 1971, 26.5; and 1972, 33.2.

authorities from totally eliminating prior deposits; as late as 1968 a plan to eliminate these deposits within a year was abandoned for that reason. On the restraining side this tool has on occasion been the only available instrument capable of rapidly stemming excessive monetary expansion, as during 1962. The practical elimination of prior import deposits during 1973, as part of the continuing liberalization process, was undertaken in the midst of an inflationary boom, and the authorities, quickly becoming fearful of the monetary consequences of that move, raised the advance deposits for buying foreign exchange as an offsetting measure.

Both prior import deposits and prior deposits required for buying foreign exchange have been relatively less effective in repressing imports than as monetary tools. The exact opportunity cost of the immobilized balances, including the advance payments deposits expressed as ad valorem tariff equivalents, is difficult to establish exactly, and given capital market imperfections it is likely to differ considerably among firms. Some companies may obtain foreign suppliers' credits for that purpose (it has even been argued that the 1959–60 increases in prior deposits led to an inflow of "hot money" into Colombia), others can obtain credit from their banks, but still others, particularly smaller ones, may suffer severe hardships in raising the needed cash. Colombian businessmen, who complain constantly about shortages of working capital, find the prior deposits particularly obnoxious. Alberto R. Musalem has estimated the ad-valorem-equivalent incidence of prior import and advance payments deposits at 11 per cent, on average, for 1960–67.[13] For more recent years the corresponding figure is lower, below 5 per cent. An across-the-board tariff increase of a few percentage points or a slightly faster rate of exchange depreciation seems like a small price to pay for the elimination of prior deposits, whose regressive incidence accentuates the concentration of economic power in Colombia.

Prior import deposits during January–May 1971 ranged from 1 to 130 per cent ad valorem. As shown in Table 4-4, on average, items on the prohibited list bore the highest rates (as with tariffs) and those on the free list had the lowest rates. As noted when discussing the tariff, the tendency to penalize "luxuries" and encourage "necessities" frequently prevailed over the policy of choosing between alternative, nonduplicating instruments to restrain imports. The spread in prior deposits was somewhat narrower than for tariffs, and the ranking by incidence on different commodity categories was also slightly different. Capital goods, for example, whose tariff rates are roughly in line with those for industrial raw materials and semimanufactured products, bore lower prior deposits on average.

As with tariffs, there are many exemptions from prior import deposits, including aid-financed imports, those made by the government and public entities, some capital goods, imports from LAFTA, and most nonreimbursable imports. Prior import deposits are regulated by the top monetary authority, the Junta Monetaria, presumably in coordination with the Consejo de Política Aduanera, which is in charge of the tariff, and with INCOMEX, which manages import controls. In fact, many inconsistencies exist in the use of these instruments; for example, in some cases, the prior deposit for inputs is higher than for the finished products using those inputs, while the tariff situation is more normal. Those cases are reviewed on an ad hoc basis, as producers complain of the situation to the Junta Monetaria.

THE AVERAGE EXCHANGE RATE APPLICABLE TO MERCHANDISE IMPORTS

By 1971 the exchange rate applied to imports had in real terms reached its highest sustained postwar levels, as can be seen in Table 4-8. The basic single nominal rate had also been unified with the rates applicable to minor exports (excluding CAT) and to capital transactions; minor statistical discrepancies show up nowadays only because of timing differences in the recorded transactions. As indicated in the second column of Table 4-8, the real rate has also been quite stable around a gently rising trend since the reforms of March 1967.

Matters were not always this tranquil and orderly. There were times, as during the 1965–66 liberalization episode, when two major rates were applied to imports: a preferential rate of 9 pesos per U.S. dollar, the old rate, and a new intermediate rate of 13.50 pesos, to which all imports were gradually transferred, while most private capital transactions took place in an uncontrolled free market. An earlier switch, from the precarious exchange stability of the mid-1950s to more realistic levels after mid-1957, can also be observed in Table 4-8.

The crucial hesitations in exchange policy which occurred during 1958–59 can also be seen in this table. During late 1957 and 1958 a relatively high import rate was achieved by means of a fluctuating basic "certificate" rate, combined with, for most imports, a 10 per cent remittance tax, which can be incorporated into the exchange rate. From April 1958 until early 1959, that tax had to be paid with U.S. dollars purchased in the fluctuating free market. In January 1959, importers were given the option of making payments through the free market, in which case they were exempted from the 10 per cent remittance tax. In May 1959 that tax was absorbed, in principle, into customs duties, with the first ten percentage points of the duty insofar as applicable, being payable in U.S. dollars. The wise de facto flexibility which had existed for the average effective import rate during 1958 and early 1959 was dead. After May 1959, the basic selling certificate rate of 6.4 pesos, which had been reached by October 1958 after attaining a high of 6.8 in June 1958, became the

TABLE 4-8

Nominal Exchange Rate (NER) on Merchandise Imports, 1948–72

	Average NER (pesos per U.S. dol.)	PPP-NER (1963 prices)	Instability Index
1948	1.75	5.64	—
1949	1.95	5.58	—
1950	1.95	5.13	—
1951	2.36	6.43	—
1952	2.50	6.74	—
1953	2.50	6.25	—
1954	2.50	5.87	2.61
1955	2.50	5.77	0.98
1956	2.50	5.39	2.59
1957 I	2.50	5.10	2.31
II	2.51	4.64	3.89
III	5.33	9.26	28.24
IV	5.74	9.80	28.90
1958 I	6.48	10.80	31.16
II	7.43	11.79	31.19
III	7.23	11.30	7.34
IV	7.11	10.77	7.06
1959 I	6.87	10.36	5.46
II	7.64	11.02	4.76
III	6.40	9.10	8.07
IV	6.40	9.03	7.09
1960 I	6.40	9.01	6.20
II	6.64	9.22	5.19
III	6.70	9.31	1.08
IV	6.70	9.18	1.23
1961 I	6.70	9.02	1.61
II	6.70	8.59	2.22
III	6.70	8.59	1.98
IV	6.70	8.59	1.63
1962 I	6.70	8.59	1.19
II	6.70	8.48	0.32
III	6.70	8.48	0.32
IV	7.30	9.13	2.24
1963 I	9.00	10.00	4.62
II	9.00	8.91	7.03
III	9.00	8.74	7.50
IV	9.00	8.41	6.53

TABLE 4-8 (*concluded*)

	Average NER (pesos per U.S. dol.)	PPP-NER (1963 prices)	Instability Index
1964 I	9.00	8.04	5.25
II	9.00	7.56	4.02
III	9.00	7.56	3.54
IV	9.00	7.56	2.59
1965 I	9.00	7.58	1.56
II	9.00	7.34	0.86
III	9.37	7.54	1.54
IV	12.21	9.25	7.21
1966 I	12.42	9.12	7.50
II	12.68	8.88	7.36
III	13.13	9.22	7.64
IV	13.53	9.31	2.21
1967 I	13.32	9.03	2.61
II	13.68	9.12	2.21
III	14.34	9.45	2.15
IV	15.05	9.80	2.83
1968 I	15.64	10.17	3.03
II	15.96	10.14	2.85
III	16.26	10.35	2.46
IV	16.50	10.53	1.97
1969 I	16.78	10.68	1.38
II	17.02	10.64	1.40
III	17.30	10.75	1.14
IV	17.65	10.78	0.78
1970 I	17.79	10.92	0.75
II	18.08	10.82	0.88
III	18.37	11.02	1.09
IV	19.10	11.28	1.61
1971 I	19.44	11.32	1.37
II	19.82	11.28	1.23
III	20.30	11.37	0.97
IV	20.80	11.38	0.40
1972 I	21.32	11.60	0.79
II	21.82	11.57	0.77
III	22.23	11.55	0.61
IV	22.71	11.47	0.76

SOURCE: Average nominal exchange rate is obtained by dividing import peso value, c.i.f., by import dollar values. The purchasing-power-parity-

Notes to Table 4-8 (*concluded*)

adjusted rate (PPP-NER) is obtained by dividing the nominal rate by the ratio of Colombian to U.S. wholesale prices. The index of instability of the purchasing-power-parity-adjusted rate is computed as in Chapter 2, i.e., it is the average of the absolute value of quarter-to-quarter percentage changes for four consecutive quarters. When the index is given for a year, it covers the four quarterly changes during that year; when it is given for a quarter, it refers to the percentage changes during that quarter and the preceding three quarters. Basic data were obtained from IMF-IFS; figures for 1958, 1959, and 1960 have been revised frequently in that publication. Those shown here include the temporary remittance tax for those years; all others include only the nominal exchange rate.

---

pegged effective import rate. This rate was below the rates reached during 1958; even after it was raised to 6.7 pesos, in 1960, it remained substantially below the late-1958 de facto levels.

It is noteworthy that such a return to "stability" was partly promoted by those who after 1967 became champions of the crawling rate. The reasons given for the new pegging in 1959 were the usual ones: fear of inflation, need for "stability," and the impact of a more devalued peso on public and private foreign debts denominated in dollars. Naturally, as erosion of the *real* or purchasing-power-parity import exchange rate continued from its 1958 levels, increasing use was made of prior deposits, tariffs, and import controls, until, late in 1962, the pressures became too great. The unfortunate 1962 episode will be reviewed in detail later; here it is enough to note that its origins can be traced back to the misguided repegging of 1959. From the end of 1962 until September 1965, the mirage of a stable import rate was again sought; the pegged 9-peso rate was buttressed primarily by tight import controls.

Primarily because of the existence of import controls applied with fluctuating severity in different periods, there is little systematic link between the real effective import exchange rate and actual imports. Correlations between percentage changes in imports and in the exchange rate and the stability index presented in Table 4-8, similar in structure to the regressions presented in Chapter 2 for minor exports, yield only insignificant coefficients and very low R^2s, whether the period is considered as a whole or is broken up into subperiods.

The first two columns of Table 4-9 contain annual summaries of the quarterly data shown in Table 4-8. In column 3, the nominal import exchange rate is also compared to that prevailing in the legal free or capital market; the latter was often pegged. The comparison shown in column 4 is with rates that were always free, if not always legal; the source for that column is *Pick's Currency Yearbook,* which publishes black market rates. The figures in the

TABLE 4-9

Characteristics of the Average Import Exchange Rate, 1956–72

Year	Average PPP-NER for Merchandise Imports (pesos per U.S. dol.) (1)	Instability Index (2)	Legal Free or Capital Market Rate as Per Cent of Col. 1 (3)	Free, Capital, or Black Market Rate as Per Cent of Col. 1 (4)
1956	5.39	2.59	198.4	200.8
1957	7.20	28.90	157.0	160.2
1958	11.17	7.06	107.5	107.5
1959	9.88	7.09	112.7	113.3
1960	9.18	1.23	104.7	104.2
1961	8.70	1.63	123.9	124.3
1962	8.67	2.24	133.3	134.0
1963	9.02	6.53	111.3	112.6
1964	7.68	2.59	115.9	116.4
1965	7.93	7.21	170.1	168.5
1966	9.13	2.21	131.1	134.9
1967	9.35	2.83	115.6	136.1
1968	10.30	1.97	101.6	112.6
1969	10.71	0.78	—	110.6
1970	11.01	1.61	—	118.5
1971	11.34	0.40	—	118.2
1972	11.55	0.76	—	109.6

SOURCE: Figures in columns 1 and 2 are from quarterly data in Table 4-8. Exchange rates for the *legal* capital or free markets, used in column 3, from A. R. Musalem, *Dinero, Inflación y Balanza de Pagos: La Experiencia de Colombia en la Post-Guerra* (Bogotá: Talleres Gráficos del Banco de la República, 1971), Table XXIV, p. 160. Exchange rates used in column 4, which also include black market rates, from *Pick's Currency Yearbook,* various issues. Figures in both columns 3 and 4 are based on monthly data, although their timing may not be identical. In 1968 the official capital market was merged with the certificate market.

last column should always be equal to or greater than those in the third column; the anomalous observations for 1960 and 1965 are due to differences in the timing of monthly observations on which the data are based.

The course of the rates in the last two columns of Table 4-9 clearly signals troubled years, such as 1956–57, 1961–62, and 1965–67, but that in the last column also reflects the success of the crawling peg instituted in 1967.[14]

The bureaucratic agencies officially in charge of establishing exchange rate policy have differed from time to time. During the Lleras Restrepo administration, the President himself kept a close watch over the exchange rate. According to Decree Law 444 of March 1967 (Article 21), the Junta

Monetaria, acting through the central bank, is charged with regulating the market for foreign exchange. The key personalities in the junta are the Minister of the Treasury and the manager of the central bank. The certificate or basic rate is typically modified (raised) twice a week, by small amounts.

Monthly changes in the certificate rate since the reforms of March 1967 are shown in Table 4-10. At the start of the new system, the monthly changes were fairly irregular, apparently in an attempt to establish the principle that this was indeed a fairly unregulated market, closer to "dirty floating" than to a crawling peg system, and that it could even appreciate, as it did during January 1968. These early exchange-rate movements were anxiously watched by Colombia's creditors and aid donors, who doubted the firmness of the Colombian commitment to a crawling peg. It is said that the slowdown in the rate of depreciation during December 1967 and January 1968 caused telegrams to fly between Washington and Bogotá, and fear was expressed that once the certificate rate reached the capital market rate (which had been pegged at 16.3 pesos since the capital market replaced the free market early in December 1966) and was unified with it, there would be a return to a fixed 16.3-peso peg. The unification point was reached in June 1968, but the upward crawling continued, although not without an unusually low depreciation rate during that month, which must have caused a few jitters. But the low depreciation rates of June, July, and August 1968 apparently had more to do with the endeavor of creating a calm atmosphere for the visit of His Holiness Pope Paul VI to Colombia, during August 22–24, than with any attempt to return to a fixed peg. Similarly, the difficult political situation that developed between the election and inauguration of President Misael Pastrana Borrero (April–August 1970) seems to account for the slowdown in the depreciation rate observed in those months. After the new President was inaugurated, the rate of depreciation became steadier, seldom falling outside a range of 0.6 to 0.9 per cent per month. The acceleration of inflation since 1971, and the improvement at the same time of Colombian terms of trade, led some to call for a slower upward crawl in the exchange rate, as part of anti-inflationary policies. It remains to be seen whether the crawling peg will work as well (or will be allowed to work) under conditions of accelerating inflation, as it did when inflation rates were low or decreasing.

It is not clear how much the demand for import licenses and for imports on the free list influences the decisions to alter the exchange rate. It is said that foreign creditors, and in particular the IMF, annually agree with Colombian authorities on a minimum target for imports so as to decrease any temptation to slow down the depreciation rate and tighten import controls. It is known that authorities also try to maintain some sort of link between depreciation and inflation in Colombia and abroad but, given the weaknesses of price indices (and of the rigid purchasing power theory), that link is deliberately kept loose.

TABLE 4-10

Monthly Percentage Changes in the Certificate Rate, 1967–73

	1967	1968	1969	1970	1971	1972	1973
January	0	−0.13	0	0.39	0.63	0.76	0.75
February	0	0.95	0.59	0.67	0.57	0.71	0.52
March	0.07	0.57	0.71	0.89	0.93	0.89	0.52
April	2.81	0.75	0.18	0.27	0.67	0.75	0.52
May	2.23	0.81	0.47	0.38	0.41	0.74	0.43
June	1.97	0.12	0.58	0.55	0.81	0.74	0.43
July	1.24	0.62	0.46	0.43	0.91	0.50	0.64
August	2.39	0.43	0.92	0.54	0.85	0.73	0.84
September	1.93	0.73	0.06	0.70	0.74	0.59	0.75
October	0.92	0.85	0.40	0.75	0.79	0.76	0.96
November	1.36	0.84	0.51	0.48	0.88	0.62	0.78
December	0.70	0.36	0.73	0.74	0.97	0.80	1.31
Average	1.73[a]	0.58	0.47	0.57	0.76	0.72	0.70
December-to-December change	16.74	7.11	5.75	7.00	9.53	8.94	8.78

SOURCE: Certificate rate quotations taken at the end of each month. Basic data from IMF-IFS. (The buying rate or "other export rate" has been used; the principal selling rate behaves almost identically.) Fourth-quarter to fourth-quarter percentage changes in Colombian and U.S. price indices (averages for the quarter; basic data from IMF-IFS) have been as follows:

	Colombia		U.S.	
	Wholesale Prices	Consumer Prices	Wholesale Prices	Consumer Prices
1966–67	6.0	6.9	0.4	2.9
1967–68	5.2	5.7	3.0	4.7
1968–69	9.2	12.8	4.6	5.8
1969–70	6.3	3.3	2.8	5.6
1970–71	11.7	13.5	3.4	3.5
1971–72	21.0	17.2	5.6	3.4
1972–73	31.5	18.9	15.4	8.4

a. April through December only.

Note, however, how the depreciation rate accelerated during 1971 and 1972 as the Colombian inflation picked up. It appears that broad depreciation targets are set on a yearly basis, depending on expected inflation, imports, exchange earnings, and other factors, and from then on the monthly rate is determined "by ear." On the whole, once inflation is taken into account the policy has more in common with that based on a firmly pegged exchange rate, under conditions of price stability, than with one allowing a freely fluctuating rate. So far, the results of the policy appear to have been favorable.

NOTES

1. See particularly Luis Ospina Vásquez, *Industria y Protección en Colombia, 1810–1930* (Medellín: E.S.F., 1955).

2. It is easily forgotten that high internal transport barriers so fragmented the Colombian markets for goods and factors of production that, until fairly recently, aggregate data for the whole nation had a misleading synthetic quality. Even today, just as the abrupt Colombian geography generates a myriad of microclimates, it continues to hamper factor and commodity price equalization within the country.

3. This paragraph is based on David S. C. Chu, "The Great Depression and Industrialization in Latin America: Response to Relative Price Incentives in Argentina and Colombia, 1930–1945" (Ph.D. diss., Yale University, 1972), Chap. 2 and App. B-2; and on UNECLA, "The Economic Policy of Colombia in 1950–66, *Economic Bulletin for Latin America,* October 1967, especially pp. 90–95. The protectionist intent of pre-1930 Colombian tariffs, however, is probably underestimated in the literature.

4. According to Departamento Administrativo de Planeación y Servicios Técnicos, *Plan Decenal de Desarrollo Económico Industrial, 1960–1970* (Bogotá, n.d.), Chap. IV.

5. According to Benjamin I. Cohen, "An Analysis of Colombia's Exports," mimeographed (AID, September 22, 1965), p. 3. Toward the end of 1959, according to the data presented in ECLA, "Custom Duties and Other Import Charges and Restrictions in Latin American Countries: Average Levels of Incidence," mimeographed (n.d., E/CN.12/554 and Add. 1-11), the arithmetic means of customs duties and other charges (including the cost of financing prior deposits) in ad valorem equivalents in Colombia were as follows (in percentages): total, 41; unprocessed foodstuffs, 68; raw materials, 31; intermediate products, 36; processed fuels, 11; capital goods, 27; processed foodstuffs and tobacco, 138; chemical and pharmaceutical products, 31; durable consumer goods, 101; and other consumer goods, 57.

6. In his influential article "Protectionism and Industrialization in Latin America," *Economic Bulletin for Latin America,* March 1964, pp. 61–101.

7. See David Morawetz's writings on this subject, particularly "Common External Tariff for the Andean Group," mimeographed (Cambridge: Harvard Development Advisory Service, 1972). Colombia apparently succeeded in obtaining a minimum common tariff close to its own in exchange for going along with a common code for direct foreign investment that was tougher than it wished.

8. Other tariff summaries confirm, in general, these conclusions. See in particular, Instituto para la Integración de América Latina, Banco Interamericano de Desarrollo, "Instituciones e Instrumentos de Política Económica Colombiana en Materia de Comercio Exterior," mimeographed (November 1968), Table 2; and David Morawetz, "Harmonization of Economic Policies in Customs Unions: The Andean Group, mimeographed (Cambridge: Harvard Development Advisory Service, December 1971), p. 11a.

9. See Richard A. Musgrave, President, and Malcolm Gillis, Editor, *Fiscal Reform for Colombia: Final Report and Staff Papers of the Colombian Commission on Tax Reform* (Cambridge: Harvard Law School, International Tax Program, 1971), especially Chaps. 12 and 13. Important tax reform measures were adopted during the second half of 1974.

10. See, for example, *El Tiempo* of September 10, 1971, where it was reported that the Executive had asked Congress to eliminate the heavy consumption tax on imported cigarettes decreed in Law 19 of December 1970, arguing that otherwise smuggling could not be stopped. The Minister of the Treasury sensibly argued that " . . . public and ostentatious smuggling weakens national morality, weakens the prestige of public institutions, and discredits the country in the eyes of foreigners." In 1971, national tax revenues from cigarette imports were running 60 per cent *below* those of 1970, as a result of the *higher* tax.

11. In a remarkable move, the Director of Customs called a press conference during August 1971 to denounce widespread corruption and inefficiency in the nation's customs administration and its harbors, particularly in those of Buenaventura. He announced measures to control such ills, but complained that import and sales taxes provided very strong stimuli to contraband, referring in particular to Law 19 of December 1970, whose approval he had opposed. He denounced conditions in the harbor of Buenaventura, where there were ten known organizations dedicated exclusively to stealing goods in transit, often in complicity with public employees in customs, the railroad, and harbor. Even eighty tons of steel were stolen! Such raids are often sponsored by the owners of the merchandise, so that they can obtain insurance payments as well as new import licenses. See *El Tiempo,* August 26, 1971.

12. See Luis J. Garay S. et al., *Análisis de la Estructura de Control a Las Importaciones en Colombia,* 2 vols. (Bogotá: FEDESARROLLO, August 1974). This valuable study was based on a large sample covering about 75 per cent of all items in the tariff. The data refer to imports actually realized, i.e., those for which permits had been obtained from INCOMEX, a procedure the authors regard as underestimating nominal and effective protection (I, 63). The calculations take into account only tariffs plus an estimate of the opportunity cost of prior import deposits; the latter, however, accounts for only about 10 per cent of the ad valorem rates mentioned in the text.

13. It appears that Musalem computes the opportunity cost of the idle deposits at the rate of inflation *plus* average yields on the Bogotá stock exchange. The latter, however, may already allow for inflationary expectations, in which case the figures overestimate opportunity cost. See Alberto Roque Musalem, *Dinero, Inflación y Balanza de Pagos: La Experiencia de Colombia en la Post-Guerra* (Bogotá: Talleres Gráficos del Banco de la República, 1971), p. 154. In his calculations Musalem also includes the opportunity cost of the prior deposits required before the central bank hands over the foreign exchange needed to pay for imports. In the FEDESAR-ROLLO study mentioned earlier in this chapter, it is estimated that the ad valorem equivalent opportunity cost of prior deposits for imports that had been granted licenses was 4 per cent in 1972 and 3 per cent in 1974.

14. During 1972–74, the narrowing of the gap between the official and black-market rates, coupled with the CAT, gave rise to charges of fake export registrations with INCOMEX and BdlR. Thus, one could buy dollars in the black market at rates, say, 10 per cent higher than the certificate rate. He could then go to the authorities to register exports (such as pieces of glass), surrendering the dollars, for which he would obtain the certificate rate *plus the CAT.*

Chapter 5

Import Controls

We now come to the cornerstone of the Colombian system for restraining the demand for imports: the controls mandating registration of all imports with a specified agency—during 1971, it was INCOMEX—authorized to prohibit or to require prior approval of import transactions. I will first explain the terms in the Colombian import licensing system, and follow this by a sketch of its historical evolution. The core of the chapter is a detailed examination of how the system worked in about 1970–71. On the basis of that description, I will advance some hypotheses regarding the biases arising from the import-licensing process, which I will test in Chapter 6. Finally, I will take a look at some of the effects of the joint operation of the several import-repressing mechanisms.

SOME KEY DEFINITIONS AND CLASSIFICATIONS

The Colombian government records the import process at several points: it first requires the *registration* with INCOMEX of all intentions to import goods except for "minor" imports; these intentions become registered only after they are approved; they are recorded at f.o.b. values. For items on the free list approval is granted almost automatically. When the goods come into the country and clear customs, they are recorded at *customs* at c.i.f. values. Finally, when the importer or his bank draws foreign exchange from the central bank, those *exchange disbursements* are noted. To obtain foreign exchange, the importer must present proof that the goods have cleared

124

TABLE 5-1

**Merchandise Imports: Registrations, Customs Values, and Exchange Disbursements,
1963–72**
(annual averages in millions of current U.S. dollars)

	1963–66	1967–70	1971–72
Total registrations (f.o.b.)	552.1	706.2	843.4
Reimbursable	484.4	596.1	748.1
Ordinary draft	390.8	414.9	639.4
Compensation agreements	38.8	60.0	45.5
AID credits	20.2	86.0	18.1
Other credits	27.0	16.9	13.3
Special import-export systems	7.6	18.3	31.9
Nonreimbursable	67.6	110.1	95.3
With foreign loans	18.9	71.7	56.2
Other	48.7	38.5	39.1
Merchandise imports (customs, c.i.f.)	555.0	645.2	847.0
Exchange disbursements for imports (f.o.b.)	371.0	475.3	633.7

SOURCE: BdlR-RdBdlR, various issues, and IMF-IFS, various issues. See text for explanation of terms and classification.

customs. In Table 5-1 these three different magnitudes are shown for recent years. Allowing for lags, registrations and customs values are roughly equal. It appears that the c.i.f.-f.o.b. differential is offset by cancellations, postregistration discounts, and nonuse of some registrations. Exchange disbursements are lower than import values for the simple reason that many imports are financed by foreign credits or covered by compensation agreements; the servicing of such debt is recorded under other items.

The lag between application for an import license and its approval, which implies registration for goods on the prior list, has fluctuated considerably since World War II. During 1970–71 it averaged between one and one and a half months. The lag between registration and the time the goods actually go through customs depends, of course, on the nature of the commodity; it is said to average four or five months. The lag between arrival and exchange disbursement, for those imports not financed by long-term credit, ranges between one and twenty months.

The average link between actual imports *(CUSTOMS)* and registration *(REGISTR.)* can be seen in the following regression, using annual dollar data for 1951 through 1972 (*t* statistics are in parentheses):

$$(CUSTOMS)_t = 94.18 + 0.55\ (REGISTR.)_t + 0.31\ (REGISTR.)_{t-1} \qquad (5\text{-}1)$$
$$(2.19) \quad (5.30) \qquad\qquad (2.70)$$

$$R^2 = 0.88;\ F \text{ statistic} = 71.58;\ DW = 2.92$$

From 1962 through 1969 this regression yields alternating under- and overestimates of actual imports. Thus, predicted customs imports for 1963 are 7 per cent above actual ones; for 1964, 6 per cent below; for 1965, 16 per cent above, and so on. The missing explanatory variable could well be past, actual, and expected exchange-rate behavior, as expectations of devaluation, say, would induce holders of registered licenses to speed up the arrival of and payment for the merchandise. But experiments in which lagged and leading exchange-rate changes were entered in regression 5-1 yielded on the whole poor results. In some regressions, the actual percentage of changes in the real average import exchange rate a year ahead had a positive sign and t statistics of about 1.2, presumably picking up realized expectations about its movements. But clearly, in any given year there are ad hoc factors influencing the lag between customs flow and registration; for example, a plausible reason for the 1964 underestimate of 6 per cent in regression 5-1 relates to doubts that the condition of relative import ease would last long, provoking a quick realization of registered intentions to import. And once this happens in a given year, the opposite can be expected in the next. Tight domestic credit conditions, on the other hand, will induce the postponement of import arrivals and payments, a procedure facilitated by the relative ease of obtaining rollover of import credits. The variability of the lag between licensing, arrival, and payment has often caused short-run disturbances in credit and exchange management.

Regression 5-1 indicates that 55 per cent of registrations are, on average, turned into actual imports within the same year, suggesting an average lag between licensing and arrival of five to six months. Note, however, that the coefficients for both registration variables add up to only 0.86, and that longer lags yielded insignificant results.

INCOMEX and its predecessors have classified registrations according to type of *payment* to which they give rise, type of *importer*, and particular regime to which the *imports* are subject.

The classification of payments used during 1970–71 for imports is presented in Table 5-1. The distinction between reimbursable and nonreimbursable imports is less helpful than it appears, because although all nonreimbursable imports are financed by long- or medium-term credits, or involve imports of direct foreign investors or gifts and donations, not all reimbursable imports are covered by current exchange earnings. The distinction turns out to hinge on whether the foreign exchange used to pay for imports is or is not at the disposal of the Banco de la República, directly or indirectly. Thus, imports financed by AID credits deposited with the central bank are reimbursable, while those financed by loans from IBRD or IADB, whose cash is kept in Washington, are considered nonreimbursable. Imports from countries with which Colombia has bilateral payments agreements, as well as those from LAFTA, come under the reimbursable category, as reciprocal credit deals are directly handled by the central bank. That part of foreign investment directly involving machinery imports is nonreimbursable; other parts, which may involve a dollar inflow deposited in the central bank to pay for other imports, would be reimbursable.

The distinction according to type of importer is of more general interest. Published import registrations are subdivided into three categories: industry, commerce, and official. For internal use, INCOMEX has a somewhat more complicated classification entailing a fourth major group, "occasional" requests, made up mainly of import applications from construction firms, professionals, private individuals, and even some public agencies, as well as other minor subdivisions. In published registrations, "industry" includes imports to be transformed and used directly by those requesting the license; "commerce," those to be resold by established commercial firms, without substantially altering the imported item. Approved "occasional" requests appear mainly under "commerce" in published registration reports. The "official" category covers imports destined for the public sector; however, INCOMEX subdivides these applications into commercial and industrial categories for internal use, and published data also contain under "industry" imports of some public enterprises. Partly as a result of foreign "tied aid" and partly because of protectionist pressures, all official imports must by law go through the prior-licensing procedure, i.e., they are excluded from the free list.

Colombia has no state trading agencies outside the quasi-official Coffee Growers' Federation (in principle a private group) and IDEMA, in charge of distributing basic foodstuffs, such as wheat. The former handles directly a major share of coffee exports, while the latter frequently imports in bulk, particularly from countries whose export trade is in state hands. IDEMA has from time to time been the recipient of large government subsidies.

Only approved (registered) license requests are published; during 1971, of all registered reimbursable imports 56 per cent fell into the industry category; 24 per cent, into commerce; and 20 per cent, into official; and for 1970 the corresponding figures were 53, 29, and 19 per cent. It may be estimated that during 1971 total requests, including those rejected, followed a roughly similar breakdown, with the share for commerce slightly higher than the shares for industry and official. Data problems do not allow a clear determination of long-term changes in the shares of these categories.

The large share of import demand and of actual imports accounted for by direct users, whether private or public, is remarkable and reflects the small share of consumer goods in the import bill. Note also that because of what is known about import prohibitions and INCOMEX policies, a large fraction of potential importers do not bother to apply for permits. Furthermore, many small entrepreneurs and individuals not used to dealing with government bureaucracies may get discouraged even when their potential applications have a good chance of being approved.

All importable items fell under one of three regimes or lists: prohibited, free, or prior license.[1] It will be seen that the coverage of these lists fluctuated considerably during the 1960s. During 1971, about 16 per cent of all items (including subcategories) to which the Colombian tariff is applicable were placed on the prohibited list. The figures in Table 5-2 show that the list included candidates for agricultural protectionism in rich and poor countries alike (e.g., meat, corn, dairy products, etc.), luxury products (e.g., furs, precious metals, jewelry, velvets, etc.), and many items for which prohibitions appeared redundant (e.g., coffee, cocoa, sugar, clothes, wood manufactures, etc.). An eccentric who wished to import coffee into Colombia in 1971, incidentally, would have faced not only a flat prohibition, but also a duty of 85 per cent if the bean was unroasted, or 170 per cent for roasted beans, plus a prior deposit of 130 per cent. The list also included items such as arms and habit-forming drugs. Note that while among the tariff chapters identified in Table 5-2, which account for two-thirds of all prohibited items and contain mainly consumer goods, the percentage of prohibitions was 66, for the rest of the tariff only 6 per cent of the categories were prohibited. Under special circumstances goods on the prohibited list can be imported, as under the Vallejo Plan. During 1971, for example, nearly 1 per cent of all registered reimbursable imports were on the prohibited list. It may be noted that some goods are prohibited for most purposes, but subject to prior licenses for a few others, e.g., some types of paper, prohibited except for use by the printing and publishing industry. On the whole, the prohibited list included many items which could be regarded as actual or potential exportable goods.

The free list, besides Vallejo Plan and LAFTA imports, included in August 1971 only about 150 items, or 3 per cent of all categories in the tariff. However, free-list items accounted for 29 per cent of all registered reimbursable imports in 1971 and 23 per cent of all registered imports (the free list was limited to reimbursable imports). Free-list items can be brought into Colombia without prior license; all that is required, in principle, besides payment of duties and prior deposits is the registration of these imports with INCOMEX. Typically, that process is routine, but INCOMEX can challenge the dollar prices appearing in the registration; such control is justified on grounds of

TABLE 5-2

Examples of Tariff Chapters with Many Prohibited Items, About 1971

Chapter Number and Description	Total No. of Items in Chapter	Prohibited Items
2 Meat and edible offal	20	20
3 Fish, shellfish, and mollusks	18	10
4 Milk and dairy products, eggs, honey	16	13
7 Edible legumes, vegetables, plant roots, tubers	24	20
8 Edible fruits and peels	74	69
9 Coffee, tea, and spices	26	10
11 Milling foodstuffs, malt, starches	34	29
12 Oilseeds, sundry seeds, industrial and medicinal plants, fodder	61	27
15 Animal and vegetable oils, fats	88	54
18 Cocoa and its products	7	6
19 Pastries, products based on flour, cereals, etc.	10	6
20 Preserves of vegetables, plants, fruits	24	21
21 Sundry foodstuffs	18	11
22 Beverages, alcoholic drinks, vinegar	33	11
41 Furs, leather, and their manufactures	26	11
44 Wood and its manufactures	35	25
58 Rugs, felts, ribbons, embroidery, velvets, tulle, etc.	61	49
60 Knitted goods	25	24
61 Other clothing and apparel	23	22
68 Ceramics, glass, cement, and their manufactures	46	15
71 Precious stones, metals, and their manufactures	38	16
Subtotal	707	469
Other chapters	3,643	235
Total	4,350	704

SOURCE: Data from *Arancel de Aduanas* (see Source note to Table 4-4).

combating overinvoicing, and can lead to denial of registration even of items on the free list. The threat is not just theoretical; e.g., some book imports were held up in about 1972 for this reason. INCOMEX can also use a number of bureaucratic excuses to delay processing free-list registrations for a few days. Neither the "prohibited" nor the "free" list has always been true to its name!

Goods on the free list included primarily some spare parts, certain raw materials and intermediate products, scientific and medical equipment, and other capital goods. Examples of the latter are harvesters, helicopters, chicken incubators, some electrical generators, tractors, and many types of engines. The remainder of the items on the lists included unmanufactured copper, lead, zinc, aluminum; some types of steel and nickel sheets; and newsprint. Of all tariff items (528) in chapters 84 and 85, which include most electrical and nonelectrical machinery and equipment, excluding transport, nearly 10 per cent were on the free list. As with the tariff, import controls are biased against the importation of used goods; it is explicitly stated in the regulations covering the free list that only new and unused merchandise can be brought in under the list. [2]

Goods on neither the prohibited nor the free list were subject to prior licensing, which covered the bulk of imports. Items could be moved from one list to another by a simple decision of INCOMEX. So long as a given commodity remained on the free list, it could be said that its demand depended only on income, prices, tariffs, etc.; but in reality this was so only so long as that demand stayed within the limits foreseen by the authorities. It has not been unusual in the past for the control authorities to curtail or eliminate the free list when demand pressure became too great; that is one reason why in Chapter 3 no distinction was made among prohibited, prior license, and free import lists when deriving the over-all import function.

There was a further distinction, primarily applied to industrial requests, between *global* licenses and ordinary or regular licenses. Global licenses, started in 1965, applied basically to imports of capital goods for projects exceeding U.S. $40,000, involving the creation, modernization, or expansion of capacity, and, if granted, were simply an approval in principle to import. After obtaining a global license, an importer was typically given about three months to apply for ordinary licenses. Extensions, however, were possible; and longer time limits were also given, depending on the nature of the project. When a company is planning new investment, for example, it submits a description of the project, in the form of a feasibility study with a nineteen-page questionnaire, together with estimated import requirements to INCOMEX, which has a special section for analyzing these projects. The motivation given for global licenses is to avoid a situation in which projects are delayed by having, say, 90 per cent of import requirements approved but a few critical requests rejected. Once a global license has been obtained, the normal expectation is that all required licenses, which must still be presented for each individual item, will be approved.

Global licenses are not obligatory for investment projects, but highly convenient; they give the government an important tool for controlling private capital formation, and entrepreneurs a way of committing the government to the realization of a project. In the difficult year of 1967, global licenses worth U.S. $48.4 million were approved and license applications worth U.S. $7.4 million were rejected. In 1969, approvals reached U.S. $110.2 million. The corresponding figure for 1970 was $84.7 million. In contrast, actual imports of all capital goods during 1969–70 averaged U.S. $346.1 million annually.

A HISTORICAL SKETCH OF THE IMPORT CONTROL SYSTEM[3]

In spite of an increase in the dollar value of Colombian exports from $81 million in 1938 to $284 million in 1948, more than a threefold increase in ten years, foreign-exchange reserves declined during 1946–48, and the import and exchange controls which were first put into effect during the Great Depression became increasingly detailed and complex. As noted in Chapter 1, exchange-rate policy appears to have become frozen by the peculiar circumstances during and following World War II, leading to an overvaluation trend.

By 1949, import licenses were granted up to the limits of individual exchange quotas computed on the basis of the importer's production, sales, and other criteria. During 1950, the allocation of exchange quotas to individual importers began to be determined on the basis of their capital, expenses, and total personnel. For some commodities, such as drugs and pharmaceuticals, import licenses were issued without regard for the exchange quotas. Thus, the nonreimbursable category was already in use, and at that time it probably included many imports financed with dollars acquired in the black market. Furthermore, licenses for the purchase of certain imports were given preferential treatment.

This system was conducive to tinkering and proliferation of multiple rates, and up until March 1951 numerous adjustments were made to exchange taxes, to proportions in the mixed rates, and to goods which could be imported outside individual exchange quotas. Apparently there was considerable criticism of the efficiency, fairness, and honesty with which the system was run, and one of the directors of the control mechanism was even assassinated.

In March 1951, when the basic import rate was devalued to 2.5 pesos per U.S. dollar, a prohibited list of about 1,200 specified luxury or locally produced items was created. But practically all licensing restrictions on imports were removed, and major exchange taxes as well as mixed or multiple rates were abolished. Imports still required registration, but this became a routine matter; if the application met all legal requirements registration was automatic. A minor stamp tax of 3 per cent was collected on all registrations; a few imports required prior approval of certain ministries (e.g., for health reasons, as in many industrialized countries). Some items on the prohibited list could be imported if they originated in countries having either a balanced trade or barter and payments agreement with Colombia. Other prohibitions were lifted if "export vouchers" (introduced in August 1952) issued for certain minor exports were used to finance importation of the items otherwise prohibited, so long as both the exports and imports related to the same foreign country. During part of 1954 even the prohibited list was abolished and replaced with a flat 40 per cent tax.

As the domestic boom got out of hand and coffee prices began to waver, late in 1954, the authorities reintroduced exchange taxes and regulations without, however, restricting most import registrations. First in October 1954 and then more thoroughly in February 1955 imports were reclassified and stamp taxes on import registrations were drastically increased, while prohibitions were once again enforced. Six import categories were created: preferential (raw materials for essential industries); other raw materials and essential products; essential durable and semidurable goods; less essential goods, importable only from certain countries; specified nonessential goods; and prohibited (luxury) goods. Stamp taxes ranged from 3 to 100 per cent. Imports of some foodstuffs were to be handled only by a special corporation. And late in 1954 the granting of exchange for import payments was made contingent upon arrival of the merchandise in Colombia, a regulation which had been abolished in November 1951.

The payments situation continued deteriorating during 1955 and 1956; it appears that at that time attempts at control relied mainly on indirect measures, such as stamp taxes and the free-market rate, plus exchange control. In other words, "essential" imports continued being registered freely and flooding into the country, and they continued to make up the bulk of the import bill,[4] while the queues waiting to buy foreign exchange for 2.5 pesos at the central bank became longer. By June 1956 authorities gave importers waiting for exchange authorizations the option of buying exchange immediately at the official rate of 2.5 pesos per dollar for half of the value of their pending applications, if they obtained the other half in the free market, where the rate at that time stood at about 4.7 pesos. By the end of 1956 that rate was 6.5 pesos. In October 1956, the payments crisis had provoked the closing of the exchange registration office, except for consideration of applications for vital imports. It was reopened, with tighter regulations and prohibitions, in January 1957. Most import registrations were also suspended during those months, and their easy granting came to an end; from January 1957 on, import control became the first and major hurdle faced by potential importers before they reached the exchange window.

Under the stabilization plan of June 1957 all imports were still subject to registration, and lists of prohibited, free, and prior license imports were established. This control system, which with further refinements was the one still in effect during 1971, was consolidated by Law 1 of January 1959.

Beginning in 1957, prior exchange registration was also enforced systematically for import payments, requiring submission of an import registration plus evidence that the goods had entered Colombia. Importers were given the choice of paying through a free market (at 6.2 pesos at the end of 1957) in which case they were exempted from the 10 per cent remittance tax. Establishment of higher import exchange rates and tougher standards for prior import deposits made it possible to relax import-licensing requirements for some commodities; during the second half of 1957, for example, two-thirds of all import registrations were on the free list, and only one-third (mainly capital goods) fell under the prior license list. But the rate of refused requests for goods in the prior license list is said to have been high, nearly 40 per cent by value of requests during those difficult months.

After the commercial arrears had been liquidated, and the payments crisis and inflationary pressures dampened by the austerity measures of 1957 and 1958, growth began to pick up again in a climate of stability. Throughout 1959, 1960, and even 1961, import controls remained stringent but fairly steady. Some even saw a trend toward liberalization as exchange reserves recovered. Certainly imports rose steadily from their 1958 low.

Difficulties in the world coffee market continued to be used as the major justification for rigorous import controls. By 1960 it was felt that about one-fourth or one-third of potential import demand was restricted by the licensing system, and that this was done more by flat prohibitions, frequently of protectionist intent, than by rejection of license applications. About half of the items in the tariff were at that time on the prohibited list. Among registered imports, the share of those on the free list had declined slightly to 60 per cent from about 65 per cent in 1959. The value of import license requests rejected as a percentage of the value of all license applications fluctuated at about 15 per cent throughout 1958, 1959, and 1960. These rates of rejection underestimate the strength of import demand not only because of the existence (and changing size) of the prohibited list, but also because the Superintendency of Imports, and later INCOMEX, made it a practice to discourage applications doomed to failure by reacting negatively to informal inquiries. The depressed conditions of the world coffee market also led Colombian authorities about this time to use the licensing mechanism to discriminate by source of imports, as part of bilateral barter deals involving mostly new coffee exports. Imports not normally permitted were occasionally allowed from bilateral partners (e.g., motor vehicles, giving Colombian roads an ecumenical assortment which included Russian, Polish, East German, and Czech vehicles) in exchange for coffee sold at de facto discounts perhaps as high as 20 per cent. During 1961 about U.S. $30 million of imports were licensed under barter and bilateral agreements.

In Chapter 7, I will discuss in detail the events surrounding the 1962 devaluation and the 1965–66 liberalization episode. Here it will be sufficient to note that import controls went through spasmodic tightening and loosening cycles: the free list, which by mid-1965 was vanishing, covered 80 per cent of all registered imports in October 1966. By December 1966 there was no free list. Throughout 1967 import controls were rigorously enforced; there was practically no free list, and it is said that of the total number of import license requests presented, about 40 per cent were rejected. In terms of value, about 25 per cent of total requests were turned down; the percentage was lower for global and nonreimbursable requests, and higher for reimbursable ones. Steep prior import deposits were reintroduced, and exchange controls were tightened. Imports dwindled; their customs value in 1967 was 26 per cent below 1966, while the drop in registrations was 18 per cent. Only after May 1968 did the free list regain some significance: free-list registrations were only 4 per cent of all reimbursable import registrations in 1967, rising to 12 per cent in 1968. The liberalization rock continued to be pushed uphill, slowly, once again. By 1970, the free list had reached 20 per cent of all reimbursable registrations (17 per cent of all registrations).

Growing foreign-exchange earnings, due both to the success of export-promoting policies and to favorable world market conditions, coupled with inflationary pressures induced a quickening of the liberalization trend during 1972–74. In August 1973 the prohibited list was eliminated, placing the 705 items then in that category under the prior license list. During 1973 and 1974, about 1,400 items under the prior license list were transferred to the free list; these were mostly items for which import permits had been readily granted during earlier years. During the first half of 1974 about 93 per cent of import requests under the prior list were being approved; rejections involved either protectionist motivation or simply a careless presentation of the request in the eyes of the authorities. It was expected that by the end of 1974, 50 per cent of all imports would be entering Colombia under the free list. On the other hand, while inflation stimulated the relaxation of import controls during 1973 and 1974, it also led to a large number of *export* prohibitions of both rural and industrial commodities.

THE OPERATION OF IMPORT CONTROLS DURING 1971

Beginning in March 1967 the import and exchange-control system took the basic shape it had in about 1971. It should be borne in mind, however, that the description contained in this section provides a snapshot of a system evolving in the direction of liberalization, and still engaged in administrative "fine tuning."

The Processing of License Requests.

All potential importers must present INCOMEX with a detailed description of the goods they wish to purchase, including intended means and timing of payment, and must also complete a questionnaire (following Resolution 15 of 1967) giving company information on payroll, number of workers, capacity, imports during current and previous three years, income and sales taxes paid during current and previous three years, minor exports for the same period, previous imports of the products intended to be imported, inventories of these products and their expected life, and some additional data. A separate form must usually be completed for each commodity, although exceptions to this rule are possible; slightly different forms of request are prescribed by Resolution 15 for industry, commerce, and government.

The INCOMEX staff first checks to see whether all the required documentation and information have been presented fully and accurately. Besides the import description and the Resolution 15 form, importers must show evidence of tax settlements and that they have made the required prior import deposits. In principle, then, the mechanism of import control can reinforce the Treasury's efforts to reduce tax evasion, particularly among commercial houses. At this stage, import applications can be returned (not officially rejected) on grounds of improper completion of forms. INCOMEX[5] argues that such devolutions are done on purely technical grounds (e.g., because the description of the proposed import is sketchy, which may lead to trouble at customs when it arrives in the country) and complains that the company employees who carelessly completed the forms then call such devolutions rejections to protect themselves. Problems arise particularly with new or complex products. In fact, the punctiliousness with which INCOMEX insists on the quality of information on import requests can be adjusted depending on the pressure of import demand. Whether an import request is returned or rejected, the potential importer can submit a new one at once. During 1971, it was estimated that of the total value of requested imports, only about 3 per cent were returned because of insufficient information or procedural mistakes.

If the application is satisfactory in form, the INCOMEX staff next examines whether products similar to those requested are produced locally. Extensive files on domestic production have been built up during the last few years. There is at this point a frank and clear protectionist bias; in case of doubt, the presumption is that local goods are indeed fully satisfactory candidates for import replacement, at least in their physical attributes. Prospective importers whose requests have been turned down on these grounds bear the burden of demonstrating to INCOMEX that the local product is in fact different from the proposed imports because of quality, product specification, or other reasons. Price differences, unless extreme, are not considered valid grounds for importing. INCOMEX occasionally brings together the prospective importer and the local import-competing producer, to iron out serious disagreements regarding prices, quality, and specifications. INCOMEX officials occasionally visit plants of import-competing firms to verify their capacity, output quality, and other characteristics, a time-consuming, subjective, and ad hoc practice.

As a third step, the INCOMEX staff looks closely at the unit dollar price of the potential import. The point here is *not* to keep track of margins between Colombian and world prices but to control overinvoicing of raw materials and parts, particularly by subsidiaries of foreign companies buying from their parents. INCOMEX and other Colombian officials argue, for example, that pharmaceutical companies operating in Colombia but owned abroad have been shown to have inflated the value of their imports of raw materials as a way of disguising profit remittances.[6] Thus, import control emerges also as a tool for regulating intracompany transfers of profits, particularly by foreign investors in the import-competing sector. The need for such regulation, of course, would disappear if these companies did not receive protection against imports of *finished* products. Even items on the free list may be held up if there is a suspicion that dollar prices declared in the registration request are out of line with world prices.

Since much direct foreign investment consists of imports of machinery and equipment, their registered value later on becomes part of the base on which under Colombian regulations allowable profit remittances abroad are computed. It is thus important for the control system to check on the real (international) value of the machinery, which is typically brought in with nonreimbursable licenses. Stories are told of gross overvaluation in some license requests, designed to inflate the value of foreign investment.

All the above procedures are handled by the Junta de Importaciones staff, whose members do not have the power to reject or accept the applications (although, as noted above, they can return applications on procedural grounds). That power, including the option of approving an application in part, lies in the Junta de Importaciones itself, a body of five permanent members, including the head of INCOMEX. Decisions on all prior license applications, totaling roughly 150,000 per year, must be made by this body, which handles about 500 applications per day. The work load is even higher than implied, as the daily tasks are carried out typically by only three members of the junta, since the other two, particularly the INCOMEX head, have other duties. The technical staff of the junta is also small, with about fifteen professionals plus supporting employees. In spite of this staggering burden, the junta is kept deliberately small to minimize the danger of corruption. The same reason is given for keeping its operations in Bogotá, in spite of pressure from various regions to decentralize the junta's decision-making powers. The junta decisions are, in principle, public. Under Article 75 of Law 444 of March 1967, INCOMEX must publish weekly all import permits granted, as well as other data on its operations. Decisions on rejections have been published off and on; publication of rejections stimulated fraudulent activities for a while by individuals who offered the unlucky applicants false contacts which presumably would improve their chances in future applications. Since 1967 the turnover of junta members has been low: for the three slots which are not ex officio there have been only eight members during the last five years (two died on the job). The junta is widely respected for its hard work and honesty; it does lead a fishbowl existence.

Each month, the Junta de Importaciones receives from the Junta Monetaria, the top monetary authority, an over-all foreign-exchange budget for all imports, which is determined on the basis of actual and expected exchange earnings. The import junta then regulates its approvals to keep within that limit. It may also be noted that it dislikes public announcements of changes in the budget, on the grounds that to do so may disturb its method of operation. In particular, rumors of a cut in the monthly limit are said to produce sharp increases in license applications.

Criteria for Evaluating License Requests.

The junta members are the first to admit that they follow no fast and rigid rules when deciding on applications (although unhelpful lists of "criteria" can be found in the relevant legislation, as in Article 77 of Law 444) and that the process is highly subjective. There are no quotas for particular products, nor for firms, nor for regions. The major criterion is a protectionist one, but occasionally imports are permitted if the quality of domestic output deteriorates markedly, or if domestic prices become unacceptably high. While junta members say all the right things about scaring local monopolistic positions by such actions, the implementation is ad hoc, with protectionist sentiment dominating. Throughout the 1960s, imports on the prior license list have been informally subdivided into three groups: those for which licensing depends on local supply conditions of competing products, those generally approved, and those generally disapproved, but which are kept on the prior list to discourage monopolistic practices by domestic producers. The protectionist bias also showed in the occasional practice during the 1960s of transferring items from the free to the prior license or prohibited category as soon as a new plant began to produce locally a previously importable good (that transfer was often done before the plant began to operate, to ward off inventory accumulation). During more recent years, however, the number of items transferred to the prohibited list dwindled. But the import control mechanism remained a key tool for protecting large new ventures, such as the automobile industry, for which special regimes and policies were established. Junta officials defend their protectionist bias bluntly: Given other policies and circumstances outside their control (exchange-rate policy and coffee prices, for example) and given the need to ration foreign exchange, what better procedure can they follow than to ask potential importers whether or not they have checked to see whether the product they wish to bring in can be found within Colombia? Junta officials say that when in doubt it is better to deny a request on protectionist grounds, a decision which after all can be reversed, than to allow imports damaging to a local producer, a decision more difficult to offset. A last argument given by the junta members in favor of their protectionist stance may baffle the pure trade theorist: Since very few firms export their entire output, they say, weakening the local base of most firms by allowing "excessive" competition from imports will hurt their exporting capacity. As I noted in Chapter 2, this argument has short-run validity in a setting of monopolistic competition; its validity for the long run, however, is doubtful under standard assumptions regarding firm behavior.

The process of establishing whether or not there is domestic production of a given item is not without complications and loopholes. A given large company, for example, can have a subsidiary declare that it does *not* produce a given product locally, so that the mother company may be allowed to import it. The same subsidiary may, however, declare to INCOMEX that it does produce the particular item when a competitor of the large company requests a license. Given the limited staff of the Junta de Importaciones, it is not always possible to check on these ambiguities. It is said that, particularly during 1965, subsidiaries were used in the way described. For some commodities, such as machine tools, it becomes difficult to establish whether local production of the right quality and design is available, as goods of that kind are often made to order.

Some junta members admit favoring applications from less developed regions within Colombia, and from firms with good records in nontraditional exports (with or without the Vallejo Plan). As discussed below, the granting of global licenses typically involves negotiations regarding export targets. Firms with large tax payments are allegedly favored over those paying few taxes, even if there is no evidence of tax evasion. The argument given is that the government has a fiscal interest in channeling imports toward those firms that are good tax-yielding partners of the public sector, which chooses to use large tax payments as prima facie evidence of efficiency in the use of imported inputs. Although the junta looks closely at past imports of firms requesting fresh licenses, it claims to take into account the needs of new importers, again "by ear." Installed capacity is looked at, but so is employment; there is no obvious a priori reason to expect such a subjective process by itself to lead to a bias in favor of capital-intensive activities greater than one in favor of labor-intensive firms. Some junta members claim that their decisions are also influenced by the state of labor relations in the firm requesting a license. Since good labor relations are likely to be associated with high wages (and a relatively small labor force), a bias in favor of capital intensity may be introduced this way.

The Junta de Importaciones also examines the actual and expected inventory levels of applicants and turns down a request if stocks are deemed excessive. Inventories for four to six months of production are considered reasonable, and are encouraged to save INCOMEX the paper work involved in more frequent requests associated with lower inventories.

Biases in the Evaluation Process.

This gentlemanly case-by-case style of import control leads to biases not always fully recognized by those in charge of its operations.[7] Given the burden of work and the speed with which applications must be handled, there is an inevitable tendency to accept without much analysis most "reasonable" requests from established, well-known (i.e., large) companies and to examine more closely and reject, in case of doubt or exchange stringency, those of less well-known, smaller newcomers, many of which may not even bother to apply. The junta prides itself, with good reason, on remaining open to complaints from importers, and incredibly its members find time to listen to an unending stream of petitioners, whether powerful or not. Furthermore, it argues that at times of exchange stringency, proportional cuts in import requests are larger for bigger than for smaller firms, and that it tends more readily to overlook faulty request forms from small than from large importers.

But on balance, the larger and better-known importers find it easier than others to communicate with the junta. Given the Colombian milieu, potential small importers may actually exaggerate in their own minds the complications of dealing with INCOMEX, housed incidentally in imposing offices on some of the highest floors of the tallest building of Bogotá.[8] Some junta officials candidly admit that this may be so, but because of their strong belief in the necessity of control, they argue that there are no other practical ways of handling the enormous mass of actual and potential applications. What is so wrong, they ask, with tilting in favor of applications from long-established corporations, with honorable records, and of being skeptical of new and unknown applicants, who may turn out to be no better than phony industrialists, disguised smugglers, and black-market operators? In the Colombian social setting, where most people who count know each other directly or indirectly, it is not difficult for control officials to persuade themselves that all legitimate requests are sooner or later handled appropriately. Another justification given for a bias against some small import requests is the fear that such requests are simply a way of seeking legal window dressing for contraband. A shop, it is alleged, may rely mainly on smuggled imports but use an approved import license as a cover-up for its mostly illegal activities. A similar argument was sometimes given to justify flat prohibitions of some imports, because that way it was possible to know for sure that if those goods were found in Colombia, they came from contraband. In fact, however, the customs office often auctions off wholesale confiscated contraband items, thus providing window dressing items covering up shadier deals.

The argument is also heard that large firms can use some imported capital goods at fuller capacity than small ones. For example, import requests for computers from small and medium-sized firms are known to have been denied on the grounds that they could not use computers at full capacity. Similar requests from larger firms have been approved. It is also argued, not without reason, that bulk-buying abroad by large firms leads to dollar unit values for imports lower than those which would be obtained by small firms.

The junta keeps files of importers, including black or gray lists of those caught in what it regards as illegal or undesirable practices. The total number of importers is said to reach about 12,000; it will be seen in Chapter 6, however, that the number of *major* importers is considerably less. Among major private importers receiving particularly careful and sympathetic attention by the junta, incidentally, are those associated with mass communications, such as the press, radio, and television.

Ultimately, of course, the junta can argue that the pattern of imports simply reflects industrial, financial, and geographical concentration in Colombia, which they neither reinforce nor weaken significantly. The elimination of import controls by itself is unlikely to change those structural facts, they add. To this difficult issue we will return in the next chapter.

Given the location of the junta in Bogotá, Bogotá-based companies have an edge in access over those located elsewhere. The presence of large numbers of "Antioqueños" in top INCOMEX positions suggests that requests by firms located in Medellín are also likely to receive an especially sympathetic hearing. Pleas from other cities, Cali in particular, for regional offices with the power to decide on prior license imports have been turned down mainly on the grounds that such offices would be more subject to pressures originating in feelings of regional solidarity or in baser motives. At present, only a few items on the free list can be registered at the 27 INCOMEX regional offices outside Bogotá. The shuttling between provincial centers and Bogotá is regarded as a small price to pay for maintaining uniform national standards and minimizing the chances of corruption creeping into the decision-making process.

In a memo to the Minister of Development in December 1969 a group of businessmen from the Cauca Valley (where Cali is located) complained about excessive centralization of all governmental functions in Bogotá, leading to "innumerable trips to arrange trivial details." They argued that as a result, many corporate headquarters, if not whole plants, were being moved from that valley to Bogotá, depriving the foimer of many important ancillary activities, such as insurance, consulting, and publicity. INCOMEX was listed as the government office causing the largest number of trivial trips; there were others, however, such as the Superintendency of Prices, the Superintendency of Corporations, IFI, and the ministries of Health, Agriculture, Labor, and the Treasury (Tax Department). Centralized paper work associated with import licenses was the main target. In the memo, it was urged that six regional offices be given exchange quotas and be empowered to decide on license requests for spare parts, raw materials, and other inputs essential to keeping production going, but it was conceded that decisions on new capital goods or peculiar cases should remain centralized in Bogotá. It is noteworthy that this group of businessmen asked for the decentralization of import controls, not their abolition.

It may be seen in Table 5-3 that, according to the 1967 industrial census, Bogotá-based industrial firms did use on average more imported raw materials relative to their gross output than firms in the rest of the country. The textile and paper industries of Antioquia, clustered in and around Medellín, as well as those producing rubber products and electrical equipment in Cali and surroundings, however, surpassed Bogotá firms in these activities in their relative use of imported inputs.

It is generally admitted that requests under "commerce" are scrutinized more rigorously and rejected more frequently than those under "industry." This is partly due to the bias in favor of big, established firms, but also to a feeling that items requested under commerce are less essential than the others. Commerce, it is also argued, brings in a general variety of imports to add to more or less ample stocks, and some delay is unlikely to harm very much of anything, while industrial requests are of a specific nature and the materials sought are expected to be put into the production process with little delay. At any rate, the pressing nature of industrial needs is easier to demonstrate than that of commercial requests. Whatever the real reason, the effect of the difference in treatment is further to reinforce the bias against smaller industrial firms, which rely more on commercial intermediaries (often large ones) for imported inputs than do the larger firms.

To summarize some of the problems of the small industrial firm, particularly one located outside Bogotá: In spite of its more difficult access to credit, its inventories as a percentage of sales tend to be higher than those of the larger firms; attempts to lower inventories of imported items by relying on commercial intermediaries will be hampered by the greater difficulties of the latter in obtaining permits, and by their charging premium-inclusive prices for

TABLE 5-3

Imported Raw Materials as Percentages of Value of Colombian Gross Manufacturing Output, Total and Selected Regions, 1967

	All Colombia	Bogotá	Antioquia	Valle del Cauca
Foodstuffs	7.9	16.4	7.8	6.5
Beverages	3.7	3.9	3.2	3.0
Tobacco products	2.5	3.3	2.0	2.3
Textiles	5.9	4.3	7.2	2.0
Clothing	0.6	1.2	0.3	1.4
Wood products except furniture	2.0	8.5	3.4	1.9
Furniture (wood)	0.4	0.5	0.2	0.1
Paper and products	18.1	8.7	25.9	18.8
Printing and publishing	20.1	27.6	14.2	16.1
Leather products except shoes	5.0	5.1	6.0	5.5
Rubber products	33.6	21.3	12.3	40.5
Chemical products	28.3	33.5	33.5	27.0
Petroleum and coal products	4.9	44.4	0	0
Nonmetallic mineral products	7.4	5.0	5.4	4.6
Basic metal industries	9.1	51.2	10.5	7.6
Metal products except machinery	22.3	21.5	14.0	21.7
Nonelectrical machinery	13.6	20.2	13.7	5.6
Electrical machinery and appliances	27.6	25.2	20.0	34.3
Transport equipment	31.4	38.1	23.7	19.1
Other industries	21.5	24.2	14.0	22.0
Total manufacturing	12.2	19.2	9.8	14.2

Source: DANE, industrial census for 1967.

those items for which permits have been obtained; attempts to lower imported inventories involve the risk of stopping production at times of crisis if INCOMEX fails to handle license requests quickly.

Applications in the "official," i.e., governmental, category are in principle subjected to the same procedure as others. As they involve duty-free imports, special efforts have been made recently to ensure that goods which are also produced locally are not brought into the country by this means. Attempts to influence the junta by open flexing of political muscle appear to be surprisingly limited. Import requests from the armed forces, the police, and Congress, of course, receive sympathetic treatment, and rejections of these requests are documented particularly well. But there *are* occasional rejections of applications from these sources (often, alas, on ultraprotectionist grounds), as well as from other powerful public agencies. On balance, however, there is a presumption that official requests should be given priority, and they are said to fare better than private requests, particularly at times of exchange stringency.

Traditionally, nonreimbursable license requests are said to have had better chances of approval than reimbursable ones, simply because they did not involve immediate claims against the central bank for foreign exchange and typically involved capital goods not produced in Colombia. Frequently, they also involved large public-sector projects and international commitments. More recently, however, both protectionist and equity considerations have led to higher rates of refusal for nonreimbursable requests. The budding Colombian capital goods industry has exerted pressure in this direction, also pointing out the low duties and frequent exemptions on capital goods imports. Local entrepreneurs have also loudly complained when direct foreign investors have been allowed to bring in under nonreimbursable licenses machinery whose importation is not possible when requested under the reimbursable category. It is correctly felt that such a situation puts the local industrialist at an unfair disadvantage when competing in the local market with foreign-owned firms. It may be noted that INCOMEX claims to follow a policy of nondiscrimination between import requests from locally and foreign-owned companies located within Colombia. At a more pedestrian level, the possibility of importing automobiles under nonreimbursable licenses, for example, would lead according to INCOMEX to all kinds of illegal triangular deals. The tendency, therefore, is to apply the same protectionist or equity criteria whether or not the license request is reimbursable.

Searching for equity among established firms, the junta often handles several import requests from different companies for a given product, particularly critical raw materials, in one bunch. For example, when several beer companies apply for imported hops, their requests are considered together, so as to avoid giving one company advantages over the others simply on the basis of a temporarily better access to imported inputs. In the case of newcomers to the industry, projected output is taken into consideration. For others, the record of past levels of imports provides a first approximation to actual needs. When some important raw material is both imported and produced locally, and the latter is more expensive or of a lower quality than the former, mixing rules are enforced; i.e., for each imported pound each company must purchase two locally, again to avoid giving companies unfair advantage based on better access to superior imported inputs. When there are no obviously equitable arrangements possible there is a tendency to deny all requests; it is argued that it is better for all to do without imports than for a few to benefit from unfair advantages arising from a lucky access to the goods. Such favoritism, even if random, would cast doubt on the honesty and fairness of the junta. Like

Caesar's wife, the junta knows that it must not only be honest, but appear honest, even at the risk of being stern and unpleasant. The possibility of auctioning off licenses is not considered to lie within the rules of the game.

Global Licenses.

In the case of requests for global licenses, covering investment projects, the authorized department of INCOMEX is supposed to coordinate its study of those projects with the National Planning Department. The Committee on Global Licenses, which began operating during 1969, includes besides INCOMEX and the Planning Department, the ministries of the Treasury and of Development plus IFI, a public body that finances and sometimes runs industrial projects. There have been occasional episodes of bureaucratic rivalry among the committee members. The Junta de Importaciones retains the ultimate power to accept or reject the applications, and there have been cases where the junta has taken decisions contrary to the resolutions of the mixed Committee on Global Licenses. The data required for global license requests are extensive, and potentially permit a fairly comprehensive cost-benefit study of each project. The general impression, however, is that such studies are not carried out, or at least not very thoroughly. There are only five professionals in the Division of Global Licenses, each of whom is supposed to study about five projects per week.[9] However, this mechanism has been increasingly used to ensure that new projects, particularly those granted tax or other advantages, commit part of their expected output for exports; for several projects specific export targets have been laid down at the time of their approval by INCOMEX in the form of formal contracts. It is not in the INCOMEX style to insist rigidly on exact compliance with such targets, but the companies know that systematic departures from these promises can lead to a displeased and colder INCOMEX in the future. Until at least the completion of this study, once a global license had been obtained, ordinary requests charged against it were typically granted almost automatically. Furthermore, changes in the specifications of equipment to be imported were allowed with relative ease. The processing of the global license request itself took an average of about two months, although not surprisingly, there were substantial variations from this average, depending on the nature of the project. It may be noted that in reviewing global licenses INCOMEX examined the proposed ways of financing the imports and could suggest modifications.

The 19-page questionnaire which must still be completed in applying for a global license is admittedly terrifying for a small entrepreneur, who in all likelihood needs to hire a consultant to fill it out. INCOMEX has been considering requiring a briefer questionnaire for smaller businessmen, but as of September 1971 this had not been done.

In many cases, at the same time that a project is being processed by INCOMEX with an eye to import demand, it will also be analyzed by other members of the Committee on Global Licenses and by the Committee on Royalties—responsible for supervising royalty payments abroad—which have other major preoccupations besides import demand. For example, all major direct foreign investments in Colombia must by law be approved by the Planning Office. Projects financed by IFI will of course be examined by that institution. As noted above, the coordination among different public agencies in this area leaves much to be desired; overlap and conflict abound.

The mechanism for granting global licenses, originally designed among other things to save paperwork and to avoid complications at customs, and the associated *gravamen único* (single import duty) have come under increasing fire from within the government not only for lacking sufficient coordination in their administration with bodies outside INCOMEX but also for excessive generosity in reducing tariff rates on capital goods.

Other Operating Practices.

Ordinary and global licenses were normally examined by INCOMEX following the chronological order of their presentation. Ordinary licenses were decided on usually within a month or a month and a half of presentation, while for global licenses the waiting period was naturally longer and less predictable. Extensions and modifications of ordinary licenses took less than a month. INCOMEX claimed that urgent requests were handled even faster, if necessary in a day, say, in cases where imported parts were essential to prevent production breakdowns. Rejections of applications were accompanied by the reason or reasons given by the junta for such a decision; seventy-two possible reasons were listed by the junta. Frequently, particularly during times of severe exchange shortage, a reapplication will be rapidly made following the rejection, but during more relaxed times, as during 1971, the few rejections were taken more seriously. Once approval was secured, and imports had cleared customs, there was no particular difficulty in obtaining the foreign exchange for payment. With memories of the pile-up of commercial arrears in 1955–56 and of the less dramatic situation in 1966–67 still fresh in their minds, the authorities have been careful in recent years not to issue import licenses beyond expected exchange earnings.

INCOMEX did not handle the further steps an importer had to take to obtain foreign exchange to pay for his goods once they arrived in Colombia. This was the responsibility of the central bank, with which the importer had to make a deposit in pesos equal to 95 per cent of the needed exchange, twenty days before making an application for an exchange registration. Proof that goods had cleared customs also had to be presented. At this stage the request for exchange was granted quickly; the exchange disbursements took place between one and twenty months after the merchandise had gone through customs. The central bank, however, could double-check with INCOMEX on unit dollar prices to prevent overinvoicing.

It is part of the INCOMEX style to avoid if possible having to issue a formal refusal; so, particularly with global licenses, negative signals are often sent informally, and the applications are seldom registered as rejections. Furthermore, as its policies are by now fairly well known, many potential importers do not even bother to apply, saving themselves time, trouble, and expense.[10]

Ordinary import permits were good for only five months;[11] if imports were not brought in within that time, a new permit or a three-month extension of the old one had to be secured. It had been argued that such limitations put the Colombian importer at a bargaining disadvantage vis-à-vis foreign suppliers, who shade their prices upward because they are aware of the time pressure faced by Colombians wanting to shop around. It is INCOMEX's expectation that goods imported in the industrial category will be used only by the company to which the license has been issued. When INCOMEX was questioned about the legality of resales of merchandise imported for industrial companies, its answers were surprisingly fuzzy. The license itself is clearly non-negotiable, as it is issued only to a specific company or person. The reselling of the imported items by industrial users is apparently not strictly illegal, but it is frowned upon by INCOMEX, if only because it implies that normal requirements stated in the Resolution 15 request form were misleading or false. Companies shown to be systematically selling part of their imported industrial inputs to others are punished by INCOMEX with total or partial rejection of future requests. Similar punishment is dealt out to individuals or companies discovered trying to import under several social or private names. INCOMEX's point is that it wants to know exactly how many imports can be traced to each industrial firm or individual. INCOMEX, however, does not punish temporary swapping or lending of imported items among industrial firms. Indeed, it finds such a practice quite reasonable, particularly if done during periods of stringency and in a "nonspeculative" manner. Apparently, during 1971 very little reselling or swapping of noncommercial imports took place, although some INCOMEX officials indicated that that practice was widespread during difficult years, e.g., 1967. Since most imports are purchased directly by companies that use them as inputs in the production of other commodities, arm's length market prices for these inputs are not observed in Colombia. Consequently, it is difficult if not impossible to establish exactly the premiums attached to import licenses, premiums which in any case are very likely to fluctuate sharply between years (e.g., between 1967 and 1971).

It also follows that it is difficult to establish the meaning of price control for imported industrial inputs. In the case of commercial imports, according to regulations INCOMEX should theoretically coordinate its activities with the Superintendencia de Precios (Price Control Board) to determine the margin at which imported goods are resold, i.e., to control the premiums derived from licenses. Such control, however, is very sporadic and unsystematic, and takes place mainly when somebody makes public a scandal about excessive margins. Nevertheless, INCOMEX claims that import controls are superior to tariffs, among other reasons because they avoid making imports more expensive, a doubtful claim in view of the loose control over the license premiums. Conventional wisdom in Colombia regards the profitability of large importing commercial houses as very high; in particular, hardware stores selling imports are popularly considered to be "gold mines." Nevertheless, the junta argues that it tries to spread out import permits among commercial importers as much and as fairly as it can.

There are more or less subtle ways by which the junta discriminates according to country of origin of potential imports. Requests to import television sets from Spain, for example, are said to have a better chance of approval than requests to import from the United States, both because Spain has a bilateral payments agreement with Colombia and because the authorities consider that the local industry will have an easier time competing with Spanish than with U.S. sets. Even where there are no explicit bilateral agreements, the junta de facto administers "gentlemen's agreements" with countries such as Japan, which make purchases from Colombia that are outside coffee agreement channels in exchange for Colombian commitments to import their goods. These games, of course, are also played by countries without explicit generalized import controls, even if they preach multilateral trade, particularly to partners with whom their balance-of-payments account shows a surplus. Some Colombian officials complain that socialist countries with which Colombia has bilateral payments agreements that are typically in surplus do not advertise their goods as vigorously as they might among potential importers. Often, the junta has to nudge importers so that they will divert their purchases to those countries; requests for licenses to import from those countries are granted more readily than requests to import from, say, the dollar area. But the quantitative importance of such trade remains small. As shown in Chapter 3, during 1967–69, less than 3 per cent of Colombian imports came from socialist countries.

As the Colombian foreign-exchange position improved during 1971 and 1972, the role of U.S. tied aid declined. The use of import controls to enforce tying also declined accordingly. In earlier years, however, INCOMEX and related institutions took strong measures to divert purchases toward U.S. products. These included favorable credit conditions, exemption from prior deposit requirements, and direct pressure on importers to buy from the United States. Those were the days of bitter wrangling over "positive" and "negative" lists, and "additionality."[12] U.S. officials were in the awkward position of simultaneously urging Colombians to liberalize import controls, to use controls to enforce tying, and to stop using controls to divert imports toward bilateral partners, such as Spain and the socialist countries.

The Treaty of Cartagena, which created the Andean group, calls for the elimination of administrative import restrictions among member countries. Colombia has been keeping her side of that bargain, and only routine registration requirements are required for imports from Andean countries.

The INCOMEX Image.

The INCOMEX performance in about 1971 was generally praised by industrial entrepreneurs interviewed during the middle part of that year. In almost all cases they compared it very favorably with the pre-1967 situation, about which stories were told that typically associated delays, corruption, and inefficiency with import controls. The flexibility, efficiency, and honesty of INCOMEX were also compared favorably with those of customs. It should be borne in mind, however, that most of these entrepreneurs came from relatively large companies, and that the foreign-exchange situation was quite relaxed during 1971, especially in contrast with 1967 and earlier years. The major complaint against INCOMEX deals with imports of spare parts, for which delays of even one month in the handling of import requests are a nuisance. Frequently, small spare parts are simply smuggled into the country by employees sent specially for that purpose to Miami and New York. It may be noted that the free- or black-market peso rate during 1971 was only about 15 per cent above the certificate rate and less than that during 1972; so using exchange from this source was not very expensive. INCOMEX, of course, is aware of these goings-on and has been considering ways of legalizing the situation, such as expanding the "minor" import category, under which imports worth less than $20 (less than $40 for books) are now allowed without prior license or registration.

Entrepreneurs, particularly those in charge of large companies, find INCOMEX on the whole a bulwark against foreign competition and at the same time an even more reliable supplier of cheap imported inputs. During 1971–72, the few controversies between entrepreneurs and INCOMEX dealt more with imports the latter had allowed to come into the country than with denials of import requests.

Apart from the smuggling of spare parts and some consumer goods, such as furs, perfumes, jewelry, and cigarettes, INCOMEX feels that the system is relatively free of leaks and well organized, in the sense that importers know what to expect. Its officials argue, not without reason, that the combination of moderate tariffs plus import controls forms a more powerful barrier to smuggling than a situation with higher tariffs and no import controls. A key element in their reasoning is that, as more items are shifted from the prohibited list to the prior license list, more uncertainty will be planted in the minds of would-be smugglers, whose profit margins could be reduced or wiped out if INCOMEX suddenly permits imports of moderately taxed goods.

The performance of the INCOMEX import control system has a good reputation even outside Colombia; officials from other Latin American countries have visited Bogotá to study it for possible application in their own countries.

One may wonder how well the INCOMEX import control system, which some observers find even more centralized than Soviet-type planning, would have performed during 1967–72 if foreign exchange had been less plentiful, or the quality of the members of the Junta de Importaciones had not been as high as it was. In a way, INCOMEX during the years under study represented some of the positive facets of elitist rule in Colombia. A more decentralized import control system, more open to rising entrepreneurs, would have led in all likelihood to an informal auctioning off of licenses by extralegal means.

SOME EVIDENCE OF THE COMBINED OPERATION OF THE IMPORT-REPRESSING MECHANISMS

The presence of duties, prior deposits, and import controls has led to a substantial gap between the domestic and world market prices of importable goods. That part of the gap corresponding to the premium attributable to import licenses has fluctuated sharply from year to year and from product to product, but data on its exact magnitude are scanty. The most systematic comparison between Colombian and world prices has been carried out by Thomas L. Hutcheson[13] for a sample of commodities during 1969. Evidence from this study on the resource allocation effects of the Colombian system of protection will be analyzed in Chapter 8; here the evidence on the interaction of tariffs and import controls and on the average gap between domestic and foreign prices will be discussed.

In the sample of 385 products, the average gap between domestic and foreign prices at the going import exchange rate was 47 per cent, as may be seen in Table 5-4. On balance, there was "water" in the tariff, as the average duty was 71 per cent. But such water was concentrated in goods produced by the more traditional and established branches of Colombian manufacturing, such as those producing foodstuffs, clothing, and leather products. Neverthe-

TABLE 5-4

Tariffs, Import Regimes, and Gaps Between Domestic and International Prices, 1969

	Excess of Domestic over International Prices	Ad Valorem Import Duty	Import Regime Classification[a]	Number of Observations
Mainly foodstuffs and beverages	25%	85%	2.7	52
Textiles, clothing, furniture, leather, and paper products	47	113	2.5	89
Chemical, rubber, glass, and other nonmetallic mineral products	46	56	2.1	79
Other manufactured goods	55	52	2.0	165
All products	47	71	2.2	385

SOURCE: Computed from data kindly made available by Thomas L. Hutcheson.

a. Dummies for import regime classification are as follows: 1 for the free list, 2 for the prior license list, and 3 for the prohibited list.

less, at least for this sample and on average, the premiums generated by the import licensing system even for less traditional items such as those under "other manufactured goods" were small during 1969.

Since regressions intended to explain the domestic-international price gap as a function of import duties and a dummy for the import regime (see Table 5-4, note a) yield very poor results, the averages shown in Table 5-4 should be taken with great caution. The only t statistics higher than 1.0 are those for the tariff variable in the group of other manufactured goods (a positive t ratio of 1.38) and for the import regime dummy in the group of chemical, rubber, glass, and other nonmetallic mineral products (a positive t ratio of 1.53). These data, however, confirm a strong positive correlation between the import duty and the stringency of the import regime for the whole sample and for each of the groups considered except for other manufactured goods.

NOTES

1. The lists are formally approved by the Superior Council of Foreign Trade (Consejo Superior de Comercio Exterior) on the advice of INCOMEX, which acts as its technical secretariat. That council is presided over by the Minister of Development, and also includes the ministers of Foreign Relations, the Treasury, and Agriculture plus the head of the Planning Office, the manager of the central bank, the manager of the Coffee Growers' Federation, the manager of IFI, the director of PROEXPO, and the director of INCOMEX. This group also forms the core of the Council of Economic Policy, which includes also the President of the republic and the

ministers of Public Works and of Labor. These two councils plus the Junta Monetaria form the three key policymaking bodies in the economic field. The director of INCOMEX is a member of the three bodies. Within INCOMEX, which covers all aspects of foreign trade, the Junta de Importaciones handles the import control system.

2. Resolution 22 of September 22, 1970, also limits the free list to the reimbursable category and to commodities originating in the same country where they have been purchased. The free list applicable to LAFTA countries is somewhat larger than that described above.

3. This section is heavily based on the IMF's annual *Report on Exchange Restrictions* and on interviews with Colombian officials and with officials in several inter-American and international institutions.

4. All import registrations were divided as follows:

| | *Official Market* | | *Free* |
	Government	*Private*	*Market*
1955	21%	75%	4%
1956	21	58	21
1957 I	18	67	15

5. My remarks on INCOMEX usually refer both to formal regulations and informal opinions of INCOMEX officials interviewed during July–September 1971 and August 1972. In fact, the Junta de Importaciones is only one part of the INCOMEX organization, which also covers other aspects of foreign trade.

6. The impressive evidence on overinvoicing in pharmaceuticals and other industries is discussed in Constantine V. Vaitsos, "Transferencia de Recursos y Preservación de Rentas Monopolísticas," *Revista de Planeación y Desarrollo* (published by the National Planning Department, Bogotá), July 1971, pp. 35–72. For the pharmaceutical companies in the sample overinvoicing averaged 155 per cent. Overinvoicing is also said to occur in items such as books and machine tools, for which it is more difficult to ascertain exact prices because of quality differences and heterogeneity of specifications. Exchange control is used by Colombian authorities to keep close tabs on payments for patents and royalties.

7. There are similarities between the Colombian style of import controls and the operating manner of committees in charge of undergraduate admissions in places like Yale University, where demand also exceeds supply. At both places there is great resistance to formalized quotas, regarded as rigid, and a tendency to fudge criteria until they become shapeless—a subjective Jell-O. Those making the control decisions resent any attempt at defining clear-cut objective rules, which are easily enough shown to be unable to cover fairly all possible cases, even when those rules would yield the same results as the committee's judgment in 95 per cent of all cases. For the sake of that 5 per cent of power, the administrators prefer gentlemanly ambiguity.

8. In July 1973 a spectacular fire destroyed the INCOMEX offices there, including import control records. Since then, however, INCOMEX has found new offices, not as high but just as plush.

9. INCOMEX argues that, even though its staff may not have time to carry out careful cost-benefit studies, the process of requesting massive data from entrepreneurs planning a new project will force businessmen to rethink their venture carefully. This is but one example of the somewhat paternalistic attitude often found among INCOMEX officials. In some cases the study of a given project is reduced to a quick visit to the plant proposing an enlargement. INCOMEX expects that requests for global licenses will involve projects in a fairly advanced state of study by the firm.

10. In 1971, all requests for import licenses had to be accompanied by a 100-peso fee and, more recently, by an additional 50-peso charge (a total of about U.S. $7). The paperwork required for making an application must also represent a small but significant expense for companies,

particularly in the case of global licenses. Such an expense is likely to be proportionally higher for smaller firms. INCOMEX finances itself partly out of the import license fees, which give it additional autonomy in contrast to government agencies more dependent on the national budget.

11. When approval is granted to an import request, copies of the import registration are sent to the central bank, the Customs office, and the Colombian consul nearest the foreign city from which the goods are to be shipped. The Colombian consul may not issue the required shipping authorization without that document.

12. See Thomas L. Hutcheson and Richard C. Porter, *The Cost of Tying Aid: A Method and Some Colombian Estimates,* Princeton Studies in International Finance 30 (Princeton, N.J.: Princeton University Press, March 1972), particularly pp.17–20. The infamous "additionality" clause in U.S. aid was abolished during the visit of President Carlos Lleras Restrepo to the United States in June 1969.

13. The results of his work are summarized in Thomas L. Hutcheson, "Incentives for Industrialization in Colombia" (Ph.D. diss., University of Michigan, 1973). I am most grateful to Hutcheson for making his unpublished basic data available to me. For a description of those data, see Appendix B of his thesis.

Chapter 6

Import Controls in 1970-71: Some Quantifiable Features

A description of the procedures followed by Colombian authorities in granting or rejecting import requests produces an impression of overwhelming complexity, particularly to market-oriented economists. It seems hard to understand how a handful of authorities, aided by a small staff, can cope with the estimated 150,000 import requests per year, and even harder to see how such requests can be processed in a sensible and systematic manner.

In this chapter, an attempt will be made to throw some light on this question by analyzing 1970 registered imports according to size of importers. It will be seen that because the import control authorities are familiar with about 500 major private importers, they are able to be reasonably sure about the destination of half the total value of registered imports. It is not farfetched to suppose that those 500 major importers make up the core of the Colombian socioeconomic system, and that they and the INCOMEX authorities know each other fairly well. With half of the imports going to 500 companies, and about 20 per cent going to the public sector, only 30 per cent has to be distributed in retail fashion.

An attempt will also be made in this chapter to quantify some aspects of INCOMEX behavior in accepting or rejecting import requests, as revealed by its handling of a sample of such requests during 1971.

Basic data for the type of exercise tackled in this chapter are not easily available. The data submitted to INCOMEX with import requests are rich, and potentially constitute a running census of at least the major Colombian industrial and commercial enterprises. It is a pity that such an opportunity for an up-to-date and continuous flow of information is largely wasted. Resolution

153

15 forms are thrown out shortly after INCOMEX decides on the import request, and only summary information on import registrations and requests appears to be maintained. Putting all of the data contained in Resolution 15 forms into a properly programmed computer would provide INCOMEX with a systematic and accessible source of information regarding importers as well as of other valuable data for decision-making, and would give the country a clearer idea of its economic structure. Coordination of import controls with tax enforcement and price controls would also become a more practical possibility. Perhaps the analysis in this chapter will illustrate how rich the data available to INCOMEX are.

During the second half of 1971, INCOMEX officials kindly allowed me to examine about 2,500 license requests in the commercial and industrial categories. The sample included cases of several requests from the same company. The requests had been either accepted or rejected, totally or partially, by the Junta de Importaciones of INCOMEX. A smaller sample (199) was also taken of requests in the official category. In choosing the requests, no refined sampling method was followed; basically I tried to get information on those requests that were around at the time, and were made available for examination. As relatively few applications were being rejected during the second half of 1971, I made a special effort to obtain data on rejected requests. There was also a bias in favor of obtaining requests from as many different companies as possible. There does not appear to be any major seasonal pattern to license requests, except a decline in numbers in December and January; so the exclusive use of the half-year of information should not introduce any bias.

From the license requests two types of information were obtained: a censuslike coverage of imports, employment, and other characteristics for each company (*not* plant) in 1970, and data on the specific import request during the second half of 1971 (amount, rejection or acceptance, and reasons for rejections).

The former type of information will be discussed first. It should be added that the information obtained in my sample did not include all data made available in the import requests, because of obvious constraints on research facilities. For example, import and tax data in the forms were given for four years (1968 through 1971). Other information, such as local purchases of goods similar to the requested imports, was so spotty that a decision was made to ignore it.

MAJOR COLOMBIAN IMPORTERS IN 1970

Following INCOMEX categories, major private importers can be subdivided into an industrial and a commercial group. Industrial importers use imports in their production process; commercial importers resell the foreign goods to local buyers. While Resolution 15 forms give no information on the ownership of the company making the import request, a somewhat rough-and-ready separation was also made according to presumed nationality.[1] In general, it was presumed that a company was Colombian-owned unless there was firm evidence to the contrary. Only companies for which foreign ownership came to 50 per cent or more were treated as foreign-owned; all others were regarded as national. There were, however, relatively few joint ventures in the sample. Note that the definition of foreign-owned companies used here is considerably weaker than that used in the Andean code on foreign investment. Lack of reliable and up-to-date data was the major reason for my choice of the definition, which implies a higher share of national ownership.

Table 6-1 contains a summary of major industrial[2] importers, classified according to their ownership status (domestic or foreign) and the value of their registered imports during 1970. Data are also presented on the number of their

TABLE 6-1

Major Industrial Importers in Colombia, 1970

No. of Cos.	Industrial Cos. Classified by Ownership and Value of Imports	Registered Imports, 1970 (mill. U.S. dol.)	No. of Employees (thous.)	Minor Exports, 1970 (mill. U.S. dol.)	Income and Sales Taxes Paid in 1970 (mill. pesos)
	Imports of more than $1.0 mill.				
49	Foreign owned	167.22	25.50	20.02	563.02
31	Domestic	107.49	48.34	18.98	966.38
80	Total	274.71	73.84	39.00	1,529.40
	Imports between $0.5 mill. and $1.0 mill.				
27	Foreign owned	19.76	12.25	3.58	127.92
36	Domestic	23.59	19.02 [a]	7.23 [b]	221.99
63	Total	43.35	31.27	10.81	349.91
	Imports between $0.1 mill. and $0.5 mill.				
58	Foreign owned	15.43	12.73	3.19	127.58
119	Domestic	27.99	42.11	45.90 [b]	456.08
117	Total	43.42	54.84	49.09	583.86
320	Grand total	361.48	159.95	98.90	2,463.17
134	Foreign owned	202.41	50.48	26.79	818.72
186	Domestic	159.07	109.47	72.11	1,644.45

SOURCE: See text.

a. Refers to only 35 companies.

b. Includes sugar exports. A total of six sugar companies included in this table exported $40.0 million.

TABLE 6-2

Major Commercial Importers in Colombia, 1970

No. of Cos.	Commercial Cos. Classified by Ownership and Value of Imports	Registered Imports, 1970 (mill. U.S. dol.)	No. of Employees (thous.)	Minor Exports, 1970 (mill. U.S. dol.)	Income and Sales Taxes Paid in 1970 (mill. pesos)
	Imports of more than $1.0 mill.				
6	Foreign owned	14.06	0.88	0.67	55.78
14	Domestic	25.38	9.52^a	1.05	16.43
20	Total	39.44	10.40	1.72	72.21
	Imports between $0.5 mill. and $1.0 mill.				
5	Foreign owned	4.07	0.83	0	22.69
20	Domestic	13.33	2.02	0.78	25.81
25	Total	17.40	2.85	0.78	48.50
	Imports between $0.1 mill. and $0.5 mill.				
13	Foreign owned	3.30	2.01	0.15	15.64
122	Domestic	25.53	13.04	17.1 ^{b}	56.50
135	Total	28.83	15.05	17.32	72.14
180	Grand total	85.67	28.30	19.82	192.85
24	Foreign owned	21.43	3.72	0.82	94.11
156	National	64.24	24.58	19.00	98.74

SOURCE: See text.
a. Refers to only 13 companies.
b. Includes exports of association of banana growers.

employees, value of their minor exports, and amounts of income and sales taxes they paid. Three subdivisions according to size are made: companies that imported more than $1 million in 1970; those importing between $0.5 million and $1 million; and those whose imports ranged between $0.1 million and $0.5 million.

Table 6-1 shows that there is a striking degree of concentration, which helps explain the relatively smooth operation of the Colombian import control system. Thus, just 80 industrial companies captured in the sample and assigned to the first group accounted for 30 per cent of all 1970 registered imports. In that year, those same companies accounted for 21.2 per cent of all income and sales taxes paid in Colombia, and employed 19.2 per cent of all those engaged in manufacturing.[3] Given the way the data were obtained, some large importers may have been missed. Therefore, the estimates presented in

TABLE 6-3

Major Commercial and Industrial Importers in Colombia, by Value of Imports, 1970

No. of Cos.	Classification	Registered Imports, 1970 (mill. U.S. dol.)	Share in Total Registered Imports	Share in Total Income and Sales Taxes, 1970
100	Imports[a] of more than $1 mill.	$314.15	34.1%	22.2%
88	Imports[a] between $0.5 mill. and $1 mill.	60.75	6.6	5.5
312	Imports[a] $0.1 mill. and $0.5 mill.	72.25	7.8	9.1
500	Total	447.15	48.6	36.8
158	Foreign owned	223.84	24.3	12.6
342	National	223.31	24.3	24.2
	Addendum: officially registered, reimbursable imports	145.20	15.8	—

SOURCE: Tables 6-1 and 6-2.
a. Covers both foreign-owned and domestic companies.

Table 6-1 and subsequently, for both import concentration and degree of foreign control, may be regarded as *minimum* ones. Further, there could be cases in which several companies are under the control of a single conglomerate or family group.

Note that, even neglecting data problems, it would not be easy to interpret the information presented in Table 6-1. Neither comparable cross-sectional nor time series data are available for Chenery-like tests of "normality." Even if they were, further analysis involving variables such as industrial structure would be required before establishing whether the degree of concentration shown is more or less than could be expected if import controls did not exist.

Table 6-2 contains parallel data for the commercial category, and the data there and in Table 6-1 are summarized in Table 6-3. There were in 1970 at least 100 companies importing more that $1 million worth of goods (with an average of $3.1 million each), accounting for 34 per cent of all registered imports. Fifty-five foreign-owned companies in this group alone represented 20 per cent of all Colombian registered imports in 1970.

The degree of concentration falls off rapidly once companies with imports worth less that $1 million are considered. Thus, the 88 companies, foreign and national, industrial and commercial, that were found to have imports worth between $0.5 million and $1 million accounted for only 7 per cent of all imports in 1970, while the 312 companies having imports worth between $100,000 and

$500,000 represented an additional 8 per cent of the import bill. In round numbers, as noted earlier, 500 companies handled at least half of Colombian imports. The same companies accounted for 37 per cent of all income and sales tax payments, and 32 per cent of those employed in "modern" commerce and manufacturing.

Because of the economic importance of those firms importing more than $1 million, their names and presumed major activity are given in an appendix to this chapter. This appendix and other data (not shown) indicate the heavy concentration of import-intensive foreign investors in chemicals, pharmaceuticals, and metal-mechanic industries, which are typically associated with fairly recent import substitution. Colombian-owned companies are more spread out among different activities.

The 80 industrial companies importing more than $1 million a year in 1970–71 hired an average of 923 employees. An additional 63 companies, importing between $0.5 million and $1 million, had each an average of 496 employees. Finally, the 177 industrial companies in the third category had an average of 310 employees each. A comparision of these figures with data reported by the Colombian Ministry of Labor and Social Security suggests that the sample succeeded in registering at least the largest Colombian firms, if it is assumed that most of the largest firms according to employment are also the largest importers.[4]

Table 6-1 reveals major industrial exporters among the major importers. It has been estimated[5] that registered Colombian manufactured exports (excluding items such as sugar) reached $76.7 million during 1970; the 80 largest importers would thus account for 50 per cent of these exports. The largest 314 industrial importers (excluding several sugar mills) would account for 77 per cent of manufactured exports.

A ranking of major importers by level of exports permits a more accurate measure of industrial export concentration. The 14 largest national industrial exporters in the sample (excluding sugar mills) had registered industrial exports of $26.89 million in 1970, while the 10 largest foreign-owned exporting industrial companies had $20.41 million of exports in 1970. Thus, 24 industrial companies accounted for 62 per cent of all (nonsugar) industrial exports. Foreign-owned companies alone supplied at least 27 per cent of all Colombian industrial exports in 1970.

Some important characteristics of major industrial importers-exporters are highlighted in Table 6-4. Average wages decline with company size as measured by annual imports, but in each size category foreign-owned companies show higher wages than national firms. Foreign companies also have higher imports per employee in each size category than do national companies, with imports per employee declining with size for both groups. The 49 foreign-owned industrial companies importing more than $1 million worth each show an astounding level of $6,557 worth of imports per employee, and

TABLE 6-4

Some Characteristics of Major Industrial Importers, 1970

Classification	Wages per Employee (pesos)	Imports per Employee (U.S. dol.)	Per Cent of Companies in Bogotá	Per Cent of Companies in Medellín	Per Cent of Companies in Cali	Employees per Company	Exports per Employee (U.S. dol.)	Income and Sales Taxes Paid per Employee (pesos)
Imports of more than $1.0 mill.								
Foreign owned	3,731	6,557	65.3	4.1	18.4	520	785	22,077
Domestic	2,040	2,224	54.8	25.8	16.1	1,559	393	19,991
Imports between $0.5 mill. and $1.0 mill.								
Foreign owned	2,810	1,613	70.4	25.9	3.7	454	292	10,442
Domestic	1,729	1,206	44.4	25.0	16.7	544	370	11,345
Imports between $0.1 mill. and $0.5 mill.								
Foreign owned	2,151	1,212	58.6	5.2	27.6	220	251	10,038
Domestic	1,537	665	50.4	19.3	9.2	354	1,090	10,830
Large industrial exporters								
Foreign owned (10 cos.)	2,867	3,232	40.0	10.0	40.0	944	2,161	10,562
Domestic (14 cos. excl. sugar mills)	2,063	1,528	35.7	21.4	14.3	1,801	1,066	9,002

SOURCE: See text.

although their exports per employee are higher than those of national firms in the same import size category, their "trade deficit" remains far superior to those in any other category. As a rule, large foreign-owned companies are more concentrated in Bogotá than large national firms. In a later section of this paper, these characteristics will be re-examined for the total sample of companies.

Among the most striking facts about the 24 major exporters, 10 foreign-owned and 14 national, are: (a) the persistence of a "trade deficit" and (b) the large average size of these companies (see the last two rows of Table 6-4). Neither fact fits well with an image of firms producing labor-intensive manufactured exports. Rather, the suggestion of both facts is that many of the same companies which in the past benefited, and which still benefit, from import-intensive import substitution now benefit from the newer export-promotion policies. It is nevertheless encouraging that these companies are less concentrated in Bogotá than other groups shown in the same table.

Income and sales taxes paid per employee, like wages and imports per employee, appear to decline with company size. In contrast to the cases of wages and imports, the national companies show higher tax payments per employee in the two smallest size categories. In spite of their large average size, the 24 large exporters show relatively small cash tax payments, a fact which may be explained by Colombian export subsidy schemes.

In summary, a picture of substantial concentration emerges from this review of major 1970 private importers. It is not possible to determine from the data whether such concentration is higher or lower than in other countries, nor whether it is encouraged or discouraged by the import control system (more on this below). But the data do help explain why the management of import controls is not as impossible a task as it appears at first sight when one is told that a handful of authorities decide on about 150,000 import applications per year. Some 500 private companies play a major role not only in the import field, but in exporting and as tax collectors for the government. Note that only income and sales tax data have been discussed; the same 500 companies must also pay a very large share of all import duties.[6]

REVEALED INCOMEX CRITERIA
FOR ACCEPTING OR REJECTING
IMPORT LICENSE REQUESTS

The analysis of characteristics of license requests approved or rejected (partly or totally) by INCOMEX during the second half of 1971 can shed some light on the question of biases created by the import control system as compared with a regime without quantitative restrictions. Table 6-5 presents a tabulation

TABLE 6-5

**INCOMEX Reasons for Rejecting Applications for Import Licenses and Tabulation of Sample
of Rejected Licenses During July–December 1971**
(per cent of all reasons given for rejection in each category)

	Category of Applicant		
	Commercial	Industrial	Official
1. Commodity is produced within Colombia	24.5	15.9	13.3
2. Requested item can be replaced by similar Colombian goods	5.5	3.2	3.6
3. Quantity requested is excessive	0.6	0.3	1.2
4. Foreign price is excessive	0.6	4.8	2.4
5. Quantity and/or value requested is excessive relative to past record	0.9	2.1	0
6. Import or approval category temporarily restricted	2.5	0.8	4.8
7. Inadequate information given to justify need for requested import, modification, or addition	1.3	1.4	4.8
8. Inadequate product description (lack of catalogues, etc.)	6.1	9.0	3.6
9. Lack of exact and detailed product specification in the request, per existing regulations	10.2	11.5	12.0
10. Adequate stocks of products are found domestically	0.6	0.1	0
11. Requests by applicant for indentical or similar products have been recently approved	13.4	4.6	1.2
12. There is shortage of foreign exchange	0.1	0	0
13. Requested imports out of proportion to taxes paid	5.7	0.8	0
14. Tax information missing	0.2	0.4	0
15. Data on imports provided by applicant do not agree with those of INCOMEX	0.5	0	1.2
16. Excessive expenditures	0.2	0.1	1.2
17. Data on sale prices, intended for price control agency, are lacking	0	0	0
18. Other special reasons	9.4	11.3	44.6
19. Percent of request granted	17.6	33.5	6.0
20 per cent	(0.4)	(0.3)	(0)
25 per cent	(0.1)	(0.6)	(0)
30 per cent	(2.4)	(0.7)	(0)
40 per cent	(3.2)	(3.7)	(1.2)
50 per cent	(5.1)	(16.2)	(4.8)
60 per cent	(3.4)	(6.1)	(0)

TABLE 6-5 (*concluded*)

	Category of Applicant		
	Commercial	Industrial	Official
70 per cent	(0.2)	(0.3)	(0)
Unspecified	(2.8)	(5.6)	(0)
Total, lines 1–19	100.0	100.0	100.0
Addendum:			
Requests for which more than one reason was given for rejection (totally or partly)	81	75	14
Total of reasons given for rejecting requests (totally or partly), including partial approvals	849	710	83

SOURCE: See text. See also Table 6-6 for total number of requests and their average values.

of the reasons given by INCOMEX for rejecting import requests in the sample; more than one reason is frequently given. The potential importer is handed a mimeographed sheet on which are listed 18 possible reasons for rejection, with those applying to his request bearing a check mark.

Many rejections are only partial, particularly under the industry category, as indicated by item 19 in the table. More serious rejections appear to be based on protectionist grounds, as reflected in reasons 1, 2, and, very likely, 8 and 9. For the commercial category these four items account for 46 per cent of the reasons for rejection, while for industry the corresponding figure is 40 per cent. The commercial requests also seem to be closely scrutinized for "excessive" imports (reason 11) and tax evasion (reason 13). Industrial requests are scrutinized for overinvoicing (reason 4). In this area INCOMEX claims to have saved the country several million dollars by keeping foreign-owned companies, especially those in the pharmaceutical field, from remitting excessive profits to their headquarters abroad by overinvoicing. Such claims appear to be substantially correct, as noted in Chapter 5. Closer analysis is handicapped because roughly one-tenth of the rejections in the industrial and commercial categories and almost half of those in the official category are justified by "other special reasons" (line 18).

The average characteristics of approved, rejected, and partially rejected import requests in the industrial and commercial categories are laid out in Table 6-6. Note first that our sample contains (by design) a higher average of rejected requests than seems to have been typical during the second half of

TABLE 6-6

Average Characteristics of Approved, Rejected, and Partially Rejected Import Requests of Sample Taken During July–December 1971
(standard deviation in parentheses)

	Industrial Category			Commercial Category		
	Approved	Partially Rejected	Wholly Rejected	Approved	Partially Rejected	Wholly Rejected
No. of employees per company	518	407	331	194	126	194
	(1,181)	(870)	(570)	(701)	(377)	(691)
Import registrations in 1970	1,252	1,168	781	779	617	660
(thous. U.S. dol.)	(3,338)	(2,639)	(2,066)	(3,293)	(2,603)	(2,557)
Unused 1970 import registrations	9	16	11	8	5	7
(thous. U.S. dol.)	(28)	(50)	(40)	(44)	(16)	(25)
Value of requested 1971 sample license	9.0	20.9	12.0	1.9	9.3	5.9
(thous. U.S. dol.)	(27.5)	(28.9)	(24.7)	(9.6)	(16.0)	(12.9)
Income taxes paid in 1970	3,682	2,960	2,269	1,010	1,068	1,155
(thous. pesos)	(10,126)	(8,743)	(7,091)	(3,774)	(4,411)	(4,760)
Sales taxes paid in 1970	4,763	4,064	2,422	961	694	795
(thous. U.S. dol.)	(31,604)	(33,380)	(26,332)	(4,592)	(3,648)	(3,583)
Minor exports in 1970	391	122	252	20	28	53
(thous. U.S. dol.)	(2,144)	(429)	(1,403)	(94)	(129)	(695)
Aver. monthly wages	2,465	2,594	2,256	2,436	2,650	2,451
(pesos)	(1,710)	(1,671)	(1,641)	(1,687)	(3,080)	(2,118)
Per cent of licenses in non-reimbursable group	18.2	0	2.5	17.8	0.4	6.2
	(38.6)		(15.5)	(38.3)	(6.6)	(28.6)
Number of requests						
In sample	747	212	325	466	232	517
From foreign-owned companies	267	96	112	75	43	91
From Bogotá or Medellín	556	165	216	373	177	384

SOURCE: See text.

1971. While at that time it was said that only about 15 per cent of all requests were being turned down, 25 per cent of the industrial requests and 43 per cent of the commercial ones appear to have been totally rejected. The companies in the sample are on average larger than those in the whole industrial and commercial sector. While this fact in itself is not surprising, it is also probably true that the sample is biased in the direction of overrepresentation of larger importing firms and larger import requests.

The large standard deviations shown in Table 6-6 warn of the difficulty of generalizing with confidence about the characteristics of accepted, rejected, and partially rejected requests. Note also that because of lack of data, some very important features of import requests are omitted; for example, the questions of whether the proposed import was competitive with some local product and whether it originated in countries having preferential trade agreements with Colombia.

In spite of these limitations, an attempt has been made to establish which characteristics of the import requests, and of the companies making them, made INCOMEX more likely to accept such petitions. As some important independent variables are left out of the analysis, we cannot expect to obtain good fits. A less ambitious goal will be to isolate characteristics which significantly influence INCOMEX in the decision to accept or reject each application, ceteris paribus. The analysis may be interpreted as measuring an INCOMEX supply function for import licenses, while neglecting the demand function for such licenses, or assuming, as a not unreasonable first approximation, that the demand for licenses is perfectly elastic at the going transaction costs involved in applications.

The dependent variable that is to be statistically explained is somewhat unusual. If all applications are divided simply into those accepted or rejected, the variable will only take values of zero for rejections and 1 for approvals. Under these dichotomous circumstances, multivariate probit analysis is known to be a superior technique to the usual least squares multiple regressions.[7] In our sample, applications partly rejected present an intermediate case, which can be handled in different ways. In what follows, the probit analysis will be applied in three ways: leaving out partial rejections, treating them as total rejections, and also treating them as total approvals. The dependent variable for partially rejected requests can also be expressed as a fraction of the value of the license granted by INCOMEX; in that case, there will be intermediate observations between zero and 1. Ordinary least squares will be used to analyze this form of the dependent variable.

The best results obtained are shown in tables 6-7 and 6-8, best being determined by the number of coefficients that had interesting values relative to their standard errors. Several other independent variables, not shown, were

TABLE 6-7

**Industrial Category: Regressions for Approval (1) or Rejection (0) of Import Requests
in Sample**
(ratio of coefficients to their standard errors in parentheses)

	Least Squares Regression	Probit Analysis		
		Partial Rejections Omitted	Partial Rejections as (1)	Partial Rejections as (0)
Constant	0.303	−0.900	−0.937	−0.246
		(1.60)	(1.95)	(0.50)
Nonreimbursable (1) or reimbursable	0.247	1.101	0.927	1.404
(0) category	(6.57)	(5.87)	(5.11)	(7.31)
Log of value of all import	0.010	0.038	0.042	0.026
registrations in 1970	(1.17)	(1.24)	(1.42)	(0.91)
Log of no. of employees	0.013	0.049	0.050	0.025
per 1970 imports	(1.13)	(1.09)	(1.23)	(0.62)
Log of value of requested imports	−0.042	−0.134	−0.046	−0.229
	(6.52)	(5.12)	(1.91)	(9.58)
Log of 1970 income and sales taxes	0.014	0.050	0.031	0.053
paid per 1970 imports	(2.81)	(2.83)	(1.90)	(3.34)
Log of 1970 minor exports per 1970	−0.013	−0.054	−0.041	−0.045
imports	(2.56)	(2.79)	(2.30)	(2.65)
Log of average wage	0.043	0.162	0.153	0.100
	(2.43)	(2.28)	(2.55)	(1.59)
Per cent of 1970 import	−0.000	−0.001	0.000	−0.001
registrations unused	(0.50)	(1.52)	(0.14)	(1.49)
Bogotá or Medellín (1) or elsewhere (0)	0.054	0.195	0.215	0.119
	(2.06)	(2.06)	(2.44)	(1.37)
R^2	0.103	—	—	—
F statistic	16.32	—	—	—
−2.0 × log of likelihood ratio	—	118.20	75.01	229.51
No. of observations	1,284	1,072	1,284	1,284

unsuccessfully tried. On the whole, it will be seen that the different techniques used to analyze the data yield similar qualitative results.

Import requests in the nonreimbursable category, i.e., those which do not involve an *immediate* claim on foreign-exchange resources, clearly have a much better chance of being approved than those under the reimbursable category, in both the industrial and commercial classifications. In both classi-

TABLE 6-8

Commercial Category: Regressions for Approval (1) or Rejection (0) of Import Requests in Sample

(ratio of coefficients to their standard errors in parentheses)

		Probit Analysis		
	Least Squares Regression	Partial Rejections Omitted	Partial Rejections as (1)	Partial Rejections as (0)
Constant	0.739	1.134	0.676	1.023
		(2.73)	(1.92)	(2.58)
Nonreimbursable (1) or reimbursable (0) category	0.115	0.421	0.220	0.535
	(2.98)	(3.14)	(1.74)	(4.02)
Log of no. of employees	0.026	0.093	0.056	0.098
	(2.60)	(2.32)	(1.72)	(2.65)
Log of value of 1970 import registrations per employee	−0.002	0.001	−0.016	0.006
	(0.27)	(0.04)	(0.57)	(0.19)
Log of value of requested imports	−0.116	−0.490	−0.208	−0.539
	(15.55)	(14.22)	(7.96)	(16.90)
Log of 1970 income and sales taxes paid per employee	0.010	0.023	0.034	0.015
	(1.43)	(0.87)	(1.50)	(0.60)
Log of 1970 minor exports per employee	0.016	0.042	0.054	0.037
	(1.91)	(1.23)	(1.93)	(1.16)
Log of average wage	−0.007	−0.048	−0.014	−0.043
	(0.51)	(0.86)	(0.28)	(0.79)
Per cent of 1970 import registrations unused	−0.000	−0.000	−0.000	−0.000
	(0.05)	(0.29)	(0.18)	(0.04)
Bogotá or Medellín (1) or elsewhere (0)	0.063	0.205	0.183	0.210
	(2.20)	(1.86)	(2.01)	(2.03)
R^2	0.197	—	—	—
F statistic	32.90	—	—	—
−2.0 × log of likelihood ratio	—	281.74	84.98	417.87
No. of observations	1,215	983	1,215	1,215

fications, smaller import requests also clearly have a better chance of being approved than larger ones. When partial rejections are counted as approvals (third column of Table 6-7) on the supposition either that the company will be happy to have obtained a share of its perhaps inflated request or that it can always present a new request later on, the significance of the coefficient for the absolute size of the import request declines but remains high. As seen in Table 6-6, the average value of license applications that were partially rejected was higher than that for complete approvals and rejections. For reimbursable industrial requests, a breakdown of the requests into ten groups according to the size of requests shows the negative relation between complete approval and size of request to be quite smooth, with the percentage of total approvals declining steadily from 77 per cent for the smallest to 36 per cent for the largest. In the commercial category, the decline in the acceptance rate is even steeper. On the whole, these facts indicate that INCOMEX authorities, besides their protectionist guidelines, still operated during the second half of 1971 with an eye (somewhat myopic) to rationing foreign exchange.

Do large firms have a better chance of obtaining desired licenses than smaller firms? Size was measured in two ways: number of employees and value of 1970 import registrations. Both measures gave substantially the same results; those using 1970 imports are shown in Table 6-7 for industrial requests, while those using employment levels are shown in Table 6-8 for commercial requests. The hypothesis being tested is that chances for approval increase steadily with size, even when other company and license characteristics are also taken into account. For the industrial category, the hypothesis receives only modest support; support is strongest when partial rejections are treated as approvals, which for large companies may be a quite suitable assumption. In the commercial category, the significance of the size variable is uniformly superior to that for industrials, and indicates a clear and smooth link between size and chances of approval, even after other variables are taken into account. I return to this issue below.

Company size is of course highly correlated with variables such as taxes paid and exports. Therefore, some other independent variables were defined relative to the size variable. In the case of industrial license requests, chances for approval significantly increased as taxes relative to either imports or employees increased. Somewhat surprisingly, the evidence for such a hypothesis is much weaker in the commercial group. Also surprisingly, a significant *negative* link appears for industrial requests between minor exports relative to imports and chances of approval. This result is inconsistent with the usual INCOMEX claims that industrial exporters are favored in the granting of import licenses. However, as shown in Table 6-12, below, a closer look at the data casts doubts on the robustness of this revealed negative link, at least for companies located in Bogotá or Medellín. It remains possible that some INCOMEX officials felt that large exporters, relative to their 1970 imports, were already obtaining enough fresh imports via the Vallejo Plan, under which the companies were exempted from the prior license rules. Most participants in the Vallejo Plan are large firms.

Finally, the correlation coefficients among the independent variables shown in tables 6-7 and 6-8 fail to show widespread collinearity problems. Indicating the independent variables in Table 6-7 as $X_1, X_2, \ldots, X_9$, following the order in which they are shown in that table, their correlation coefficients are as follows:

	X_1	X_2	X_3	X_4	X_5	X_6	X_7	X_8
X_2	−.01	—	—	—	—	—	—	—
X_3	.09	−.78	—	—	—	—	—	—
X_4	−.20	.16	−.16	—	—	—	—	—
X_5	.08	−.24	.37	−.08	—	—	—	—
X_6	.09	−.51	.50	−.12	.24	—	—	—
X_7	.10	.38	−.42	.06	−.07	−.13	—	—
X_8	−.01	−.02	.01	.00	.00	.02	−.02	—
X_9	.06	−.03	−.02	.09	.05	−.15	.01	.02

Similar results are obtained for the independent variables of Table 6-8. There *are* interesting relationships among the size, export, wage, and tax variables discussed for major importers in the first section of this chapter and to be further explored below for all companies in the sample, but they do not appear seriously to mar the results of tables 6-7 and 6-8.

INDUSTRIAL COMPANY SIZE AND INCIDENCE OF APPROVAL: A CLOSER LOOK

The hypotheses dealing with the links between chances of approval and size, geographical location, and generation of minor exports will be further examined in this section for industrial companies. It will be shown that the largest industrial companies, particularly those in Bogotá and Medellín, do in fact have a better chance than smaller firms of obtaining import licenses.

The data, as shown in the last columns of tables 6-9 and 6-10, indicate that the percentage of requests falling under the nonreimbursable category is noticeably higher for the largest companies. In these and the subsequent tables, only license applications that had been totally rejected or approved are considered. The link between size and share of nonreimbursables in the total request is *not* a smoothly increasing one. Indeed, as the size of the firm increases, the approval rate seems to dip before rising most clearly for the *largest* firms. It was seen earlier, and confirmed in tables 6-9 and 6-10, that requests under the nonreimbursable category have a much higher chance of being accepted than those under the reimbursable one. In other words, if no allowance is made for the relation of nonreimbursables to reimbursables, the largest companies and exporters have the best chance of all of obtaining approvals, thanks to their better access to nonreimbursable licenses, which is a consequence of their links to foreign sources of credit, including concessional ones (aid), and to foreign investors.[8]

TABLE 6-9

Industrial Category: Approvals and Complete Rejections by Employment Size and Reimbursable or Nonreimbursable Category

Number of Employees in Firm Making Request	Reimbursable		Nonreimbursable		Total		Non-reimbursables as Per Cent of Total
	Total Requests	Per Cent Approved	Total Requests	Per Cent Approved	Total Requests	Per Cent Approved	
Less than 55	196	63.8%	23	91.3%	219	66.7%	10.5%
55–122	183	68.3	20	90.0	203	70.4	9.9
123–245	193	64.8	31	96.8	224	69.2	13.8
246–466	174	59.8	26	92.3	200	64.0	13.0
More than 466	182	72.5	44	97.7	226	77.4	19.5
Total	928	65.8	144	94.4	1,072	69.7	13.4

SOURCE: See text.

TABLE 6-10

Industrial Category: Approvals and Complete Rejections by Level of Registered Imports in 1970 and Reimbursable or Nonreimbursable Category

Imports in 1970 (thous. U.S. dol.)	Reimbursable		Nonreimbursable		Total		Non-reimbursables as Per Cent of Total
	Total Requests	Per Cent Approved	Total Requests	Per Cent Approved	Total Requests	Per Cent Approved	
Less than 50	215	65.1%	40	87.5%	255	68.6%	15.7%
50–200	204	65.7	22	95.5	226	68.6	9.7
200–500	191	66.0	24	100.0	215	69.8	11.2
500–2,000	205	61.0	33	100.0	238	66.4	13.9
More than 2,000	113	76.1	25	92.0	138	79.0	18.1
Total	928	65.8	144	94.4	1,072	69.7	13.4

SOURCE: See text.

TABLE 6-11

Industrial Category: Approvals and Complete Rejections by Employment Size and Geographical Location

Number of Employees in Firm Making Request	Bogotá or Medellín		Elsewhere		Total	
	Total Requests	Per Cent Approved	Total Requests	Per Cent Approved	Total Requests	Per Cent Approved
Less than 50	159	66.0%	42	66.7%	201	66.2%
50–99	112	75.0	39	66.7	151	72.8
100–199	140	67.1	53	69.8	193	67.9
200–299	112	70.5	52	57.7	164	66.5
300–499	96	72.9	50	54.0	146	66.4
More than 500	153	81.0	64	67.2	217	77.0
Total	772	72.0	300	63.7	1,072	69.7

SOURCE: See text.

Tables 6-9 and 6-10 also show that when only reimbursable license applications are considered, the percentage approved shows no clear association with size until the largest size categories are reached. Firms with more than 466 employees or more than U.S. $2 million of imports in 1970 show reimbursable approval rates clearly above the average.[9]

The geographical pattern of approvals and rejections is explored in tables 6-11 and 6-12, in relation to employment and minor exports. Sharp differences in approval percentages between Bogotá or Medellín and the rest of Colombia emerge clearly only for the three largest employment categories and the two largest categories of minor exporters. In Table 6-12, firms from Bogotá or Medellín with at least $50,000 in minor exports in 1970 have the largest percentage of approvals, while in Table 6-11, the largest employers in Bogotá and Medellín have the most successful performance of those shown.

In the total number of import requests from Bogotá and Medellín under the industrial category, the share of requests in the nonreimbursable group is higher than the corresponding share for the rest of the country (12.2 per cent versus 8.5 per cent). The same is true for the commercial category (10.4 per cent versus 5.4 per cent). But even for reimbursable requests alone, the percentage of approvals is higher for Bogotá and Medellín for both industrial and commercial categories.

Of the total requests from foreign-owned industrial companies, 68.4 per cent came from those located in Bogotá and Medellín, while the corresponding percentage for national firms was 76.2. The share of nonreimbursable requests in total requests from foreign-owned industrial companies was almost identical to the corresponding share in requests of national firms. Regardless of how

TABLE 6-12

Industrial Category: Approvals and Complete Rejections by Registered Minor Exports in 1970 and Geographical Location

Minor Exports in 1970 (thous. U.S. dol.)	Bogotá or Medellín		Elsewhere		Total	
	Total Requests	Per Cent Approved	Total Requests	Per Cent Approved	Total Requests	Per Cent Approved
None	483	72.9%	139	67.6%	622	71.7%
1–49	154	63.0	67	70.1	221	65.2
50–399	84	79.8	54	50.0	138	68.1
400 or more	51	78.4	40	57.5	91	69.2
Total	772	72.0	300	63.7	1,072	69.7

SOURCE: See text.

requests are sliced, the percentage of approvals for requests by foreign-owned industrial companies turns out to be nearly as high as that for national firms.

The finding that very large industrial firms located in Bogotá or Medellín have a higher approval rate than all others is most clearly seen in Table 6-13 and in its underlying data. When partial rejections are omitted from the sample, the combined approval rate for firms that imported less than $2 million in 1970 *or* were located outside Bogotá and Medellín was 68.4 per cent; the corresponding rate for the big firms in Medellín or Bogotá was 83.7 per cent. The null hypothesis, i.e., that there is no relation between chance of approval and the circumstance of being a big firm located in Bogotá or Medellín, must be rejected at the 1 per cent level of significance. If partial rejections are counted as approvals, the approval rate is 86.8 per cent for big firms in Bogotá and Medellín versus 73.5 per cent for all others. The null hypothesis can again be rejected at the 1 per cent level of significance. Finally, if partial rejections are registered as total rejections, the approval rates are 67.5 per cent for the large firms in Bogotá and Medellín versus 57.3 per cent for the rest. Now the null hypothesis can be rejected "only" at the 5 per cent level of significance.[10]

It should be recalled that perhaps the most serious shortcoming of the sample data is lack of information on the characteristics of requested imports, particularly on whether or not they are competitive with local production. It is conceivable, for example, that the higher share of approvals for large companies compared to all others could be explained by their more frequent requests for imports not competitive with Colombian production, such as machinery and equipment (often brought in under the nonreimbursable category) and inputs originating in heavy industries. But while available data do not allow a test of this hypothesis, it is doubtful that it could fully explain the foregoing results.

TABLE 6-13

Industrial Category: Percentage of Approvals According to Two Key Characteristics

	Partial Rejections Omitted		Partial Rejections as Approvals	
	More Than U.S. $2 Mill. 1970 Imports	Less Than U.S. $2 Mill. 1970 Imports	More Than U.S. $2 Mill. 1970 Imports	Less Than U.S. $2 Mill. 1970 Imports
Bogotá or Medellín	83.7%	70.4%	86.8%	75.6%
Elsewhere	69.6	62.6	75.4	67.2

SOURCE: See text.

THE IMPORT-EXPORT-TAXES-WAGES NEXUS

In the first part of this chapter some characteristics of the major Colombian importers were explored. In this section, a further examination will be made of possible interrelationships among company size, imports, minor exports, and wages and taxes paid for the total sample.

One way of carrying out such an analysis is to define, say, company "import functions" as a means of explaining 1970 imports per employee on the basis of size, ownership, and other independent variables. Similar attempts can be made to explain company minor exports and taxes paid per employee and company wages. One problem with these relations is that the direction of causation is not always as clear as would be suggested by a model specifying dependent and independent variables. The results shown in tables 6-14 and 6-15 should therefore be interpreted with caution; their usefulness lies primarily in presenting in a systematic fashion the interrelations among import, export, taxes, and wages as found in the sample data.[11]

Industrial companies with high imports per employee clearly tend to pay relatively high taxes per employee and high wages; more surprisingly, they also have relatively high minor exports per employee. Once this nexus is allowed for, the size variable as measured by number of employees in fact suggests a negative link with per employee imports and exports, although such negative connection may be partly spurious. Even after the indicated nexus is taken into account, larger industrial companies appear to pay higher taxes per employee, although not higher wages. For commercial companies the results, shown in Table 6-15, are clearest regarding the per employee import-taxes link, which is particularly strong.

A traditional criticism of a system that represses imports by quotas rather than duties is that it involves public revenue losses. The data in tables 6-14

TABLE 6-14

Multiple Regressions for Imports, Exports, Wages, and Taxes per Employee
of Industrial Companies
(ratio of coefficients to their standard errors in parentheses)

Independent Variables	Dependent Variables			
	Log of 1970 Registered Imports per Employee	Log of 1970 Registered Minor Exports per Employee	Log of 1970 Income and Sales Taxes per Employee	Log of Average Wage
Constant	−2.624	−2.869	−1.804	7.830
Log of number of employees	−0.107 (3.55)	−0.452 (9.82)	0.148 (3.22)	0.011 (0.84)
Foreign owned (0) or national (1)	−1.258 (13.01)	−0.356 (2.21)	−0.090 (0.58)	−0.461 (10.90)
Bogotá or Medellín (1) or elsewhere (0)	0.137 (1.49)	−0.951 (6.68)	0.405 (2.91)	0.071 (1.79)
Log of average wage	0.524 (8.26)	0.341 (3.35)	0.287 (2.92)	—
Log of income and sales taxes per employee	0.154 (8.58)	0.102 (3.55)	—	0.023 (2.92)
Log of 1970 registered imports per employee	—	0.079 (1.81)	0.354 (8.58)	0.097 (8.26)
Log of 1970 registered minor exports per employee	0.032 (1.81)	—	0.095 (3.55)	0.026 (3.35)
R^2	0.327	0.131	0.136	0.270
F statistic	103.57	31.96	33.56	78.69
No. of observations	1,284	1,284	1,284	1,284

and 6-15 suggest that such a loss is only partial. Either because companies eager to obtain import licenses pay higher-than-average income and sales taxes, or because INCOMEX channels licenses toward especially efficient companies, or both, the indication in the third column of Table 6-14 is that a 10 per cent increase in imports per employee appears to lead to a 3.5 per cent increase in sales and income tax revenues of the government. In the commercial group, the apparent feedback elasticity is nearly twice as great.

As argued by some INCOMEX officials, these results can be viewed as the consequence of a policy of channeling the still scarce imports, ceteris paribus, toward companies that yield the government high tax returns. It is also argued that such companies "deserve" import permits, as they have

TABLE 6-15

Multiple Regressions for Imports, Wages, and Taxes per Employee
of Commercial Companies
(ratio of coefficients to their standard errors in parentheses)

Independent Variables	Dependent Variables		
	Log of 1970 Registered Imports per Employee	Log of 1970 Income and Sales Taxes per Employee	Log of Average Wage
Constant	−0.352	1.820	7.435
Log of number of employees	−0.114 (3.04)	−0.078 (1.90)	0.077 (3.56)
Foreign owned (0) or national (1)	−0.568 (4.33)	−0.580 (4.03)	−0.422 (5.60)
Bogotá or Medellín (1) or elsewhere (0)	−0.246 (2.54)	−0.111 (1.04)	0.253 (4.53)
Log of average wage	0.229 (4.63)	0.010 (0.17)	—
Log of income and sales taxes per employee	0.551 (26.30)	—	0.003 (0.17)
Log of 1970 registered imports per employee	—	0.661 (26.30)	0.076 (4.63)
Log of 1970 registered minor exports per employee	0.063 (2.19)	0.037 (1.16)	0.017 (1.00)
R^2	0.459	0.438	0.136
F statistic	170.94	156.59	31.79
No. of observations	1,215	1,215	1,215

shown themselves more efficient (profitable) than the rest, as revealed by their high taxes and wages per employee. The chain of causation, of course, is unclear, and is likely to run both ways in a manner difficult to untangle either statistically or a priori.

Companies with high imports per employee also pay higher-than-average wages. My data contain no information regarding industrial allocation or the skill composition of company labor force. Conceivably, high imports per employee may be correlated with the use of skilled labor commanding higher wages, but while such reasoning is plausible for industrial companies, it has much less force for commercial companies. Yet, in both tables 6-14 and 6-15, a strong link is shown between wages and imports. On the whole, the figures in the last columns of these two tables seem to support the hypothesis that wages are related to the profitability of each company, with access to imports being a key element in profitability.

The dummies for ownership and location emerge as significant in several regressions. Foreign-owned industrial companies have higher imports per employee than national ones and pay higher wages. The commercial ones also clearly pay more taxes per employee. The observed results, as in earlier cases, could arise from sector and skills variables not included in the regression. Foreign-owned pharmaceutical companies, for example, are likely to have high per employee imports and a skilled labor force not because they are foreign-owned, but because they are in pharmaceuticals.

Industrial companies located in Bogotá or Medellín, not surprisingly, appear to pay somewhat better wages, and have both higher-than-average imports and tax payments per employee. For commercial companies only the tendency to pay higher wages in Bogotá or Medellín remains.

The "minor export functions" yielded the poorest results, suggesting the importance of industrial classification and other variables in explaining export performance. Nevertheless, foreign-owned industrial companies and those outside Bogotá or Medellín are shown to have higher-than-average minor exports per employee. More surprisingly at first sight are coefficients for wages and per employee imports: companies with high per employee exports tend to import more and pay higher wages. Once these variables are taken into account, the size variable adopts a negative sign. But the data shown in the two bottom lines of Table 6-4, regarding the concentration of large minor exporters, cannot be gainsaid.

On the basis of the information shown in Table 6-4 and that presented in Chapter 2,[12] Colombian *industrial* minor exports in 1970 and 1971 do not emerge as obviously intensive in unskilled labor and national raw materials. Whether this is due to a failure of the Hecksher-Ohlin hypothesis in explaining the Colombian trade pattern or the result of distortions induced by domestic policy (such as the Vallejo Plan and LAFTA trade) is a matter deserving further research.

SOME CONCLUSIONS

There is substantial concentration in the distribution of Colombian imports, a concentration that makes the control system easier to manage. The control system, in turn, appears to buttress such concentration because it gives the largest companies, particularly those located in Bogotá or Medellín, a better chance of obtaining licenses. This conclusion is strengthened by the fact that it was reached without taking into account the "discouraged firm" effect. In other words, data on actual import requests were generated by a group of firms that had some hope of receiving a license; the average size of this group of companies is larger than that for all industrial firms. Discouraged firms, which do not bother to apply, are in all likelihood small ones for which transaction costs in license application loom relatively large. These smaller firms often end up buying imported items from large commercial houses.

Nevertheless, the bias toward import concentration arising *solely* from preferential treatment of the largest firms in Bogotá or Medellín, ceteris paribus, does not appear quantitatively very strong. Access to foreign credits and investments, which makes importation possible without immediate use of foreign exchange, seems a more powerful force in biasing the operation of import controls in favor of the largest (and best-connected) companies. One may speculate that much of this concentrating influence would survive a possible elimination of import controls.

In this chapter, attention was also called to the even greater concentration of minor industrial exports in 1970 than imports. Given the tendency of large import-intensive companies paying high wages, whatever their industrial activity, to use more capital-intensive methods than other firms, some skepticism regarding the magnitude and even direction of employment and income-distributional effects of minor export expansion is warranted, at least for the medium run. This, of course, does *not* mean that the encouragement of minor exports is a mistaken policy or that it will never generate more modern-sector employment than a comparable amount of import substitution. It does suggest, however, that for a given over-all growth rate, the employment difference may be only marginally superior, so long as the 1970 industrial and export structure is maintained. It may be hoped that such a structure could still reflect the early stages of industrial export promotion, one which may change as new exporters, less committed to earlier import-substituting ventures, enter the field.

While the revealed INCOMEX criteria for allocating import licenses include the historical import record of companies, no evidence has appeared that this "fair-share" approach is rigidly applied or that it is linked systematically to installed capacity. Resolution 15 forms for the industrial category do request information on maximum production capacity. But that information, provided in physical units by some companies and in value terms by others, is clumsy and less easily handled by INCOMEX than the four-year import record expressed in dollars appearing in the same form. Therefore, although the protection generated by the import control system combined with the monopolistic competition also encouraged by that system can lead to excess capacity in some import-competing sectors, a matter to be reviewed in Chapter 8, it would be difficult to argue that INCOMEX fair-share rules lead companies to create excess capacity for the sake of improving their chances of obtaining import licenses, as appears to have been the case in India and Turkey. By seeking information on company inventories of merchandise involved in the import request, as well as on the value of past requests approved but not actually used, INCOMEX attempts to limit spurious creation of import "track records," an unimportant issue at any rate during 1970–71.

The avoidance of rigid rules combined nevertheless with a style making access to import licenses far from "democratic" has probably helped reduce the real resource costs in the public and private sectors of running the import control machinery. It was seen that the bureaucratic framework of INCOMEX is quite lean. During 1970–71, large private companies did incur additional costs in trying to obtain import licenses, but even so, their marginal cost of dealing with INCOMEX was small, partly because of the clarity of the unwritten rules of the game, and partly because of reliance on company clerks who were used to dealing with *many* public agencies involved in matters such as taxation, credit, health, and other regulations. In other words, the fixed costs for a large company of keeping a Bogotá lobby could be spread out among several activities, only one of which was dealing with INCOMEX. Smaller firms outside of this circle typically would not invest resources trying to break in; under a more populistic environment they probably would, leading to a greater resource use by the import control system.[13]

APPENDIX: COMPANIES WITH IMPORTS WORTH MORE THAN $1 MILLION IN 1970

(N.B. Companies placed by INCOMEX under *both* the industrial and commercial categories are here listed only under the industrial category.)

Foreign-owned; Industrial

	PRESUMED MAJOR ACTIVITY
Abonos Colombianos, S.A. (I.P.C.)	Fertilizers
Aluminio Alcan de Colombia, S.A.	Aluminum products
Armco Colombiana, S.A.	Construction materials and welding equipment
BASF Química Colombiana, S.A.	Chemicals
Bayer de Colombia, S.A.	Pharmaceuticals
Bristol Farmacéutica, S.A.	Pharmaceuticals
Cartón de Colombia, S.A. (Container Corporation of America)	Paper products
Cela Colombiana Ltda.	Printing
Celanese Colombiana, S.A.	Textiles (synthetic fibers)

Foreign-owned; Industrial (continued)

	PRESUMED MAJOR ACTIVITY
Ciba Colombiana, S.A.	Pharmaceuticals
Colgate Palmolive, S.A.	Soap, toothpaste, chemicals
Cyanamid de Colombia, S.A.	Chemicals
Dow Química de Colombia, S.A.	Chemicals
Du Pont de Colombia, S.A.	Chemicals
Eli Lilly Interamericana, Inc.	Pharmaceuticals
Enka de Colombia, S.A.	Tires
E. R. Squibb and Sons, S.A.	Pharmaceuticals
Eternit Colombiana, S.A. (Johns Mansville Corporation)	Construction materials
Fábrica Chrysler Colombiana de Automotores, S.A.	Automobiles
Fábrica de Hilazas Vanylon, S.A.	Textiles (synthetic fibers)
General Electric de Colombia, S.A.	Electrical equipment
Goodyear de Colombia, S.A.	Tires
Hilanderías Medellín, S.A. (Branch River Wool Combing Co.)	Textiles
Hilos Cadena	Textiles
Hoechst Colombiana, S.A.	Chemicals and drugs
I.B.M. de Colombia, S.A.	Office machines
Icollantas, S.A. (B.F. Goodrich)	Tires
Industrias Phillips de Colombia, S.A.	Electrical equipment
International Petroleum Colombia Ltda. (I.P.C.)	Petroleum refining
Laboratorios Life, S.A.	Pharmaceuticals
Laboratorios Undra, S.A.	Pharmaceuticals
Monómeros Colombo-Venezolanos, S.A.[14]	Petrochemicals
Monsanto Colombiana, Inc.	Chemicals
Olivetti Colombiana, S.A.	Office machines
Organización Farmacéutica Americana (Foremost McKesson)	Pharmaceuticals
Petroquímica Colombiana, S.A. (Diamond Shamrock Co.)	Petrochemicals
Polímeros Colombianos, S.A.	Synthetic fibers, chemicals
Productos Quaker, S.A.	Foodstuffs
Productora de Papeles, S.A. (Grace)	Paper products
Química Schering Colombiana, S.A.	Chemicals
Rhinco Productos Químicos, S.A.	Chemicals
Sandoz Colombiana Ltda.	Pharmaceuticals

Foreign-owned; Industrial (concluded)

	PRESUMED MAJOR ACTIVITY
Siemens Colombiana, S.A.	Telephone material and electronics
SOFASA (Renault-IFI)	Automobile engines
Texas Petroleum Co.	Petroleum products
The Sidney Ross Company of Colombia	Pharmaceuticals
Uniroyal Croydon, S.A.	Tires
Aluminio de Colombia, Ltda. (Reynolds Metals)	Aluminum products
Productos Roche, S.A.	Chemicals and drugs

Foreign-owned; Commercial

Distribuidora Nissan, Ltda.
Distribuidora Toyota, Ltda.
Kodak Colombiana, Ltda.
Productos Químicos Esso, Inc.
Shell Colombiana, S.A.
Union Carbide Colombiana, S.A.

National; Industrial

Acerías Paz del Rio, S.A.	Steel
Bavaria, S.A.	Beer
Britilana Benrey Ltda.	Not known
Cano Isaza y Cia.	Not known
Cales y Cementos de Toloviejo, S.A.	Construction materials
Carvajal y Cia.	Printing
Casa Editorial El Tiempo	Publishing
Cementos del Caribe, S.A.	Cement
Cia. Colombiana de Alcalís	Chemicals
Cia. Colombiana de Tabaco	Cigarettes
Cia. Colombiana de Tejidos (Colte-jer)	Textiles
Cia. Pintuco	Paints
Consorcio Metalúrgico Nacional, S.A.	Metals
Corporación de Acero (Corpacero)	Steel products
David y Eduardo Puyana	Liquor and cigarettes
Detergentes Limitada	Detergents
Empresa Siderúrgica, S.A.	Steel products
Fábrica de Hilados y Tejidos del Hato	Textiles

National; Industrial (concluded)

PRESUMED MAJOR ACTIVITY

Fábrica Nacional de Chocolates, S.A.	Food products
Gaseosas Posada Tobón, S.A.	Beverages
IFI-Concesión de Salinas	Mining of salt
Leónidas Lara e Hijos	Agricultural machinery and autos
Lloreda, Jabones y Glicerina, Ltda.	Soaps, detergents
Planta Colombiana de Soda	Chemicals
Productos Fitosanitarios de Colombia, S.A.	Not known
Rosemberg Hermanos e Hijos	Toiletries and soap
Siderurgica del Pacífico, S.A.	Steel products
Vitabono, S.A.	Fertilizers
Empresa Colombiana de Cables, S.A.	Steel cables
Tejidos Leticia, Ltda.	Textiles
Facomec, S.A.	Electrical equipment
Colombia, S.A.	

National; Commercial

Almacenes Angel, S.A.
Avianca
Central Colombiana Auto-Agrícola Ltda.
Corpal
Distribuidora Química Holanda-
    Colombia, S.A.
Distribuidora Saja Ltda.
Droguería Gutiérrez
Ingenieros Civiles Asociados
Jorge Manuel Gómez (Jomago)
Nepomuceno Cartagena e Hijos
Pfaff de Colombia, S.A.
Praco Ltda.
Almacén El Motorista
Distribuidora Pantécnica, S.A.

NOTES

1. In establishing company ownership, I placed heavy reliance on information supplied by knowledgeable Colombians and on the following: U.S. Department of Commerce, Bureau of International Commerce, *American Firms, Subsidiaries and Affiliates—Colombia* (Washington,

D.C.: U.S. Govt. Printing Office, May 1970); "The Fortune Directory; The 300 largest industrials outside the U.S.," *Fortune,* August 1972, pp. 152–161; and Juvenal L. Angel, ed., *Directory of American Firms Operating in Foreign Countries,* 7th ed. (New York: World Trade, 1969).

2. In several cases, a given company in the sample had import requests listed by INCOMEX under both the industrial and commercial categories. In those cases, the company was placed only under the industrial category. The same procedure was followed in the few cases in which a company was listed under both the industrial and official categories (e.g., Acerías Paz del Rio).

3. Total income and sales taxes paid in cash during 1970 amounted to P7,220 million, as reported in the *Revista del Banco de la República.* These data, like those shown in the tables, exclude tax payments made with tax certificates issued in connection with export subsidy payments. Total national tax revenues in the same year were P12,591 million. The number of workers and employees engaged in manufacturing *and registered with the Colombian Social Security Institute* was 384,600 in December 1970. See Gabriel Turbay M., "Una Política Industrial Para Estimular Las Exportaciones y Fomentar al Empleo," mimeographed (FEDESARROLLO, May 1972), Table 9. The equivalent amount for the commercial sector was 203,000. For both commerce and manufacturing, the employment figures are limited mostly to their "modern" segments, leaving out the "informal" sector.

4. See Turbay, "Una Política Industrial," Table 9. This source reports the following number of firms in mining and manufacturing for December 1970:

Size Category	Number of Firms
More than 500 employees	84
More than 250 but less than 501 employees	143
More than 100 but less than 251 employees	487

Direct comparison of INCOMEX data with those from the Industrial Census is not possible as the latter reports on plants, not companies.

5. See FEDESARROLLO, *Coyuntura Económica,* July 1972, Table X.2, p. 87.

6. Major importers under the official category have of course a different nature than those listed under industry and commerce. In our sample of official requests the following characteristics were isolated:

Registered Import Category, 1970	Number of Institutions	1970 Registered Imports (mill. U.S. dol.)
More than $1 mill.	19	130.83
Between $0.5 mill. and $1 mill.	10	7.17
Between $0.1 mill. and $0.5 mill.	16	4.11
Total major official importers	45	142.11

The largest official importers include institutions such as municipal and national public utilities (electricity, telephones, and waterworks); public agencies marketing basic foodstuffs (IDEMA) or rural inputs (Caja Agraria); and the ministries of Public Works and Defense.

For 1970, the 119 largest industrial, commercial, and official importers combined accounted for $445 million in registered imports, or 48 per cent of the total import bill.

7. See James Tobin, "The Application of Multivariate Probit Analysis to Economic Survey Data," mimeographed, Cowles Foundation Discussion Paper 1, December 1, 1955. The condition that the dependent variable must always have a value within the interval from zero to 1 cannot be

maintained if its expected value is assumed to be a linear combination of the independent variables, as in multiple regressions. "Moreover, the multiple regression model assumes inappropriately for this case, that the distribution of the dependent variable around its expected value is independent of the level of that expected value" (Tobin, p. 2). See also Paul L. Joskow, "A Behavioral Theory of Public Utility Regulation" (Ph.D. diss., Yale University, 1972) for another application of probit analysis.

8. The average value of import requests under the industrial nonreimbursable category, however, was only U.S. $8,200, compared to $12,174 for those in the reimbursable category. In the commercial group the corresponding figures were $2,285 and $5,276.

9. When partial rejections are counted as approvals, the percentages of reimbursable licenses approved, according to size as measured by 1970 imports in U.S. dollars, are as follows: under $50,000, 70.1; over $50,000, but under $200,000, 71.3; over $200,000, but under $500,000, 71.2; over $500,000, but under $2 million, 70.7; over $2 million, 81.5.

10. The statistics used in the chi-square test (with one degree of freedom) are as follows: partial rejections omitted, 8.642; partial rejections as acceptances, 9.082; and partial rejections as rejections, 4.098.

11. Note also that the calculations in tables 6-14 and 6-15, although based only on the census-like information of my sample, have as many observations as tables 6-7 and 6-8. In other words, duplications were not weeded out, and data for a given company may appear several times. This is partly to avoid the laborious effort involved in the weeding-out process. In making the compilations, it was also noted that on several occasions what appeared to be the same company had different information in different import requests; this could be due to changes in company definitions or in time coverage or simply to errors of observation. No obvious criteria for choosing one set of information over another could be devised. As in earlier regressions, when a given company happened to have, say, zero minor exports or imports, these zeros were transformed into 1s, so that the logarithms would make sense. Finally, the simple correlation coefficients among the variables appearing in the more interesting Table 6-14 should be noted. Denoting X_1, X_2, ..., X_7 the independent variables in the order in which they are presented in Table 6-14 (extreme left-hand column), we have the following results:

	X_1	X_2	X_3	X_4	X_5	X_6
X_2	−0.26	—	—	—	—	—
X_3	−0.07	0.08	—	—	—	—
X_4	0.09	−0.45	0.01	—	—	—
X_5	0.08	−0.21	0.06	0.23	—	—
X_6	0.03	−0.47	0.02	0.42	0.33	—
X_7	−0.22	−0.11	−0.16	0.15	0.12	0.16

12. Albert Berry has also noted that data on Colombian industrial two-digit sectors for 1971 show a positive correlation between share of output exported and horsepower per worker. As of 1971, the major two-digit sectors in terms of gross value of exports were textiles, food products, chemicals, nonmetallic minerals, paper products, and leather products.

13. For a stimulating discussion of these issues placed in a general context, see Anne O. Krueger, "The Political Economy of the Rent-Seeking Society," *American Economic Review*, June 1974, pp. 291–303.

14. This is a joint Colombo-Venezuelan venture, with public sector participation. Thus, its nature is quite different from the rest of the companies on this list.

Chapter 7

The 1965-66 Liberalization Episode

In this chapter an examination will be made in some detail of the Colombian attempt during 1965–66 to eliminate administrative controls over imports and other transactions that entail purchases of foreign exchange. In earlier chapters I have already touched upon not only the Phase III episode itself but also its background and its aftermath. Here I will highlight aspects of that experience which have not been discussed earlier or which are particularly important to an understanding of the reasons why, shortly after imports had been almost fully liberalized, in October 1966, a return was announced, late the next month, to the drastic import and exchange controls characteristic of Phase II.

In previous chapters some key relationships in the Colombian economy were quantified that provide a useful framework for analyzing particular cyclical situations. However, nothing has been done so far to quantify the dynamics of Colombian inflation, a quantification which is also part of the necessary framework for short-run analysis. This will be my first task in this chapter. I will then proceed to discuss the relevant background to the 1965–66 liberalization episode, the episode itself, and its sweet-sour aftermath.

THE DYNAMICS OF INFLATION

As in almost all countries, developed and developing, Colombian balance-of-payments policies have interacted with those in the monetary and fiscal fields, which are aimed at obtaining steady growth near "full capacity" and without

184

undue inflation. Programs for reducing the rate of inflation have been typically accompanied in Colombia by policies to strengthen the balance of payments and improve economic efficiency by reduced reliance on administrative controls over imports or foreign-exchange transactions. Desirable policies, particularly regarding greater exchange-rate flexibility, have frequently been avoided or attacked on grounds of their alleged inflationary impact. It is therefore important to obtain some idea about the major factors influencing Colombian inflation, and about whether inflation during key cycles was more or less "normal" in the sense of following patterns established for the whole period.

The approach pioneered by Arnold C. Harberger in the study of inflation dynamics[1] will be useful here. That approach uses multiple regression analysis to explain percentage rates of change of different measures of the price level as a function of rates of change in several other variables assumed to be independent. The latter typically include measures of the money supply or total banking credit, wages, the exchange rate, and real supplies. Alberto R. Musalem has applied this technique for the Colombian case, with interesting results.[2] What follows builds on his work, although modifying it to better suit the purposes of this chapter and covering a different period.

This methodology has some weaknesses, mainly related to its reliance on a single equation which assumes one-way causation from the independent variables onto the dependent variable, the inflation rate. There have been circumstances in Colombia (as elsewhere) when monetary expansion could have been said to accommodate rather than cause price increases, which may have originated in sectoral maladjustments or in the foreign sector. Under those conditions a failure to accommodate price increases would have led to declines in output rather than to a severe reduction of inflation. But the construction of a simultaneous monetary model for Colombia is beyond the scope of this work, and the results of the single-equation regressions may be taken as little more than a descriptive summary of past links among ·the included variables, leaving the question of causation undecided. The best results obtained after considerable, but far from exhaustive, experimentation are presented in Table 7-1. The basic data, sources, and elaborations are given in the appendix to this chapter.

Note first that the dependent variables are quarterly percentage changes; the money, wage, and supplies variables represent yearly changes; and the import exchange rate represents a quarterly change also. The lagged money and supplies variables represent nonoverlapping yearly changes, and the lagged exchange-rate variable represents a quarterly change. In other words, to explain, say, the change in the cost-of-living index between the first quarter of 1958 and the last quarter of 1957, the relevant regression uses both the changes in money plus quasi money between the first quarter of 1958 and the

TABLE 7-1

Regressions for Quarterly Percentage Increases in Colombian Price Levels, 1958–69
(*t* statistics in parentheses)

	Cost-of-Living Index	Wholesale Price Index	Wholesale Price Index Excluding Foodstuffs
Constant	−2.87	−2.20	−0.78
	(1.81)	(2.01)	(0.83)
Money plus quasi money (yearly change)	0.08	0.08	0.01
	(1.22)	(1.75)	(0.15)
Lagged money plus quasi money	0.02	0.05	0.10
	(0.37)	(1.03)	(2.59)
Average import exchange rate (quarterly change)	0.08	0.08	0.11
	(1.52)	(2.24)	(3.32)
Lagged average import exchange rate	0.13	0.13	0.12
	(2.45)	(3.50)	(3.96)
Wage rates (yearly change)	0.19	0.12	0.05
	(4.60)	(4.16)	(2.20)
Real supplies (yearly change)	−0.03	−0.04	−0.06
	(0.87)	(1.89)	(2.92)
Lagged real supplies	0.01	−0.01	−0.03
	(0.44)	(0.67)	(1.61)
First-quarter dummy	1.41	0.52	0.61
	(1.48)	(0.79)	(1.09)
Second-quarter dummy	3.43	2.18	0.71
	(3.66)	(3.38)	(1.28)
Third-quarter dummy	−3.02	−0.72	0.65
	(3.14)	(1.08)	(1.15)
R^2	0.75	0.72	0.71
DW statistic	1.97	1.42	1.71
F statistic	10.98	9.71	9.12

SOURCE: See appendix to this chapter.

first quarter of 1957 and the change in the same variable between the first quarter of 1957 and the first quarter of 1956. It also uses both the change in the import exchange rate between the first quarter of 1958 and the last quarter of 1957 and the change for that variable between the last and the third quarter of 1957. It is not surprising that the different independent variables show varying lag structures; further experimentation would probably yield even greater differentiation.

The variables are mostly self-explanatory. Money plus quasi money worked better than just money or total credit. The wage rates refer to average hourly money wage rates in manufacturing. The real supplies variable is somewhat unusual, as it includes only merchandise imports plus agricultural and livestock output excluding coffee. The combination of these two strategic supply sources performed better in the regressions than others relying on more aggregated variables, such as the gross domestic product.

The fits are sufficiently good for our purposes, even though the regressions do not attempt to take into account expectation variables. Trends in the *world* price level are also ignored, with some justification for the period analyzed. As in the Musalem results, the story told does not support either extreme "monetarist"[3] or extreme "structuralist" explanations of the Colombian inflation. The regressions also show that changes in the import exchange rate do significantly influence changes in the price level. That influence is also quick (yearly changes for the exchange rate performed much worse than the quarterly ones) and quantitatively important. A 10 per cent devaluation would be expected to increase prices by about 2 per cent, ceteris paribus, according to these equations. It is noteworthy that when the 1956–58 period is included in the regressions, the importance of the exchange-rate variable declines. For reasons that are not completely clear,[4] the very large devaluations of those years affected the price level less than devaluations of later years. At any rate, even the 1958–69 results show that the extreme claims often heard in Colombia, which imply a value of 1.0 for the sum of the exchange-rate coefficients, are exaggerated. The combination of short lags for the price effects of devaluations, somewhat longer ones for wage-rate changes, and much longer (and less clear) ones for money, in turn influenced by fiscal and monetary policies, suggests an explanation for the popular but exaggerated identification of devaluations with inflation.

A clearer idea of the results presented in Table 7-1 may be obtained by asking what would be the net impact on the price level of a 10 per cent devaluation *and* a policy of liberalization that resulted in a permanent rise in imports also of 10 per cent, ceteris paribus. In the accompanying tabulation of the time profile of price changes (in percentages), each of the coefficients in Table 7-1 is taken at its face value; it is assumed (realistically) that imports make up 40 per cent of the real supplies variable; and devaluation and liberalization are started at an arbitrary quarter I.

Quarter	Cost-of-Living Index	Wholesale Price Index	Wholesale Price Index, Excl. Foodstuffs
I	0.68	0.64	0.86
II	1.18	1.14	0.96
III	−0.12	−0.16	−0.24
IV	−0.12	−0.16	−0.24
V	0.04	−0.04	−0.12
VI	0.04	−0.04	−0.12
VII	0.04	−0.04	−0.12
VIII	0.04	−0.04	−0.12
IX	0	0	0

If each of the price indices shown stood at 100 before devaluation plus liberalization, by the time the lagged effects had worked through the system (the ninth quarter), they would stand at 101.8, 101.3, and 100.9. Thus, the assumed import liberalization would not be sufficient to offset the price increases generated by the exchange-rate changes. According to the regression for the wholesale price index excluding foodstuffs, in which supplies have the most potent deflationary effect, it would take a sustained increase in imports of about 16 per cent to offset the inflationary impact of a 10 per cent devaluation by the ninth quarter. Even in this case the time profile, with early price increases and later declines, may mislead some into regarding the whole package as inflationary.

THE 1962 DEVALUATION: REVIEW OF SOME BACKGROUND

It will be recalled that the severe balance-of-payments crisis faced by Colombia after the collapse of the coffee boom of 1954–56 was handled by a combination of a sharp devaluation, tightened import controls, and implementation of austere fiscal and monetary policies. Between the first quarter of 1957 and the first quarter of 1959, the average import exchange rate rose by a remarkable 175 per cent, while money plus quasi money rose by a modest 23 per cent. Money wage rates, in turn, rose by 29 per cent. Thanks to the spartan fiscal, monetary, and wage policies, price increases were kept far below exchange-rate variations, yielding a substantial change in relative prices. The percentage increases in prices from the first quarter of 1957 to the first quarter of 1959 were as follows: cost of living, +32.4; wholesale price index, +31.9; and wholesale price index, excluding foodstuffs, +36.3.

It is worth remembering that while Colombia's stabilization effort was regarded sympathetically by foreign creditors, in those years there were no foreign credit facilities as flexible as the "program loans" available after 1961, nor access to Eurocredits as during the early 1970s. A good deal of civic enthusiasm, which now (middle 1970s) looks almost naive, more than made up for the scarcity of foreign assistance. The debt problem at that time involved primarily short-term suppliers' credits, which could be expected to be cleared up by a vigorous once-and-for-all effort. For the period 1957–60, changes in Colombian gross foreign-exchange reserves very closely followed movements in the balance of the merchandise trade account, which after a deficit of U.S. $106 million in 1956, yielded an accumulated surplus of U.S. $147 million during the three years 1957–59, in spite of the fall in coffee prices.

By 1959 there was an eagerness to resume a faster pace of growth; real GDP during 1958 was less than 5 per cent above that reached in 1956, indicating a fall in per capita product. Merchandise imports during 1958 were nearly 40 per cent below the 1956 levels. Inevitably, development-minded Colombians pressed for more expansive public policies. The new chapter (volume?) in inter-American relations that started with the triumph of the Cuban revolution had just been opened, and there were high hopes in Colombia for a large amount of aid from the United States.

It has been noted that, in spite of the substantial increase in the real import exchange rate between 1956 and 1959, administrative controls over imports were strengthened. In January 1959, in fact, a new law institutionalized the revised controls. In May 1959 a new customs tariff was also put into effect, intended to capture for the public treasury some of the premiums accruing to receivers of import licenses. The new tariff also included protectionist features. During 1957 and most of 1958 an essentially flexible exchange-rate policy was followed. However, after about August 1958, the certificate import rate was kept at 6.4 pesos per dollar, while the "free" rate fluctuated slightly around 8 pesos, as many influential voices called for "consolidating" monetary stability by adopting less flexible exchange rates. Indeed, as a result of changes in the average mix of certificate and free rates charged to importers, the average de facto import exchange rate *appreciated* by almost 8 per cent in the first quarter of 1959 compared with the second quarter of 1958.

By the end of 1959 this premature consolidation and appreciation of the average nominal import exchange rate had carried it to the level of the pegged certificate rate, 6.4 pesos. The expansionary fiscal and monetary policies were thus launched just as the import rate was being pegged.

Much to his credit the then Minister of the Treasury, Hernando Agudelo Villa, quickly saw the dangers of that combination, and during March 1960 he and his colleagues began experimenting with what later was to be called a "crawling peg," moving the certificate rate by less than 5 per cent to 6.7 pesos. Unfortunately, this wise policy was met by heavy opposition, particularly from the then Senator Carlos Lleras Restrepo, who, ironically, was to institutionalize the "crawling peg," under his presidency during 1967. He was already regarded as the Liberal politician most knowledgeable in economics, and had been the main author of Law 1 of 1959, institutionalizing the new import and exchange-control system. In a remarkable and friendly debate, on April 4, 1960, Lleras Restrepo and Agudelo Villa discussed this and other aspects of the government's economic policies.[5]

Lleras Restrepo challenged the notion that large imports during the first quarter of 1960 indicated the need for further devaluations. He warned against unifying the certificate and "free" rates by raising the certificate rate to the level of the latter (which was then only about 6.9 pesos), and said such action would be "incomprehensible." Hardly mentioning minor exports, he expressed the fear that the new policy would lead to gradual devaluations which would grow " . . . as the poet Jorge Rojas says, more or less insensibly, like the roses."

The reply by Agudelo Villa reads on the whole quite well, particularly in light of what came later. But politically the debate was finished after the Lleras blast. The certificate rate was to remain at 6.7 pesos until November 1962, when after much fruitless and wasteful resistance it was raised by more than 34 per cent to a new pegged level of 9 pesos. Proposals for greater flexibility were again rejected.

THE IMPACT OF THE 1962 DEVALUATION

The failure of the policies adopted in November 1962, early in the presidency of León Valencia, to achieve their objectives can be easily summarized by the following indicators, showing percentage increases between the third quarter of 1962 and the third quarter of 1963:

Cost of living	35.4
Wholesale price index	29.9
Wholesale price index, excluding foodstuffs	27.0
Average nominal import exchange rate	34.3
Money plus quasi money	21.0
Hourly wage rates	40.6

The price level increased roughly in the same proportion as the nominal devaluation, in sharp contrast to the 1957–59 experience. Based on this unfortunate incident many in Colombia reached the conclusion that devaluation "could not work." It may be worthwhile to look with greater detail at this inflationary episode, using the regressions developed in Table 7-1.

Table 7-2 contains actual and predicted quarterly price changes from 1960 through 1964; the predictions are from the regressions in Table 7-1. It may be seen, first of all, that the period from 1960 through 1962 was one of relative price stability, in spite of the more expansionary policies adopted since 1959. Real GDP rose by 4.3, 5.1, and 5.4 per cent in 1960, 1961, and 1962, respectively. Note, however, that by 1962 all three regressions were forecasting higher-than-realized rates of inflation; that was the year when attempts to maintain the 6.7 pesos rate became most intense.

When devaluation came in November 1962, the inflationary burst, following an apparently mild price response in December 1962, was concentrated in the first half of 1963, after which the rate of price increase declined sharply. Note that most, but not all, of that price explosion is predicted by our "normal" regressions. For the whole of 1963 the regressions still slightly underestimate the actual increase in the price level.

A rough indication of the explained and unexplained sources of the inflationary burst of the first half of 1963 is given by Table 7-3, in which predicted price increases are decomposed according to the current and lagged values of the independent variables. The three equations yield similar predictions of the amount of absolute inflation to be expected from the change in the nominal import exchange rate, all falling within a range of inflation of 6.1 to 6.5 per cent (the higher *share* in Table 7-3 for the inflationary contribution of the exchange rate to the increase in wholesale prices excluding foodstuffs is partly compensated by the lower inflation rate shown by that index). Clearly, other factors aggravated the inflationary pressure, although for wages and monetary expansions (particularly the former) the different regressions yield different quantitative estimates.

During both 1961 and 1962 government expenditures rose relative to GNP; the sum of all current expenditures of the general government plus public fixed capital formation rose from 10.4 per cent of GNP during 1960 to 11.7 per cent in 1961 and to 12.3 per cent during 1962. Current revenues of the national government, which in 1960 were 95 per cent of expenditures, fell to 77 per cent of expenditures in 1961 and to 72 per cent in 1962. Net banking credit to the government, which at the end of 1960 represented 20 per cent of all credit, accounted for 33 per cent of the *increase* in all such credit between the end of 1960 and the end of 1962. The deficit financed by net banking credit amounted to 0.7 per cent of GNP in 1961 and 2.2 per cent in 1962.[6] In the

TABLE 7-2

Actual (A) and Predicted (P) Quarterly Changes in Colombian Price Level, 1960–64
(per cent; averages for whole year in parentheses)

	Cost-of-Living Index		Wholesale Price Index		Wholesale Price Index Excluding Foodstuffs	
	A	P	A	P	A	P
1960 I	1.99	1.42	0	0.59	0.33	1.10
II	2.71	3.45	2.59	2.12	1.33	1.59
III	−0.88	−0.47	0.19	0.76	0.89	1.92
IV	1.77	1.62	1.45	0.80	0.83	0.59
(1960)	(1.40)	(1.51)	(1.06)	(1.07)	(0.85)	(1.30)
1961 I	3.48	3.91	2.05	1.90	1.19	1.48
II	7.71	5.64	3.69	3.38	2.13	0.93
III	−3.91	−2.08	−0.41	−0.02	0.67	1.07
IV	−0.81	1.37	0.05	0.90	0.57	0.32
(1961)	(1.62)	(2.21)	(1.35)	(1.54)	(1.14)	(0.95)
1962 I	1.64	2.67	0.27	1.63	0.97	1.08
II	1.61	5.42	1.49	3.91	1.43	2.13
III	0	−1.38	−0.09	0.67	1.41	2.03
IV	1.59	3.90	2.09	3.56	2.32	3.62
(1962)	(1.21)	(2.65)	(0.94)	(2.44)	(1.53)	(2.22)
1963 I	13.54	10.48	11.51	8.24	12.79	8.19
II	13.99	13.72	12.20	10.30	8.09	7.27
III	3.02	4.13	1.71	4.32	1.79	3.65
IV	7.23	5.39	4.18	3.98	1.93	2.64
(1963)	(9.45)	(8.43)	(7.40)	(6.71)	(6.15)	(5.44)
1964 I	3.28	4.26	4.97	2.89	2.15	1.86
II	10.23	5.49	6.11	4.29	1.66	1.79
III	−6.80	−1.32	0.21	1.19	1.76	2.34
IV	−1.63	1.76	−0.12	1.63	1.14	1.33
(1964)	(1.27)	(2.55)	(2.79)	(2.50)	(1.68)	(1.83)

SOURCE: Table 7-1.

TABLE 7-3

Share of Actual Increases in Price Level During First and Second Quarters of 1963 "Explained" by Variables in Regressions of Table 7-1

(per cent of actual total increases)

	Regression for:		
	Cost-of-Living Index	Wholesale Price Index	Wholesale Price Index Excluding Foodstuffs
Money plus quasi money	12.3	18.3	21.6
Import exchange rate	22.4	25.8	31.0
Wage rates	53.8	38.9	20.1
Real supplies	2.5	2.3	2.6
Seasonal factors plus constant	−3.3	−7.2	−1.2
Total: predicted inflation as per cent of actual inflation	87.8	78.1	74.1
Actual inflation (sum of first and second quarters)	27.5	23.7	20.9

SOURCE: Table 7-1.

context of weak monetary policy tools, described in earlier chapters, such fiscal policy was a key factor in the expansion of 42 per cent registered in money and quasi money between the last quarter of 1960 and the last quarter of 1962.

A legitimate preoccupation at a time of devaluation is how much the burden of adjustment will fall on the employed working class via decreases in real wages. Our wage rate series shows an upward trend in *real* wage rates (nominal rates deflated by the cost-of-living index) throughout 1960, 1961, and 1962. In spite of the devaluation, the upward trend continued during the early months of 1963. For the whole of 1963, *real* wage rates were 7 per cent above those for 1962, although toward the end of 1963 a downward tendency was visible, which continued in 1964. For the whole of 1964, real wages were 3 per cent below those of 1963, and about 2 per cent above those of 1962. Public policy, under intense trade union and political pressure, had something to do with at least the timing of these movements.

Early in the discussions about a new devaluation, the government had pledged to raise wages. Wages were in fact increased abruptly by a national law during the first quarter of 1963, with Congress going beyond the wage concessions suggested by the executive. The quarterly percentage changes in nominal hourly wages during 1962 and 1963 evolved as follows:

1962 I	2.1	1963 I	14.1
II	4.1	II	12.4
III	5.0	III	2.4
IV	7.1	IV	3.0

The wage legislation also provided for an escalator clause, which was later abandoned with the apparent approval of the trade unions.

According to our regressions, declines in real supplies during early 1963 contributed (slightly) to the inflationary burst. Import licensing had been severely restricted during late 1962. As a result, during the first half of 1963 the dollar value of merchandise imports was 20 per cent below the corresponding period in the previous year. The noncoffee rural GDP practically stagnated (it rose by 0.7 per cent) between 1962 and 1963 because of bad weather, thus decreasing per capita agricultural supplies. It is quite possible that our clumsy way of taking into account rural real supplies leads to an underestimation of the inflationary impact of declines in supplies during early 1963. Real GDP as a whole rose between 1962 and 1963 by 3.3 per cent, only slightly faster than population growth.

It should be added that many have reported weather as being unfavorable during early 1963, and that hurt mainly the output of key foodstuffs.[7]

As noted in Table 7-3, the actual inflationary burst went beyond that predicted by the regressions. One may speculate as to the reasons for this overshooting. A first consideration, totally ignored in the regressions, is the timing of changes in a host of government-regulated prices not only for electricity and public transportation but also for a number of "basic necessities" (milk, sugar, cigarettes) ordinarily subject to price controls and other agricultural commodities for which minimum prices are ordinarily set. During 1962 the government held a strict line on these prices, which may partly explain the size of the residuals of the regressions for 1962. Right after the devaluation, and under advice from international lenders, most of these prices were abruptly readjusted upward. Early in 1963, for example, public transportation fares were increased between 50 and 75 per cent; and gasoline prices, by 20 per cent; and price ceilings on cement, cigarettes, milk, and sugar went up between 15 and 20 per cent.

More difficult to quantify is the inflationary impact, via expectations, of the *manner* in which the government went about the devaluation. As is not unusual when it comes to moving an adjustable peg, before the November 20 decision there was considerable discussion of the forthcoming devaluation, and a clear signal of what was to come was given on November 7, when all imports were temporarily placed on the prohibited list. A politically weak government publicly discussed options as to whether and how to devalue, before November 20, adding to the climate of uncertainty and speculation.

While the regressions take into account changes in monetary conditions, the peculiar way in which money plus quasi money expanded late in 1962, at the time of devaluation, may have had greater-than-average inflationary impact because of the expectations it generated. Beginning in November 1962, as part of its agreement with the IMF, the government liquidated its sizable floating debt with domestic creditors by using bank credit. As a result, of the total net increase in money plus quasi money between the end of 1961 and the end of 1962, an astounding 78 per cent took place during the last two months of 1962. In other words, while money plus quasi money rose by 5.3 per cent between December 31, 1961, and October 31, 1962, it rose by 17.4 per cent between the latter date and the end of 1962.

After this sketchy review of the 1962 devaluation it can easily be seen why memories of its impact were a major obstacle facing those attempting after that date to use a more flexible exchange rate as a policy tool. The argument that that event was a textbook example of how *not* to manage a devaluation made little impression. The feelings of most Colombians were accurately reflected by the then President León Valencia, who throughout 1963 and 1964 would warn his economic advisers not to mention the abominable word in his presence, in spite of continuing balance-of-payments difficulties.

THE 1965–66 LIBERALIZATION EPISODE:
ORIGINS AND IMPLEMENTATION

The years 1963 and 1964 were melancholy ones for foreign trade policy in Colombia. The nominal import exchange rate was pegged and obviously overvalued once again, while that for minor exports, one peso higher, shared those two features (until the last quarter of 1964). Not surprisingly, foreign-exchange difficulties continued to plague the economy, while real GDP grew at an average rate of only 4.3 per cent per year during 1963, 1964, and 1965.

In the new cycle following the devaluation of the basic import rate in November 1962, the expected relaxation of import controls did not last long because that stabilization program failed significantly to change relative prices. The prestige of licensing as *the* tool to repress imports rose as that of exchange-rate devaluation sank. Imports on the free list as a share of total registered imports fell from 60 per cent in 1960–61 to about 35 per cent in late 1964 and lower still in early 1965. The time taken to decide on import requests lengthened, and during the last half of 1964 it reached, on average, nearly three months. Prior import deposits were kept in the central bank longer than usual, often for more than ten months. By late 1964 about 35 per cent of all license applications were being refused, and bitter and severe criticisms were again levied at beleaguered import control authorities. In December 1964 the free list was suspended, at first for 90 days, but then until September 1965, and prior exchange registration was made more difficult, resulting in a new piling up of commercial arrears. Early in 1965 prohibitions were extended, and licensing became increasingly slow and difficult, particularly for capital goods. Fresh attempts were made to divert both private and official imports toward bilateral partners, particularly with capital goods such as agricultural and construction machinery, elevators, tractors, trucks, and other vehicles. Some Colombian trading partners that felt injured by these practices, particularly the United States and the West German Federal Republic, made their displeasure known directly and indirectly.

Throughout 1964 the draining of exchange reserves for supporting the "free rate" at 10 pesos per U.S. dollar became more burdensome. It will be recalled that the rate for minor exports was pegged at that 10-peso level right after the November 1962 devaluation of the certificate import rate, under the pressing advice of the IMF, among others. Indeed, and quite incredibly when viewed in retrospect, the IMF urged at that time and throughout 1963 that the rates should be unified *at 9 pesos,* arguing that the 10-peso rate gave minor exports a privileged position and an unjustified subsidy, while generating inflationary pressures! It should be noted that at that time some Colombian officials in the executive branch apparently *agreed* with the IMF, but tried to blame Congress for the higher rate legislated for minor exports. As can be seen in Table 2-10, during 1963 the net real exchange rate applied to minor exports was below both what it had been in 1962 and what it was to be in 1970; the 1962 and 1970 rates were 15 per cent higher than the 1963 rate. As can be seen, in turn, in Table 4-7, the nominal purchasing-power-parity exchange rate applied to imports in 1958 was 24 per cent above that for 1963, while the 1970 rate exceeded it by 22 per cent.

Most cautiously, late in 1964 members of the Junta Monetaria began hinting to an embattled President the need to reconsider exchange-rate policy. At that time the President was troubled not only by memories of the 1962 devaluation, but also by a very serious political situation, which included rumors of an imminent coup d'etat. Devaluation advice was severely rebuffed. Nevertheless, in October 1964 the central bank stopped supporting the pegged free rate, apparently then less politically sensitive than the certificate rate. The free rate depreciated quickly and more or less steadily, going from an average of 10 pesos in October 1964 to a high of 19.2 pesos in August 1965. By late 1964 the IMF was also advising devaluation, and had given up at last its opposition to a dual system including a higher rate for minor exports.

While during the second and third quarters of 1965 the purchasing-power-parity effective exchange rate applied to minor exports reached, thanks to the freeing of the "free" rate,[8] high levels not reached either before or after, by the second quarter of that year the purchasing-power-parity nominal import exchange rate fell to its lowest point since early 1957. At that time, the rate was about one-third below the (almost identical) averages for 1958 and 1970. Import control administrators recall with horror the chaotic conditions of licensing during the first six months of 1965; delays and rejections of applications were at levels not seen since 1956–57. During April 1965, for example, average delays in handling import requests were said to have reached six months. The zooming free-market rate reflected widespread speculation and capital flight, also stimulated by severe political unrest. At this time, however, the increase in the price level was not particularly severe; in the third quarter of 1965, the cost-of-living index was 4 per cent above its level in the same period in 1964. The corresponding figure for the wholesale price index was 8 per cent; for the index excluding foodstuffs, the increase was 11 per cent.

At the end of June 1965, gross foreign-exchange reserves were down to their lowest levels since 1957, and were, at $56 million, only a little more than half of what they had been a year earlier. In that climate, both official and public attention first focused on the wild goings-on in the free exchange market. At the end of June 1965, in a controversial move allegedly motivated by fears of inflation, the rate applicable to minor exports was divorced from the free rate and set at 13.5 pesos, representing a sharp appreciation for minor exporters. The inflation argument was related to the obligation of the central bank to buy dollars earned by minor exports at the rate ruling the previous week in the free market to cover its commitment to importers in the certificate market. The loss from buying dollars at 18.8 pesos (the average free rate in June 1965) and selling them at 9 pesos was covered by simply printing pesos. This move, at a time when the need to stimulate new exports was obvious, can only be understood in terms of the severe political constraints under which economic policymakers operated and the weakness of monetary policy tools.

Perhaps the best thing that can be said for the 13.5-peso rate for minor exports is that, once it was created, it provided a "plausible" and sound alternative to both the 9-peso certificate rate (note that it was exactly 50 per cent higher) and the eye-catching but thin free market. As noted in Chapter 1, allegedly the President was finally persuaded to go along with the de facto gradual devaluations of the average import exchange rate, started together with the import liberalization program in September 1965, by the argument that relative to the free-market rate the move toward a rate of 13.5 pesos was really a *revaluation* which would also bring down the free rate. The fixation of public opinion with the antics of the free rate had become so intense that one cannot be sure whether the acceptance of that thesis represented economic wishful thinking or the wiles of a subtle politician with a short-term horizon. In fact, between August and October 1965 the free rate appreciated from 19.2 pesos to 17.8 pesos.

On September 2, 1965, following the advice of the Junta Monetaria, the certificate market was divided into a preferential and an intermediate section, with rates of 9 and 13.5 pesos, respectively. The preferential group included commodities such as foodstuffs, chemicals, and pharmaceuticals. Imports were to be transferred gradually from the first to the second section, with the less "essential" imports going first, while simultaneously freeing them from administrative controls. Capital goods were also quickly placed in the intermediate market, on the grounds that payments on such imports are spread out over a period of time.

The original liberalization plan called for removal of prior licensing on about half of all imports within six months, and eventually including 65 per cent of all imports. It was expected that imports of capital goods for industrial plants would be kept under control as part of the mechanism for investment planning.[9] In fact, the pace of liberalization went even faster. The free list was expanded on each of the following dates: September 8, November 11, 1965; January 27, February 22, February 28, March 17, July 29, and August 21, 1966. By this last date nearly all imports had been reclassified to the intermediate exchange rate; most imports were now either prohibited or on the free list, although some remained subject to prior licensing. Furthermore, starting in October 1965, advance import deposits were reduced every month by 5 percentage points from the rates in force on September 30. The plan called for continuing this rhythm for twenty months until those deposits were eliminated. In late August 1966, however, it was announced that the 5 per cent cuts were to be made quarterly, not monthly, starting in November 1966. It will be recalled that between September 1965 and August 1966 numerous modifications, mainly upward, were also introduced in the tariff, in principle to harmonize it with import liberalization. The temporary maintenance of a prohibited list was justified primarily on protectionist grounds. Of all registered imports during 1965 only 15 per cent had been on the free list; the corresponding figure for 1966 was 56 per cent. By October 1966 the free list covered 80 per cent of all registered imports.

Because of the lack of candor and clarity with which the liberalization plan was launched, a number of points remained ambiguous, and were to haunt policymakers a year later. In particular, the issue of raising the 13.5-

peso rate was left fuzzy. In September 1965 such fuzziness on future devaluation was used to sell the package and avoid inflationary expectation, as in
1963; but by September 1966 this was to become a source of irritation between
Colombians and international creditors. Among the latter, some were convinced in 1965 that Colombian authorities had committed themselves to
depreciating the intermediate rate if necessary, in line with a policy of
exchange flexibility, rather than stop or reverse import liberalization. In fact,
they expected such further devaluations to be necessary, suspecting that the
13.5-peso rate was too low. Other architects and sponsors of the plan, one
may speculate, probably assumed that import liberalization would inevitably
drag the authorities, unable to reverse liberalization, into further devaluations
in the future whether or not they were willing to consider such a possibility in
September 1965. By this time, it should be noted, the Monetary Board had
been given the power to make exchange-rate adjustments at any time and of
any size. The free rate was still allowed to fluctuate freely, and some hoped
that eventually an upward crawling intermediate rate would reach and merge
with the free rate. The progressive liberalization of import controls would test
the appropriateness of the 13.5-peso rate, which was to be raised if the import
surge proved to be too great. A species of "chicken" game was set up. On
such shaky foundations was based the most systematic attempt at import
liberalization attempted in Colombia since World War II.

Regardless of how a 13.5-peso rate looked in September 1965, the inflationary burst of late 1965 and the first half of 1966 robbed the gradual nominal
devaluation of a good share of its real effect, although matters were much
better in this respect than following the 1962 devaluation. By the time the new
President, Carlos Lleras Restrepo, assumed office, in August 1966, virtually
all import payments were being made at 13.5 pesos per dollar and nearly all
(nonprohibited) imports were on the free list. The price level during the third
quarter of 1966 was, however, substantially above that for the third quarter of
1965 (21 per cent according to the cost-of-living index, 17 per cent according to
the wholesale price index, and 19 per cent according to the index of wholesale
prices excluding foodstuffs).

Changes for 1965–69 in the actual price level and as predicted by the
regressions of Table 7-1 are shown in Table 7-4. It may be seen that there were
sharp price increases in the last quarter of 1965 and the first half of 1966, which
were, however, quite "normal" in the sense that they were predicted to a very
large extent by the regressions. This may be more clearly seen in Table 7-5, in
which also shares of the observed inflation are attributed to the different
independent variables according to their coefficients and concurrent and
lagged actual changes.

As in the predictions for the first half of 1963, the three regression
equations forecast similar absolute inflation rates—7.6, 7.6, and 8.1 per cent—

TABLE 7-4

Actual (A) and Predicted (P) Quarterly Changes in Colombian Price Level, 1965–69
(per cent; averages for whole year in parentheses)

	Cost-of-Living Index		Wholesale Price Index		Wholesale Price Index Excluding Foodstuffs	
	A	P	A	P	A	P
1965 I	2.09	3.29	0.56	2.37	1.98	2.85
II	3.42	4.81	3.90	4.11	2.51	3.80
III	0	−0.92	3.16	1.76	5.40	4.02
IV	5.79	4.81	5.69	5.19	6.23	6.49
(1965)	(2.83)	(3.00)	(3.33)	(3.36)	(4.03)	(4.29)
1966 I	7.81	6.83	5.02	6.03	4.90	6.13
II	7.97	5.18	5.25	3.78	3.28	2.22
III	−1.34	−2.08	0.45	0.17	3.08	1.70
IV	2.04	0.88	1.91	0.91	2.57	1.31
(1966)	(4.12)	(2.70)	(3.16)	(2.72)	(3.46)	(2.84)
1967 I	2.67	2.41	1.44	1.30	1.78	1.76
II	3.25	4.63	1.58	3.40	1.95	2.56
III	−0.63	−1.10	1.58	0.88	2.06	2.77
IV	1.27	2.22	1.31	1.88	0.90	2.08
(1967)	(1.64)	(2.04)	(1.48)	(1.87)	(1.67)	(2.29)
1968 I	2.50	3.23	1.60	2.16	1.47	2.17
II	2.44	4.42	2.93	3.28	1.72	1.67
III	−1.19	−2.03	0.17	0.55	0.48	1.55
IV	1.81	0.90	0.37	1.20	1.40	1.03
(1968)	(1.39)	(1.63)	(1.27)	(1.80)	(1.27)	(1.61)
1969 I	2.37	2.82	1.64	2.16	2.53	2.53
II	6.47	4.77	3.25	3.31	2.96	1.94
III	1.95	−1.59	1.23	0.46	2.32	1.89
IV	1.76	1.82	2.82	1.65	1.59	1.55
(1969)	(3.14)	(1.96)	(2.24)	(1.90)	(2.35)	(1.98)

SOURCE: Table 7-1.

stemming from the change in the average import exchange rate, most of which occurred during the last quarter of 1965. Inflationary monetary factors appear more important than for the first half of 1963, while increases in nominal wage rates are less so.

Contrary to the case of the 1962 devaluation, national government finances do not appear to have been the major culprit for the hefty rates of

TABLE 7-5

Share of Actual Increases in Price Level During Last Quarter of 1965 and First Half of 1966 "Explained" by Variables in Regressions of Table 7-1
(per cent of actual total increases)

	Regression for:		
	Cost-of-Living Index	Wholesale Price Index	Wholesale Price Index Excluding Foodstuffs
Money plus quasi money	27.4	45.0	44.2
Import exchange rate	35.1	47.2	56.2
Wage rates	36.2	30.5	15.3
Real supplies	−3.2	−4.4	−5.7
Seasonal factors plus constant	−17.5	−24.4	−7.1
Total: predicted inflation as per cent of actual inflation	78.0	93.8	102.9
Actual inflation (sum of three quarters)	21.6	16.0	14.4

SOURCE: Table 7-1.

expansion in money and quasi money observed in late 1965 and early 1966. Current revenues accounted for 87 per cent of government expenditures in 1964 and for 91 per cent in 1965. As liberalized imports rose, custom revenues (particularly from duties on autos) expanded sharply, and during 1966 the central budget showed a small surplus. Monetary expansion, which during the first quarter of 1966 ran 19 per cent above a year earlier, can be blamed primarily on the imperfect tools available to the monetary authorities for restraining banking credit to the private sector. Such imperfection arose in part from the power of private banks practically to ignore reserve requirements imposed by the central bank.[10] It also includes the power of the Coffee Growers' Federation to obtain credit and the effects of a coffee policy encouraging such pressures. During 1966 while the domestic coffee price was fixed, the dollar price was falling. This, together with a good crop and the desire to withhold some of it to prop up the dollar price, led to credit demands that the lame-duck Valencia government was unable to resist.

Increases in money wage rates were not encouraged by public policy during 1965–66 and were in fact modest. Real hourly manufacturing wages *declined* by 4 per cent between the first three quarters of 1965 and the following three quarters, in spite of rising imports and output. If the first three quarters of 1965 are compared with those of 1966, a decline of 5.5 per cent is observed in real wage rates. No wonder that the abrupt death of the liberalization episode in November 1966 evoked few tears from the working class.

Seasonal factors were more favorable than in 1963, and the effect of changes in real supplies was to dampen inflation, contrary to its behavior in the previous major devaluation. As may be seen in Table 3-3, merchandise imports reacted vigorously to the liberalization beginning in the first quarter of 1966; during the first half of that year the dollar value of imports was 30 per cent higher than the corresponding value for the same period in 1965, and 43 per cent higher than during the second half of 1965. Noncoffee rural output rose by 2.8 per cent in 1965 and by 3.9 per cent in 1966, figures not far from normal trends.[11] Over-all real GDP was expanding during 1966 at higher-than-trend rates, finishing that year with a 5.4 per cent increase over 1965.

During 1965–66 the large gap between the free-market rate and the rate applicable to merchandise imports was blamed by some for creating expectations contributing to inflation. As shown in Table 7-5, that gap is unnecessary to explain the behavior of wholesale prices. Its contribution to increases in the cost of living is also doubtful: a variable showing the ratio of the two exchange rates during 1958–69 was found insignificant in regressions of the type shown in Table 7-1.

In August 1966 it appeared that the liberalization program was firmly established. The new President had pledged to continue it and early in his administration, on August 21, 1966, took measures to complete the transfer of imports from the 9- to the 13.5-peso rate. The import surge was expected to abate once pent-up import demand had spent itself. According to the price dynamics of Table 7-1, the most inflationary phase of the devaluation-liberalization episode had been passed, and a net deflationary effect could be expected from the current *and lagged* effects of the expansion of real supplies, driven mainly by the import surge. Thus, taking the regression for the wholesale price index (excluding foodstuffs) of Table 7-1, the *net* percentage effect on price changes of the observed movements in the exchange rate and real supplies variables was as follows: 1965IV, +4.25; 1966I, +3.34; 1966II, −0.34; 1966III, −0.80; and 1966IV, −0.49.

BLOWUP

As already noted, back in September 1965 it was the understanding of the IMF (and some others) that if the balance-of-payments situation remained precarious after the transfer to the 13.5 peso rate had been completed, further adjustments would be made in the exchange rate. It was further understood by the IMF that the Colombian government had agreed, in its "letter of intention" of 1965, to use quarterly targets in gross foreign-exchange reserves as objective indicators of the state of the balance of payments which would, if not met, trigger automatic devaluations. At the end of September 1966 the reserve target was not met. Indeed, Colombian *net* reserves were deep in the red.

During the first three quarters of 1966, merchandise imports (dollar c.i.f. values) had run at 44 per cent above the corresponding period for 1965, while registered merchandise exports had declined slightly (by 1 per cent). The export outlook was not very promising; coffee prices had been declining since April 1966 and minor exports were sluggish and certainly below trend. For the whole of 1966 the change relative to 1965 was as follows:

Merchandise imports (dollars, c.i.f.):	48.7%
Recorded merchandise exports (dollars):	−5.8
Coffee exports (dollars)	−4.5
Registered minor exports (dollars):	1.6
Crude petroleum exports (dollars):	−20.0

Gross foreign-exchange reserves at the end of the third quarter of 1966 stood at $52 million, or $11 million less than a year earlier, and represented only 8 per cent of 1966 imports.

Under these circumstances the IMF pressed for an immediate devaluation as a condition for releasing the last credit tranche of the standby agreement signed in 1965 and renewing the standby agreement. The Colombian government, i.e., primarily President Lleras and his Minister of the Treasury, argued that such a move was not necessary at that time. Among younger government economists and technicians opposition to devaluation was not as strong. Indeed, some members of that group had argued for devaluation since early September, before the IMF recommended such a move. The higher Colombian authorities argued that both the fall in coffee and in minor export earnings reflected basically exogenous declines in world commodity prices and were to blame for the failure to achieve the reserve target. In particular, the link between the poor performance of minor exports in 1966 and the decline in the real minor export exchange rate between 1965 and 1966 was rejected. The government also insisted that the import surge had peaked and that a decline in imports could be expected. It pointed out that the liberalization program had been carried out at a faster pace than had been agreed in 1965. It rejected the idea of rigidly linking exchange-rate movements to changes in the reserve situation, using arguments similar to those used by the French in the 1973 discussions of international monetary reform. It denied that either explicitly or implicitly a commitment had been made to that notion in

September 1965, a denial supported by Colombian officials who participated in those negotiations. The government went on to say that the circumstances called not for devaluation, but for an expanded volume of concessionary aid flows to Colombia to support the liberalization program during those difficult circumstances. The critical breathing space to be purchased by aid referred not only to that needed to face allegedly temporary balance-of-payments difficulties, but also that required by the new government (inaugurated in August 1966) to get a firm hold on domestic policy tools, particularly monetary ones.

The new government was very eager *not* to repeat the performance of that other new administration which four years before, in November 1962, had undertaken a devaluation under pressure from the IMF and aid-granting organizations. Indeed, the new President was very conscious that, whether justly or not, he was being attacked as having been one of the key architects of the 1962 devaluation.

In October and November 1966, there was intense shuttling of national and international civil servants between Washington and Bogotá. The Colombian government hoped that the IMF did not represent the position of other credit institutions, such as the IBRD and AID. It also argued that it did not necessarily oppose the idea of eventual devaluations; it simply did not regard October 1966 as the right time. It noted that it had no intention of freezing the free market, then used mainly for capital and some "invisible" transactions (as well as smuggling), and which stood at about 16.4 pesos in September 1966, below the rates of a year earlier. It reaffirmed its intention of making sure that fiscal and monetary policies were under control and noninflationary *before* further devaluing the certificate rate.

The leverage which foreign aid agencies could exert on the Colombian government was still substantial in 1966. As already noted, Colombian foreign-exchange reserves were particularly low. The Colombian foreign debt, while not reaching the extraordinary levels of some other less developed countries, had been rising. Interest and amortization on that debt amounted to 12 per cent of exports of goods and nonfactor services in 1962; by 1966 that debt burden indicator had increased to more than 16 per cent.[12] It will be recalled that at that time the Washington aid agencies as a group had a virtual monopoly of medium- and long-term credit vis-à-vis countries such as Colombia, not only because of the flows they controlled directly but also because of the strong influence their judgments had on U.S. and European private banks. The competitive forces and new options generated by the Eurocurrency market were still in their infancy. Faced by a liquidity crunch, Colombia had either to give in to the combined aid agencies or take drastic austerity measures.

Things came to head late in November, apparently triggered by the announcement of AID and the IBRD to Colombian officials that their aid would be conditioned on a Colombian agreement with the IMF, including firm commitments to a devaluation timetable. The IMF-AID-IBRD group charged that the Colombian government lacked a balance-of-payments policy, and said that under those conditions they could not go on lending money to it. The Colombian government claimed to have been surprised by this collusion among foreign creditors and acted decisively. The apparently new AID position was first heard by Colombian officials on November 27 (a Sunday), and again the next day, together with that of the IBRD. A cabinet meeting showed most younger economists in favor of immediate devaluation, but the influential Minister of the Treasury opposed any such move. On November 29 (Tuesday), President Lleras went on television to announce the breakdown of the negotiations with foreign lending agencies, the elimination of the free market rate, and the imposition of rigorous import and exchange controls. Devaluation was out of the question. The import liberalization program had lasted slightly more than one year. Before attempting to draw lessons from this episode and its spectacular end, it is important to review what followed.

SISYPHUS AND LAW 444

The energetic preparation of a new comprehensive law on foreign trade and payments began about a month after the dramatic presidential announcement. Discreet contacts were also re-established with foreign creditors. On the latter front, foreign personalities more diplomatic than those who had conducted earlier negotiations, drawn particularly from the IBRD, began an important role as "honest brokers" between the Colombian government and the international lending group.

The preparation of what eventually became Decree Law 444 of March 22, 1967, absorbed most of the creative forces of the Lleras administration starting in December 1966. The new law codified and rationalized existing regulations and practices in the field of foreign trade and payments, and made a number of important innovations, as noted in Chapter 1. The more flexible exchange-rate policy, which should not have been abandoned in 1958, was reinstated. Very cautiously, moves toward import liberalization were started once again, from square one. As of early 1974, however, the import administrative regime, including both licensing and prior deposits, had not regained the freedom reached in October 1966. Since 1967, a year when imports had to be cut back drastically and the rate of growth of real GDP was below trend (at 4.2 per cent), Colombia has experienced an expansion in production and exports which by 1974 was without parallel in duration in the post-World War II period. In the next chapter, I will explore the extent to which this remarkably happy ending to the 1966 blowup was due to exogenous and endogenous factors; here, it will be sufficient to state that the new policies, particularly the crawling peg, by successfully breaking the stop-go cycles of earlier years, deserve much of the credit for the performance.

It should nevertheless be pointed out that the new policy course, now clear in retrospect, was not obviously foreseeable in March 1967 either by Colombians or by the foreign lending agencies. Those agencies were apparently caught off guard and embarrassed by the November 1966 Colombian moves, which had a very favorable political impact within Colombia and widespread repercussions and acceptance throughout Latin America. Throughout December IBRD officials had active conversations with Colombian representatives, and by February 1967 a new IMF mission was in Colombia to negotiate a fresh standby agreement that was finally signed in spite of the uncertainty regarding the *pace* at which the crawling peg was to be moved. On this score President Lleras clearly won his argument and obtained the resumption of aid without committing himself to a particular pace or timing of depreciation.

Officially, the post-March 1967 Colombian exchange rate is supposed to be the result of a reasonably free play of supply and demand, akin to "dirty floating." In fact, it is a crawling peg set daily by the government via associated banks. The peg is changed every few days. As noted in Chapter 4, there does not appear to have existed any rigid post-1967 formula for determining the pace of the crawl.

QUESTIONS AND LESSONS FROM THE 1965–66 LIBERALIZATION EPISODE AND ITS AFTERMATH

As conventionally measured, the performance of the Colombian economy since 1967 has been better than its average for the rest of the postwar period. Could all that *plus* the benefits of the import liberalization reached in October 1966 have been obtained by avoiding the November 1966 blowup? Assuming that this is the case, and leaving until Chapter 8 the discussion of exactly *how much better* performance would have been under those circumstances, the obvious question centers on the responsibility for the blowup.

With the help of hindsight, and of tables 2-9 and 4-8, it may be seen that key exchange rates were overvalued during the third quarter of 1966 (unless one wishes to argue that 1970 rates were *undervalued*). Thus, the PPP-EER for minor exports was at that time 17.6 per cent below the 1970 average; it was also below the averages registered for 1961, 1962, and 1965. The PPP-NER for

TABLE 7-6

Selected Colombian Annual Growth Rates, 1964–70
(per cent)

	1964	1965	1966	1967	1968	1969	1970
Gross domestic product	6.2	3.6	5.4	4.2	6.1	6.4	6.7
Gross domestic fixed capital formation	12.5	−5.6	8.0	6.6	15.0	2.5	13.1
Manufacturing output	5.9	4.7	6.6	3.6	6.2	7.3	8.3
Registered minor exports	18.9	35.8	0.6	17.4	34.8	21.5	1.5
BCST exports	−11.3	32.4	−11.3	56.2	27.3	2.7	−1.2
Manufactured exports	71.2	19.9	22.5	4.8	32.7	24.6	−15.6
Miscellaneous minor exports	17.0	93.2	−19.0	−25.1	75.2	69.6	42.8

BCST = bananas, coffee, sugar, and tobacco.
SOURCE: National accounts data from BdlR-CN; they are in constant market prices. Minor export data from Table 2-3; they are in dollar values at current prices.

imports in the third quarter of 1966 was 16.3 per cent below the 1970 average and below the 1958–59 rates. As dollar prices for coffee and other Colombian exports were, as claimed by the government, particularly weak during 1966 (see Table 2-5), the ex post case for declaring the 1966 exchange rates overvalued is strengthened.

The issue of the *timing* of the needed devaluation, however, is something else. Both political and economic considerations suggest the soundness of the Lleras reluctance to devalue until monetary and fiscal instruments were well under control. Foreign pressure to devalue during October and November 1966 was not only insensitive but also economically dangerous, given monetary conditions. The latter had been made more explosive by the automatic release of funds previously frozen by prior import deposits. During the first half of 1966 this had been offset by the sharp increase in imports, but during the second half it threatened to add substantially to monetary expansion.

Most observers now agree that by October 1966 stocks of imported goods were bulging, and a downturn in imports (even at the existing exchange rate) was imminent. A good share of the increase in imports during 1966 had been motivated by a speculative desire to take advantage of a liberalization not expected to last long. It can be plausibly argued that the maintenance of the external credit flow for at least a few more months would have saved the liberalization program *and* given the new Lleras administration time to prepare a noninflationary setting for the needed gradual devaluations. The decline in the GDP and manufacturing growth rates registered during 1967, as shown in Table 7-6, would presumably have been avoided.

If that had been done, would the pace of devaluations after 1966 have been as fast as that actually observed? Would the crawling peg have been maintained? It would be pleasing to answer these questions with a clear yes. Yet serious doubts must remain. As noted earlier, President Lleras, who participated in the Bretton Woods conference of 1944, had in 1960 called for an end to a short-lived experiment with the crawling peg. Six years after Decree Law 444 had been promulgated, in March 1973, former President Lleras called for an end to or at least a slowdown in the creep of the crawling peg as a way to fight inflation and eliminate excess profits in some exporting activities benefiting from the world commodity boom.[13] It seems difficult to argue that without the 1966–68 pressure of foreign creditors Colombian exchange-rate policy, particularly the pace of devaluation, would have been the same as that actually observed.

There are some fairly straightforward lessons from the 1965–66 Colombian experience. A government that does not want to be caught between the alternatives of being pushed around by public or private foreign creditors (with good or bad will is irrelevant here) or instituting drastic trade and payments policies it does not regard as desirable should avoid launching import liberalization programs with low foreign-exchange reserves *and* a commitment to a pegged import exchange rate.

The 1965–66 devaluation-plus-liberalization episode lasted little more than a year, from September 1965 to November 1966. Nearly full liberalization lasted about two months (September and October of 1966). It can be argued that such time spans only show the transitional problems of the program and few of its benefits. Nevertheless, it is worth noting that, contrary to what some of the most enthusiastic champions of liberalization have claimed in the past, there was in 1966 a dramatic upsurge neither in minor exports, nor in investment, nor in over-all growth rates. As shown in Table 7-6, the 1966 GDP, investment, and manufacturing growth rates were above postwar averages (shown in Table 1-1), but below those registered in many subsequent years. The somewhat erratic evidence on the then still thin flow of minor exports indicates no dramatic response to liberalization, apart from the response to changes in the effective exchange rate documented in Chapter 2.

It is also worth noting that a return to harsh import controls late in 1966 did not prevent substantial minor export expansion during 1967, 1968, and 1969. The Colombian experience indicates that drastic import liberalization is neither a necessary nor a sufficient condition for export growth.

The large output gains to be obtained by avoiding stop-go cycles, and the need to coordinate foreign trade and payments policies with those in the fiscal and monetary fields to avoid such cycles, are also lessons emerging from the Colombian experiences of the 1960s and early 1970s. And had the peso exchange rate been kept flexible, as it was in 1957 and early 1958, and again since March 1967, the growth and balance-of-payments performance during 1958–68 would have been clearly better. But more on this in the next chapter.

Finally, it may be noted that the circumstances surrounding Colombian trade and payments policy during the 1960s were so unique as to make it difficult to link them neatly with the Bhagwati-Krueger phases. Devaluation, stabilization, and import liberalization policies were all either carried out or promised late in 1962 and in mid-1965; so those events can be clearly labeled as Phase III episodes. The events of November 1966 through March 1967 just as clearly mark a return to Phase II. But the new phase started in March 1967 is more difficult to define. Perhaps it is best characterized as a slow-motion Phase III, which has carried Colombia almost imperceptibly (growing like a rose?) into Phase IV, which can be said to describe the last years covered in this book.

APPENDIX

The percentage changes used in the regressions of Table 7-1 are shown here in tables 7-7 and 7-8. The sources of the basic variables are as follows:

1. Cost-of-living index. Obtained from IMF-IFS, without further changes.

2. Wholesale price index, with and without foodstuffs. Obtained from BdlR-RdBdlR, without further changes.

3. Money plus quasi money. End-of-month data obtained from IMF-IFS. *Centered* quarterly series were obtained by averaging four of these end-of-month observations. The user should be warned that starting with the April 1974 issue of IMF-IFS, substantially revised monetary data appear for Colombia.

4. Average import exchange rate. Obtained by dividing the value of merchandise imports in pesos by their value in U.S. dollars. It corresponds to the rate shown in Table 4-8.

5. Average hourly wage rates in manufacturing. Refers to nominal wages in manufacturing. Basic data from DANE-BME. There is a discontinuity in the methodology used to report such average wage data in DANE publications of May 1962 or thereabouts. Where they overlap, the old series is about 14 per cent lower than the new one. That percentage was applied to earlier observations to obtain a homogeneous series.

6. Real supplies. Expressed at 1958 peso prices. Includes noncoffee gross domestic *agricultural* product plus merchandise imports. The former series is available only annually, from the BdlR national accounts. It was

TABLE 7-7

Quarterly Percentage Changes in Dependent Variables Used in Regressions Shown in Table 7-1, 1958I–1969IV

	Cost-of-Living Index	Wholesale Price Index	Wholesale Price Index Excluding Foodstuffs
1958 I	2.09	2.71	3.06
II	6.33	3.16	3.53
III	−0.97	2.11	4.82
IV	0.97	1.53	1.70
1959 I	3.86	1.61	0.96
II	2.94	4.75	2.16
III	−2.86	1.56	3.35
IV	0.93	−0.25	0.33
1960 I	1.99	0	0.33
II	2.71	2.59	1.33
III	−0.88	0.19	0.89
IV	1.77	1.45	0.83
1961 I	3.48	2.05	1.19
II	7.71	3.69	2.13
III	−3.91	−0.41	0.67
IV	−0.81	0.05	0.57
1962 I	1.64	0.27	0.97
II	1.61	1.49	1.43
III	0	−0.09	1.41
IV	1.59	2.09	2.32
1963 I	13.54	11.51	12.79
II	13.99	12.20	8.09
III	3.02	1.71	1.79
IV	7.23	4.18	1.93
1964 I	3.28	4.97	2.15
II	10.23	6.11	1.66
III	−6.80	0.21	1.76
IV	−1.63	−0.12	1.14
1965 I	2.09	0.56	1.98
II	3.42	3.90	2.51
III	0	3.16	5.40
IV	5.79	5.69	6.23

TABLE 7-7 (*concluded*)

	Cost-of- Living Index	Wholesale Price Index	Wholesale Price Index Excluding Foodstuffs
1966 I	7.81	5.02	4.90
II	7.97	5.25	3.28
III	−1.34	0.45	3.08
IV	2.04	1.91	2.57
1967 I	2.67	1.44	1.78
II	3.25	1.58	1.95
III	−0.63	1.58	2.06
IV	1.27	1.31	0.90
1968 I	2.50	1.60	1.47
II	2.44	2.93	1.72
III	−1.19	0.17	0.48
IV	1.81	0.37	1.40
1969 I	2.37	1.64	2.53
II	6.47	3.25	2.96
III	1.95	1.23	2.32
IV	1.76	2.82	1.59

SOURCE: See appendix to this chapter.

simply divided by 4 to obtain quarterly estimates. Merchandise imports are available quarterly, but quantity estimates are shaky. The quarterly series in 1958 pesos was obtained by multiplying the quarterly import data at *current* dollars by 7.06, the average import exchange rate for 1958. During 1958–69 the variation in average dollar import prices appears to have been small.

TABLE 7-8

Percentage Changes in Independent Variables Used in Regressions Shown in Table 7-1, 1957I–1969IV

	Money Plus Quasi Money (yearly changes)	Average Import Exchange Rate (quarterly changes)	Wage Rates (yearly changes)	Real Supplies (yearly changes)
1957 I	12.33	0	25.32	−25.04
II	8.40	0.40	27.16	−22.83
III	14.95	112.35	39.29	−9.33
IV	6.25	7.69	34.83	−6.33
1958 I	7.30	12.89	23.23	15.95
II	5.79	14.66	20.39	3.40
III	8.33	−2.69	7.69	−15.67
IV	16.41	−1.66	5.83	−18.02
1959 I	14.27	−3.38	4.92	−10.52
II	16.06	11.21	8.07	6.17
III	13.87	−16.23	8.73	14.96
IV	12.64	0.16	12.60	9.28
1960 I	10.89	−0.16	12.50	20.74
II	6.26	3.75	10.45	12.89
III	8.85	0.90	20.44	10.72
IV	10.66	0	18.18	13.58
1961 I	12.00	0	20.14	0.05
II	16.25	0	18.92	6.37
III	17.17	0	10.91	1.16
IV	19.73	0	12.43	6.30
1962 I	23.23	0	12.14	12.82
II	20.09	0	14.77	2.77
III	15.79	0	15.85	8.14
IV	18.32	8.96	19.47	−8.61
1963 I	15.01	23.29	33.51	−16.01
II	13.73	0	44.06	−1.17
III	20.97	0	40.57	−2.11
IV	18.78	0	35.24	11.60
1964 I	24.58	0	22.01	21.80
II	31.43	0	11.68	6.31
III	25.52	0	11.75	8.19
IV	23.79	0	11.40	3.49
1965 I	19.75	0	10.44	−8.52
II	16.95	0	9.85	−4.70
III	17.54	4.11	11.11	−11.81
IV	17.85	30.31	11.99	−8.81

TABLE 7-8 (concluded)

	Money Plus Quasi Money (yearly changes)	Average Import Exchange Rate (quarterly changes)	Wage Rates (yearly changes)	Real Supplies (yearly changes)
1966 I	18.90	1.72	13.75	12.52
II	17.58	2.09	15.13	15.36
III	15.03	3.55	13.78	29.89
IV	13.16	3.05	12.53	25.34
1967 I ·	13.09	−1.55	11.34	8.82
II	13.78	2.70	10.46	−9.86
III	12.28	4.83	9.74	−13.94
IV	14.93	4.95	9.98	−8.94
1968 I	17.97	3.92	10.63	7.45
II	19.33	2.05	10.79	22.83
III	23.32	1.88	10.39	19.02
IV	22.63	1.48	9.49	16.93
1969 I	19.74	1.70	9.00	−2.59
II	19.24	1.43	8.55	3.68
III	20.58	1.65	9.80	13.43
IV	23.27	2.02	10.02	9.58

SOURCE: See appendix to this chapter.

NOTES

1. See Arnold C. Harberger, "The Dynamics of Inflation in Chile," in Carl Christ et al., eds., *Measurement in Economics: Studies in Mathematical Economics and Econometrics in Memory of Yehuda Grunfeld* (Stanford, Calif.: Stanford University Press, 1963). For the Argentine case, the method has also been applied by Adolfo C. Diz, "Money and Prices in Argentina, 1935–62" (Ph.D. diss., University of Chicago, 1966), and by me, most recently in *Essays on the Economic History of the Argentine Republic* (New Haven: Yale University Press, 1970), Essay 7, pp. 366–377.

2. See Alberto R. Musalem, *Dinero, Inflación y Balanza de Pagos: La Experiencia de Colombia en la Post-Guerra* (Bogotá: Talleres Gráficos del Banco de la República, 1971), Chapter II.

3. "Monetarist" is used here to refer to those who would explain variations in the price level exclusively as a function of changes in the money supply. There is, of course, a neomonetarist view which argues that devaluation of the exchange rate works *only* insofar as it reduces the real value of cash balances, which requires a devaluation-induced increase in the price level. The neomonetarist view, however, typically assumes devaluation occurs from a position of equilibrium in the balance of payments and neglects the case where devaluation is accompanied by relaxation of import controls.

4. A purely numerical reason may be involved: data on the average import exchange rate for those years are likely to exaggerate the abruptness of the real transition between the old rate of 2.50 pesos per dollar, and the newer rates, which are higher. The unusual political circumstances

of 1956–58 may have also induced a restraint on the part of the importing community difficult to obtain under more normal and less euphoric circumstances.

5. The banquet at the Tequendama Hotel, sponsored by the Economic Society of Friends of the Country, where the Lleras-Agudelo exchange took place, was fully reported in the issue of April 5, 1960, of *El Tiempo* of Bogotá. Quotations in the text are from this source; translations are mine.

6. Data on general government current expenditures, public fixed capital formation, and GNP were obtained from the national accounts published by BdlR. All basic data were expressed at current market prices. Data on banking credit and on the budget of the national government were obtained from IMF-IFS, 1972 Supplement.

7. Between 1962 and 1963, output indices of some key foodstuffs fell much more than over-all noncoffee rural output; the percentage figure for rice was -6.0; beans, -6.4; corn, -1.8; potatoes, -34.2; and wheat, -44.5.

Given its importance in the diet of the Colombian masses, and its special import difficulties, the decline in the potato output is particularly noteworthy. These figures suggest that the construction of a more refined index of supplies, as suggested by Miguel Urrutia, may be desirable. (Basic data are from BdlR, National Accounts.)

8. The Banco de la República apparently intervened somewhat in the free market until April 1965, after which date it withdrew almost totally. Throughout the 1950s and early 1960s the free rate, generated by a thin market, was influenced not only by expectations and other usual factors but also by special circumstances, particularly conditions in neighboring Venezuela. Unregistered Colombo-Venezuelan transactions played an important role in the fluctuations of the free rate; they still have great influence on the black-market rate. The free rate, eliminated in November 1966, acted as a safety valve for the import control system; generally, authorities looked the other way if imports were financed through the free market.

9. Some authorities justified strict licensing of capital goods imports with the curious argument that they would simply lead to higher demand for imported raw materials in the future. Some observers thought that import restrictions weighed more heavily on capital goods than on raw materials and even consumer goods during 1963 and 1964.

10. Law 7 of 1973 finally strengthened the power of the Junta Monetaria to punish banks effectively for their failure to meet reserve requirements.

11. Output indices of key foodstuffs were as follows (with 1964 = 100):

	1965	1966		1965	1966
Rice	114	114	Potatoes	103	113
Beans	90	75	Wheat	125	169
Corn	90	92			

12. Debt service ratios obtained from IBRD, *An Appraisal of the Development Program of Colombia,* Report WH-119a, June 21, 1962, Annex I, p. 16; and IBRD-IDA, *Annual Report,* various issues. The 1962 IBRD report contained the following judgment: "The present ratio of 12 percent is already very high and a ratio of 15 percent must be considered unsafe, particularly in view of the great uncertainties about the world coffee situation" (p. 16). The 1966 debt-service ratio was the highest recorded during the 1960s.

13. As reported in *El Tiempo,* March 23, 1973. It must say something about the Colombian political system that the same ministers of the Treasury and Development who in 1960 received the Lleras criticism against exchange-rate flexibility were to receive the new criticism in 1973. The only difference was that in 1973 Agudelo Villa was Minister of Development whereas Rodrigo Llorente, who in 1960 was Minister of Development, was in 1973 Minister of the Treasury.

Chapter 8

Trade Policies
and Colombian Development

Anyone who has followed this book so far would expect to find in this last chapter a quantification of the impact of changes in Colombian trade policies on that economy's various development targets in the areas of efficiency, growth, employment, income distribution, stability, and national autonomy. The *direction* of expected changes in the various magnitudes would not be enough; ideally something should also be said about the likely magnitude of the different effects.

No such scientific and credible quantification will be presented here. Two interrelated types of difficulties stand in the way. As for most countries, no simple positive trade theory appears to explain accurately the evolving Colombian trade structure. An inelegant and qualitative eclectic appeal to elements of positive theories of location, "vent-for-surplus," Heckscher-Ohlin, and the product cycle is the best that can be done to explain Colombian trade patterns both with industrialized countries and with other developing countries, particularly those in Latin America. While these positive theories of trade agree on the misty proposition that liberalized trade policies could and are likely to improve the efficiency (and perhaps growth) of a country without monopoly power in international markets, their predictions regarding income distribution and employment effects of trade liberalization are even mistier, especially when they are applied to a world that contains more than two goods and two factors.

A fairly disaggregated quantitative model of the Colombian economy, something which as yet does not exist, could simulate responses to trade policy changes. In this chapter, the kind of information ideally desired will be

listed, and available data will be reviewed. Rough order-of-magnitude estimates of possible effects of trade policies will be made whenever possible.

In Chapter 7 it was shown how after the November 1966 collapse of the
ambitious import liberalization program launched in September 1965 a more
modest and gradual liberalization process could be said to have started in
March 1967. Thus, a review of major economic trends from 1967 through 1973
will be presented first. Then we shall speculate on possible effects of further
liberalization on efficiency, growth, income distribution, employment, stability, and national autonomy.

THE RECORD FOR 1967–73

Foreign trade statistics, other partial data, and national accounts, the latter
available only through 1972, show a notable change for the better between
1956–67 and 1967–73. But as can be seen in Table 1-1, a good share of that
contrast can be explained by the difference in behavior of the key exogenous
variable, the dollar coffee price, which after falling at a rate of more than 3 per
cent per year from 1956 through 1967, rose by more than 6 per cent per year
from 1967 through 1972.[1]

Nevertheless, a comparison of trade data for 1948–56 with those for
1967–72 confirms what is known from previous chapters: the improved performance of recent years is not simply due to exogenous factors. The rise in
coffee prices during 1967–72 has been smaller than during 1948–56, while the
expansion of registered minor exports has been larger. While in the earlier
years the share of minor exports tended to fall, it rose significantly during
1967–72. Furthermore, contrary to what would be expected for magnitudes
that start from a small base, the growth rate of minor exports rose between
1956–67 and 1967–72. Undoubtedly, many nontraditional exports benefited
from unusually high world prices, particularly during 1972–73, but in most
cases such exports had initially responded to inducements originating in
domestic policy, which stimulated activities that could so benefit.

The growth rate of real GDP has averaged more than 6 per cent per year
from 1967 through 1973, a figure somewhat higher than that for 1948–56,[2] and
sharply better, especially in per capita terms, than the average 4.6 per cent
registered for 1956–67. All major GDP components listed in Table 1-2 show
increases in their growth rate between 1956–67 and 1967–72, and all stand
above their respective averages for the whole period from 1950 through 1972.
At least for the level of aggregation shown, it does not appear that the higher
post-1967 growth is the result of pulling resources *out* of the least productive
(measured) activities and putting them into more productive ones; the growth
profile thus has a "vent-for-surplus" flavor.[3] It may also be observed that the

post-1967 expansion has a more balanced profile than that for 1950–56. Especially to be noted in Table 1-2 are the lower growth rate for construction and the higher one for primary production. (Construction, however, appears to have boomed during 1973 and early 1974.)

One way to investigate whether a significant change in the pattern of Colombian growth has occurred since 1967 is to examine how well average growth rates since World War II fit the post-1967 experience. This has been done for the output of major activities in agriculture, livestock, and manufacturing, as given in the national accounts, which are available from 1950 through 1972. Each of the output indices (y) for these activities has been fitted with the following regression: $\log y = a + bt_1 + ct_2$.

As before, t_1 denotes a time trend variable going from 1 (for 1950) through 23 (for 1972). The variable t_2 takes values of zero for 1950 through 1966 and values of 18, 19, . . . , 22, 23 for the six years included from 1967 through 1972. The b coefficient will then yield a hypothesized "normal" growth rate for the whole period; the c coefficient will give deviations during 1967–72 modifying such a trend. A plot on a semilogarithmic grid of the logarithm of y against time shows a kink and a change of slope after 1966, with both pre- and post-1966 trends represented as straight lines joining in 1966. If the coefficient c happens to be zero, the graph will show the usual straight line, whose slope yields the single average growth rate. In what follows, when the coefficient c is twice its standard error or more, it will be deemed significant, which of course does not imply necessarily that it is large. The positive or negative deviations can be due to a variety of causes, including policy changes not directly related to the trade and payments system (and to changes in the coverage of national accounts data!). It could also be argued that lack of a significant deviation from trend may result from conflicting influences that cancel each other out. But since a complete model of the Colombian economy is lacking, an obvious first step seems to be to examine the clearest departures from trend, speculating later as to their meaning.

The results of this exercise are presented in tables 8-1 and 8-2. As noted earlier, in recent years there has been a slight pickup in the mediocre growth rate for agriculture and livestock. In Table 8-1, significantly positive 1967–72 deviations from trend appear in garlic and onions, rice, potatoes, plantains, mandioc, horses (!), and "other," both in agriculture and livestock. In the Colombian context this whole group may be characterized as involving predominantly nontradable goods. Major export crops apart from coffee, such as cotton, bananas, cocoa, sugar cane, tobacco, and bovine cattle fail to show significant accelerations in their growth rates during 1967–72. However, the trend growth rates are impressive ones, particularly those for cotton, sugar cane, and bovine cattle. On the whole, it would be difficult to attribute the pickup in the agriculture and livestock growth rate after 1967 to *further* stimuli

TABLE 8-1

Agriculture and Livestock: Average Annual Percentage Growth Rates of Output for 1950–72 and Growth Rate Deviations During 1967–72
(standard errors in parentheses)

	Trend Growth Rate, 1950–72	Deviation from Trend, 1967–72
All agriculture	2.98	0.24
	(0.18)	(0.13)
Sesame	13.25	−3.57*
	(1.91)	(1.40)
Garlic and onions	2.57	2.68*
	(1.21)	(0.89)
Cotton	14.64	−1.76
	(1.51)	(1.11)
Rice	4.77	0.73*
	(0.29)	(0.21)
Bananas for export	1.98	0.69
	(1.03)	(0.75)
Cocoa	4.25	−0.16
	(0.28)	(0.21)
Coffee	2.20	−0.81*
	(0.31)	(0.23)
Sugarcane	6.00	0.41
	(0.40)	(0.30)
Rubber	5.03	1.43
	(1.28)	(0.94)
Barley	4.59	−1.80*
	(0.91)	(0.67)
Copra[a]	11.42	−1.81
	(2.29)	(1.72)
Beans	−1.48	1.53
	(1.17)	(0.85)
Corn	0.66	−0.19
	(0.47)	(0.35)
Potatoes	2.66	1.38*
	(0.78)	(0.57)
Plantains	2.82	0.65*
	(0.14)	(0.10)
Tobacco	4.31	−1.25*
	(0.73)	(0.54)
Wheat	−0.67	−2.46*
	(1.02)	(0.75)

TABLE 8-1 (*concluded*)

	Trend Growth Rate, 1950–72	Deviation from Trend, 1967–72
Mandioc	0.02	4.14*
	(0.43)	(0.31)
Panela (unrefined brown sugar)	5.65	−0.38
	(0.43)	(0.32)
Other agriculture	2.85	1.01*
	(0.19)	(0.14)
All livestock	3.68	0.18
	(0.25)	(0.18)
Bovine cattle	4.42	−0.15
	(0.56)	(0.41)
Pigs	5.05	−0.27
	(1.10)	(0.81)
Sheep	2.44	−1.22
	(1.36)	(1.00)
Goats	2.08	0.55
	(1.51)	(1.11)
Horses	0.87	0.90*
	(0.46)	(0.34)
Other livestock products	3.55	0.49*
	(0.23)	(0.17)

SOURCE: Basic data from BdlR-CN.
*Coefficient for the deviation from trend is twice its standard error or more.
a. Through 1971 only.

arising from the trade policies followed since that year. At best it could be argued that those policies helped sustain continued diversification away from coffee and impressive growth rates in several export-oriented rural activities that otherwise might have been slowed down in their performance, as in the case of some oilseeds of which production had been oriented primarily toward import substitution. Preliminary data for 1973 show that output growth for agriculture and livestock as a whole has remained somewhat above the whole postwar trend, but no sharp break in trend is apparent.

The manufacturing pattern, presented in Table 8-2, is even more difficult to characterize simply. First of all, while in Table 1-2 an increase is shown in the manufacturing growth rate for 1967–72, in contrast with that for the whole period, in Table 8-2, a slowdown is recorded in the 1967–72 growth rate for "modern" manufacturing. The sensitivity of the results to use of the depressed year 1967 as a base (as well as to the relatively slow recovery in

TABLE 8-2

Manufacturing: Average Annual Percentage Growth Rates of Output for 1950–72 and Growth Rate Deviations During 1967–72
(standard errors in parentheses)

	Trend Growth Rate, 1950–72	Deviation from Trend, 1967–72
All manufacturing	6.23	−0.12
	(0.12)	(0.09)
Industrial manufacturing	7.03	−0.23*
	(0.15)	(0.11)
Small-scale industry and handicrafts	3.26	0.09*
	(0.03)	(0.02)
Food processing	5.98	0.89*
	(0.27)	(0.20)
Beverages	4.57	0.21
	(0.26)	(0.19)
Tobacco processing	3.12	0.92*
	(0.25)	(0.19)
Textiles	6.66	−0.63*
	(0.35)	(0.26)
Shoes and clothing	8.28	−0.15
	(0.20)	(0.15)
Wood products and furniture	4.80	−1.10*
	(0.52)	(0.38)
Paper products	10.94	0.39
	(0.32)	(0.23)
Printing and publishing	7.95	−0.65
	(0.48)	(0.35)
Leather processing	4.46	0.03
	(0.29)	(0.21)
Rubber products	8.72	−1.40*
	(0.68)	(0.50)
Chemical products	8.33	−0.70*
	(0.30)	(0.22)
Petroleum and coal derivatives	9.57	−1.03*
	(0.48)	(0.35)
Nonmetallic mineral products	6.32	−0.58*
	(0.34)	(0.25)
Basic metal products	20.78	−5.67*
	(2.38)	(1.74)
Mechanical and metallurgical products	14.65	−2.60*
	(0.43)	(0.32)

SOURCE: Same as for Table 8-1.
*Coefficient for the deviation from trend is twice its standard error or more.

1968) suggests that no great weight can be attached to the apparent change in trend. Furthermore, preliminary data for 1973 indicate above-average manufacturing growth rates. On the whole, once longer time series become available, it will probably not be possible to establish that a significant break occurred in the manufacturing growth rate in about 1967, using the technique of Table 8-2.

That table also shows a complex pattern of acceleration and deceleration in growth rates for manufacturing branches. Counting small-scale industry and handicrafts as a branch, significant declines appear for eight branches, significant increases for three, and no significant changes show up in five branches. Among the eight activities with declining growth rates, several are associated with strong import-substituting efforts, including rubber products, chemicals, and basic metal products; but others, such as textiles, wood products, and furniture, are increasingly linked to manufactured exports. The three manufacturing industries with significant acceleration in their growth rates during 1967–72 are also a mixed bag: small-scale industry and handicrafts, food processing, and tobacco processing. The three sell overwhelmingly to the domestic market, but presumably have sharply different requirements for unskilled and skilled labor and capital. Some indirect information on the latter point is given in Table 8-3. Unfortunately, the categories in tables 8-2 and 8-3 are not exactly alike, and neither source provides information on recent shares of output exported. Nevertheless, from the figures in column 1 of Table 8-3 it may be assumed that activities such as tobacco and food processing have requirements for human and physical capital per unit of output which were not below the manufacturing average.[4]

Application of the technique used in tables 8-1 and 8-2 to the more aggregated national accounts indicates significant post-1967 acceleration in growth rates only for primary production (in spite of deceleration in mining, mainly petroleum), construction, and what is called in Table 1-2 Type-II services. Construction and services, of course, have a very small degree of "tradability." Thus viewed, the post-1967 acceleration in the growth rate of GDP could hardly be said to rest on a reallocation of resources, neither absolute nor relative, from nontradable goods and services into tradable ones.

On the whole, it is difficult to detect a powerful and unambiguous impact of post-1967 trade policies on the 1967–72 growth pattern. But besides the problem of untangling the effects of new trade policies from those of other policies and variables, the 1967–72 period is perhaps too short to allow for structural changes. During that period, for example, the performance of individual manufacturing activities was in many cases more influenced by the long-run import-substitution cycle than by the new export promotion policies, but such a situation, which can be seen in the residuals of several of the trend regressions, could change in the future.

TABLE 8-3

Colombian Manufacturing Activities Ranked by Value Added per Employed Person in 1967
(shares in percentages)

	Value Added per Person (thous. 1967 pesos) (1)	Share of Total Value Added (2)	Share of Total Employment (3)	Col. (2) Minus Col. (3) (4)	Share of Imports in Domestic Market (5)	Share of Exports in Domestic Production (6)
Petroleum and coal products	277.7	3.7	0.7	3.0	8.4	14.9
Tobacco products	185.0	4.0	1.2	2.8	0.2	0
Beverages	135.9	13.5	5.4	8.1	0.7	0
Chemicals other than pharmaceuticals	87.3	5.6	3.5	2.1	36.5	2.2
Pharmaceuticals and related products	87.2	7.7	4.8	2.9	9.3	1.2
Basic metal products	68.7	2.1	1.7	0.4	31.5	0.8
Paper products	64.4	2.5	2.2	0.3	25.9	11.9
Food processing	59.8	15.9	14.4	1.5	0.4	0
Rubber products	56.4	2.5	2.4	0.1	4.5	3.3
Electrical machinery except appliances	54.5	2.2	2.2	0	43.6	1.2
Electrical appliances	49.2	1.0	1.1	−0.1	2.0	0

Other manufacturing	44.2	2.7	3.3	−0.6	19.6	1.3
Textiles	43.4	13.0	16.3	−3.3	2.3	2.5
Printing and publishing	41.7	3.1	4.0	−0.9	7.7	1.2
Leather and products	41.2	1.1	1.4	−0.3	0	9.0
Nonmetallic mineral products	38.1	5.0	7.1	−2.1	3.6	6.0
Metal products	36.1	4.4	6.6	−2.2	10.5	1.9
Motor vehicles	36.0	1.9	2.9	−1.0	37.0	0.5
Mechanical machinery	32.0	1.2	2.0	−0.8	87.0	13.7
Nonelectrical appliances	26.6	0.2	0.3	−0.1	0	0
Wood and products	25.1	1.0	2.1	−1.1	1.3	15.4
Clothing and footwear	23.9	4.2	9.5	−5.3	1.2	0.4
Ceramic products	21.7	0.5	1.3	−0.8	7.5	5.6
Furniture and fixtures	19.8	0.6	1.7	−1.1	1.2	1.1
Transport equipment except motor vehicles	19.8	0.7	1.9	−1.2	80.2	0
All manufacturing	54.4	100.0	100.0	0	15.8	2.3

SOURCE: Basic data are from DANE unpublished estimates, and were obtained from IBRD unpublished documents. See also World Bank, *Economic Growth of Colombia: Problems and Prospects* (Baltimore: Johns Hopkins University Press, 1972), pp. 490–491. "Domestic market" is defined as domestic production plus imports less exports. It may be noted that the definition of manufactured exports excludes slightly processed foodstuffs such as sugar. The IBRD report estimates manufactured exports at $55.6 million in 1967.

The good 1967–73 growth performance may be best explained by the following mechanism. Higher growth rates in foreign-exchange receipts, primarily derived from merchandise exports, allowed the government systematically to follow more expansionary fiscal and monetary policies than had been possible during 1956–67. Such stimuli, and the positive reactions they triggered in private expenditure, led to a higher level of resource utilization almost *across the board* within the Colombian economy. Widespread pockets of underutilized labor, capital, and land were gradually brought into production without any major sector being required to contract so as to release resources for better use elsewhere. The foreign-exchange scarcity of 1956–67 forced fiscal and monetary policies sporadically to apply severe limits on aggregate demand; these restrictions were clumsy in the sense that nearly all sectors suffered, whether or not they were heavy users of foreign exchange.

If this interpretation is correct, recent growth should have been not only higher but also more stable than before 1967. In the following tabulation, simple year-to-year growth rates were taken for 1968–72 and for the previous five years (1963–67), and the means of *absolute* deviations from average growth rates for both periods were compared.

	1963–67	1968–72
GDP at constant market prices:		
Average growth rate	4.52%	6.28%
Average absolute deviation	0.99	0.38
Real domestic gross capital formation:		
Average growth rate	3.09	9.37
Average absolute deviation	10.80	7.37
Dollar merchandise imports, c.i.f.:		
Average growth rate	1.85	11.46
Average absolute deviation	24.34	8.07

Deviations around the average growth rate were smaller from 1968 through 1972 not only relative to average growth but also in absolute amounts. A more plentiful supply of foreign exchange since 1967 made possible the elimination of erratic stop-go policies, improving both the growth rate and domestic stability.

The process of bringing into production resources left idle by past stop-go policies has clear limits. Some types of land and of relatively unskilled labor may remain in "surplus" even after the 1967–73 expansion, although it is doubtful that supply is perfectly elastic even in their case. The "venting" of those resources with low opportunity costs via exports will remain a key ingredient for a successful growth policy, but domestic expansion will be sustained by fewer pockets of other underutilized resources than during 1967–73. Investment rates, which did not change much between 1963–67 and 1968–

72, will probably have to increase merely to maintain the recent growth rates. But more on this in the section dealing with trade policies and future growth.

The quality of the available data on 1967–73 changes in income distribution, employment, and degree of foreign ownership and control is poorer than the data I used for the output indices. In spite of this limitation, in the rest of the chapter, an attempt will be made to answer the question, What can we expect, viewing the matter during 1974, from further Colombian trade and exchange liberalization? This will involve reviewing (and some guessing) as to what has actually been happening to key variables during 1967–73. Guessing will also be necessary regarding the future trend of world prices for Colombian staples. If the world prices reached by coffee, cotton, sugar, and all other tradables in 1973 are sustained, the case for further real effective peso devaluations would become quite doubtful, and the ideal liberalization policy (as well as its urgency) would be different from that which would result if it is expected that prices of coffee (and other staples) will collapse as they did in 1956–57.

EVIDENCE ON STATIC EFFICIENCY EFFECTS OF COLOMBIAN TRADE POLICIES: REVIEW AND OUTLOOK

Colombian postwar trade and exchange policies induced static inefficiencies in the sense that some of the foreign exchange saved by import substitution could have been obtained more cheaply, i.e., at lower domestic resource costs, by using in export activities Colombian resources that have low opportunity costs, primarily natural resources of various kinds, and to a lesser extent, unskilled labor. This formulation does not imply that resources not used in those export activities but which "could have been" used, or could have been developed much earlier than they in fact were, found their way into the import-substituting sector. In the Colombian case it is more accurate to regard a good share of these low-opportunity-cost resources as remaining untapped, as with natural resources, or blending into a murky nontradable or "informal" sector. The blocking effect of trade and exchange policies in the vent-for-surplus process will be discussed in the next section, on the assumption that foreign nonpreferential demand for many actual and potential nontraditional Colombian exports is high. Such a key assumption is also made in this section, which will focus on prima facie evidence of static inefficiencies.

In earlier chapters, documentation was provided for the assumption that during the postwar period world demand for Colombia's actual and potential nontraditional exports was highly price-elastic. Such a statement is of course easier to make ex post than ex ante. The process of finding new foreign markets is much more complex than is implied by the small-country assumption, and it is surrounded by considerable uncertainty both for individual export products and for the whole export drive. Nevertheless, on balance it appears that excessive elasticity pessimism dominated Colombian policy after the Second World War.

As a result, postwar public policy offered, on the whole, greater encouragement to import substitution than to exporting activities. Detailed studies on the exact incidence of such incentives are few, and available only for the more recent years. The most complete is a study carried out by Thomas L. Hutcheson,[5] who used various assumptions and methodologies to calculate effective rates of protection in 1969 for several manufacturing and primary activities. In that study, he relied on comparisons between Colombian and foreign prices for his calculations; his data came predominantly from Colombian producers and consisted of comparisons of their domestic price with their export price.[6]

Some of Hutcheson's major results are presented in Table 8-4. Taking as a yardstick an exchange rate 34 per cent higher than that observed during 1969, Hutcheson argues that any activity listed in Table 8-4 that received less than 34 per cent in effective protection was relatively disfavored, while those receiving more were protected. The 34 per cent devaluation involves a "guesstimate" about the adjustment which would have been necessary to maintain external balance if the protective structure had been removed.

The theoretical and empirical difficulties in this type of calculation are well known. Nevertheless, a major robust conclusion emerges from Hutcheson's results, based on the large variance observed in the protection received by different sectors in 1969. Thus, the generalization that, on average, manufacturing is protected while primary production is not can be supplemented with the generalization that protection varies considerably from industry to industry. Indeed, if comparable data were available, they would almost certainly show that net protection also varies sharply according to size of firm or farm.

Tariffs, import controls, export subsidies, and exchange rates are only part of the state's arsenal of policy instruments. Tax and credit incentives or direct official participation can be of greater importance for some projects. Furthermore, the exact incidence of the whole array of policy instruments can change from year to year, depending on such things as the actual and expected relative price structure being signaled to Colombia from world markets in a given year. Nevertheless, Hutcheson argues that his measures of effective protection are significantly and positively related to growth rates of different industries in the manufacturing sector.[7] He concludes that protection, particularly as measured by the Balassa method, made a difference in the pattern of growth within manufacturing. He argues that the structure of protection has contributed to slow economic growth and increasing unemployment. Propos-

TABLE 8-4

Effective Rates of Protection by Groups of Traded Sectors, 1969
(per cent)

	Balassa Method	Corden Method
Coffee	−45	−45
Mining	−8	−6
Sugar	−23	−19
Primary except coffee and mining	0	1
Food products except sugar	2	11
Beverages	121	103
Tobacco	95	84
Textiles	5	8
Shoes	−22	−10
Clothing	4	13
Wood products	−11	1
Furniture	−25	−11
Paper products	12	14
Leather products	11	16
Rubber products	−31	−26
Chemical products	61	56
Refinery products	−5	4
Nonmetallic mineral products	−8	0
Basic metals	151	39
Metal manufacture	47	43
Nonelectrical machinery	−7	12
Electrical apparatus	a	668
Transport equipment	610	319
Diverse industries	117	89
All manufacturing	44	29
All manufacturing except tobacco and beverages	40	25
All manufacturing except sugar	50	33
Primary exports except coffee and mining	18	18
Manufactured exports except sugar	21	21

SOURCE: Adapted from Thomas L. Hutcheson, "Incentives for Industrialization in Colombia" (Ph.D. diss., University of Michigan, 1973), Table 3.5, p. 68.

a. Value added is negative.

ing a policy of uniform protection, he expects that there would be much reshuffling within each sector as specialization occurred, but few cases of outright disappearance of sectors.

Comparison of a few new export activities with some import-substituting industries as they stood in about 1971 also reveals large differences in domestic resource costs (DRCs) between the two groups, on the order of two to one. For example, while exporters of carnations and of some leather products had respective DRCs of 18 and 17 pesos per dollar received, a firm producing specialized textile products and benefiting from prohibitions against competition from imports had DRCs of 36 pesos per dollar.[8] These examples serve a useful pedagogical purpose, but more needs to be said about the prevalence of extremes in DRCs among Colombian sectors producing tradable commodities.

Although the extraordinary expansion of nontraditional exports during 1967–74 was aided by favorable world economic conditions, it has demonstrated that a large number of varied Colombian activities have DRCs no higher than about the exchange rate plus the CAT. By 1973, minor exports had reached between 5 and 6 per cent of GNP, and that placed an upper limit on those lowest-DRC activities. Given an annual growth rate in the dollar value of these exports of about 15 per cent, it is difficult to imagine scenarios for which the share of minor exports in GNP could have been *much* higher than that achieved. The static assumption of almost perfectly elastic world demand for Colombian minor exports implies that much higher shares (even 100 per cent?) of Colombian resources could have been directed into low-DRC minor exports "quickly." However, it can be argued that once uncertainty, costs of obtaining information about foreign markets, and high marginal costs for abrupt changes in production plans are taken into account, it becomes questionable whether expansion rates for minor exports higher than those observed are feasible (or even optimal). By 1970, in fact, minor exports had reached levels close to those foreseen in 1962 by observers who assumed that Colombia would follow "correct" policies during 1962–70.[9]

At the other extreme, the manufacturing activities found by Hutcheson to have the highest effective rates of protection, say 40 per cent and above, account for about one-third of value added in manufacturing at domestic prices, or between 6 and 7 per cent of GNP. A more precise identification of the "horror stories" of import substitution can be given. Prime candidates include the automobile industry, which received government impetus during the late 1960s; petrochemicals and some other chemicals, particularly pharmaceuticals; electrical appliances, such as refrigerators and washing machines; artificial fibers; and some alcoholic beverages, particularly whiskey. Such sectors represent somewhat less than a third of manufacturing value added; what is remarkable is how much of Colombian manufacturing operates near world prices.

On the other hand, as emphasized by Francisco Thoumi, the share of manufacturing investment captured during the last fifteen years by the horror-story industries is an impressive one. It is estimated that between 1962 and 1967 gross investments in petroleum derivatives, including petrochemicals, amounted to one-fourth of all manufacturing investment.[10] David Morawetz reports that over $100 million was invested in petrochemicals in Colombia in the 1960s, and another $120 million was scheduled to be invested during the 1970s.[11] Such projects have also taken up an important share of the limited pool of highly skilled professionals and workers. One should note, however, that sensible cost- and employment-conscious criticisms of petrochemical investments have been made to look less than farsighted because of the unusual events occurring in world markets during 1973–74. However, substantial direct and indirect commitments to the automobile industry have not yet found a redeeming historical accident.[12]

It may be added that the participation of direct foreign investment in many of the horror-story industries, such as automobiles, pharmaceuticals, and artificial fibers, is large. The horror in those stories involves not just high real costs due to low production runs, unsuitable factor combinations, and other standard reasons, but also untaxed quasi rents or excess profits earned by foreigners, and made possible by the protective system. On its own and in partnership with foreign or local investors, the public Institute of Industrial Development (IFI, Instituto de Fomento Industrial) has also involved its long-term credit facilities in several ill-starred import-substitution schemes, including Forjas de Colombia, making foundry products and rolling equipment, and COLCARRIL, producing railroad cars. IFI participated with Renault in the expansion of the automotive industry, and with public Venezuelan capital in the creation of a large plant for producing caprolactam, a sophisticated petrochemical (Monómeros Colombo-Venezolanos).

The gradual lifting of import restrictions which has taken place since 1967, and which accelerated during 1973 and early 1974 under the pressure of bulging foreign-exchange reserves and extraordinary domestic inflation, has probably removed static inefficiencies involved in excessive precautionary as well as speculative holdings of inventories of importable goods. Such inventories usually involve spare parts, intermediate products, and raw materials, but could also include installed but unused imported machinery and equipment. Interviews with businessmen during 1971 indicated that uncertainties about access to imports led them to carry stocks they regarded as excessive compared with those of, say, Venezuelan businessmen. Musalem[13] has shown that the early stages of import liberalization programs were accompanied by a rush to build up inventories of importable goods, in the expectation that such liberalization efforts would be reversed. So both the level and the fluctuations in inventories were in all likelihood influenced by the import control system, especially before 1967, in a manner conducive to inefficiencies.

A strong a priori case can be made for linking LDC import-licensing policies to generalized excess capacity in industry. But in Colombia such a link appears weak. Thoumi, who did major research on the utilization of fixed industrial capital in Colombia, concluded[14] that capacity utilization in recent years had been relatively high compared with that in the few other countries for which there is any information. Hours of capacity use are related to long-run structural variables, including management quality, which are influenced by trade policy only indirectly. Stop-go cycles related to the foreign-exchange bottleneck have influenced capacity utilization, particularly during 1956–67, and excess capacity in the horror-story industries can also be found, but no strong general link appears to exist between import licensing as practiced in Colombia and excess capacity. The protective system can, of course, be blamed for excess capacity in the most misguided import-substitution projects, whether because one plant was built with full knowledge that the domestic market could not absorb its full output for many years (and export markets could not be found), or because the combination of extravagant protection and easy entry led to industrial organizations characterized by monopolistic competition, with many plants working at far less than full capacity, as in washing machines and automobiles. It may be noted that "easy entry" was often the result of pressure from foreign interests. If a firm from country X entered a juicy import-substituting industry, the embassy of country Y would complain if its firms were not allowed to share in the spoils.

Although some major import-substitution projects whose efficiency was far from obvious were launched after 1967, in the most recent years the reluctance of the public sector to support similar schemes has been growing. Remember that such attitudes will be reflected not only in the tariff and the management of import controls but also, and often mainly, in the promises made or withheld regarding credit, taxes, and long-term public support. This new ambience in public development offices, including IFI and other public credit agencies, has perhaps been more important for what it has kept from happening than for any tangible achievements.

If extravagant and massive new ventures into import substitution appear on the decline, it remains true that the import control mechanism is still vigorously used for protecting existing (and some new) activities. Even with foreign-exchange reserves reaching $600 million during the first quarter of 1974, import controls remained more restrictive than during January–October 1966. At the beginning of 1974 the free list still accounted for less than half of reimbursable imports. The biases described in Chapter 6 remained, and under the circumstances prevailing in early 1974, it was difficult to make a good economic case for import controls as then administered. Their retention could be justified only in special cases such as those involving dumping, health hazards, and threats to public safety, for which tariffs may be insufficient. Elimination of most import controls should bring about gains in efficiency and competitive pressures, and would probably improve access to imports for medium and small businessmen and for those located outside Bogotá and Medellín. Announcement of a decision to eliminate controls gradually (barring a world depression), accompanied by measures to be discussed below, should signal an even firmer government commitment to expanding the export sector.

The maintenance of some forms of exchange control may be found necessary, however, less for balance-of-payments reasons than to execute other Colombian policies, such as vigilance over some kinds of capital flows, particularly flows of direct foreign investment. Even for balance-of-payments reasons *standby* controls can be justified in a country like Colombia that is still vulnerable to unexpected changes in a far from stable world economy, and not so rich in policy tools that it can afford to throw away one still widely used in industrialized countries. Whether standby tools can be kept either from getting rusty or from being used by bureaucrats "because they are there" is a moot question which I gladly refer to the wisdom of political scientists. It may also be noted that Colombian trade with nonmarket socialist economies may require some types of trade and exchange control.

By signing the Cartagena Agreement creating the Andean Common Market, Colombia committed herself to a gradual loss of purely national control over her tariffs. A common external Andean tariff is to be agreed upon by 1976 and should be fully implemented by 1980.[15] The common *minimum* external tariff agreed upon in December 1970, and toward which Colombia is already moving, is not very different from the one in effect in Colombia at the start, and could be described as on the whole lower and less varied than prior national tariffs. The hope has been expressed that the eventual common external tariff will be no higher on average than the *minimum* one, whose average is about 50 per cent. The outlook is not clear, but Colombia has been reported as opposed to higher duties.

Ad hoc industrial complementation agreements among Andean countries, under which temporary monopolies will be granted, could also involve Colombia in intra-Andean import-substitution schemes. Some of these could have the effect of rationalizing existing and mostly inefficient industries (e.g., steel), but not all of them would be desirable from an efficiency viewpoint. Progress has been slow in the negotiation of such agreements, which involve laborious and detailed parceling out of plants among countries. It is also reported that Colombia is on guard against the gestation, under these agreements, of white elephants of Andean dimensions.

By 1980, tariffs and controls over most commodity imports into Colombia from the Andean countries should be eliminated. The effect should be to generate some efficiency gains and a salutary competitive pressure on industry. Contrary to a widespread misconception, there is room for trade creation within the Andean group (see note 15). It could be argued that the political solidarity which may develop among the Andean nations could provide effective mechanisms for smoothing adjustment burdens generated by growing trade. Thus, specialization would be encouraged to a larger extent than is done by trade with the rest of the world, which remains subject to sudden and uncompensated shocks.

If import controls on trade are entirely eliminated and purely Colombian management of import tariffs disappears, exchange-rate policy will become even more important in keeping possible balance-of-payments pressures from leading to inefficient trade policies. The point is reinforced because there is growing recognition of the advisability of revamping the system of export subsidies. As discussed in Chapter 2, the CAT scheme has contributed to the expansion of minor exports, but it shows technical faults generating some inefficiencies and has become increasingly expensive in terms of badly needed tax revenues forgone. Its gradual elimination, compensated by a faster upward crawl in the exchange rate, could leave exporters no worse off, on average, than during early 1974 while providing more uniform incentives and increased tax revenues.[16] It would be desirable to relax import controls, as discussed above, to help offset at least for the long run the upward pressures on the domestic prices of importable goods that would be generated by the proposed exchange-rate policies. Available information makes it difficult to be precise on this point, however, providing a further reason to handle the whole package in gradual steps, at the same time bringing under control the inflationary pressures that existed during the first half of 1974. The gradual elimination of both import controls and export subsidies may reduce frictions and quarrels with both trade partners in the Andean region and those elsewhere.[17]

Since the crawling peg system was adopted, in 1967, most observers sympathetic to import liberalization have felt that the crawl was too slow, citing as ultimate proof the continued need for licensing to repress imports and CAT to stimulate minor exports. High and rising foreign-exchange reserves during 1973 suggested that the degree of peso overvaluation may have been substantially reduced, and it may even be questioned whether overvaluation still exists. But the events of 1973 and early 1974 show the complications of overvaluation calculations: much hinges on what is assumed about the future of coffee and other commodity prices and about detailed elasticities in Colombian trade with different geographical areas. The latter is necessary as the peso followed the U.S. dollar after August 1971 and was therefore devalued with respect to key nondollar currencies. Sustained inflation in industrialized countries, of a type which may not be accurately reflected in wholesale price indices, reduces confidence in purchasing-power-parity calculations such as those presented in chapters 2 and 4.[18] One has to fall back on observation of the trend in foreign-exchange reserves as import controls and the CAT are gradually removed to verify the degree of present and future overvaluation. It also remains to be seen whether the crawling peg will be as successful under accelerating inflation as it was while Colombian inflation was diminishing in the context of a relatively stable world price level.

A removal of export subsidies and import controls compensated for by exchange-rate adjustments will tend to reduce existing discrimination against service exports, which include tourism and were never eligible for CATs, and in favor of service imports, on which no duties are paid and which have been benefited by overvalued import exchange rates. Service imports include many items that are doubtful candidates for subsidies, such as profit remittances, travel, and remittances to middle- and upper-class children studying abroad.

Adoption of the policy package described above would complete the trend started in 1967, and put Colombia fully into the Bhagwati-Krueger Phase V. The impact of such a step on GNP growth, say over the following ten years, is again difficult to quantify. Note that now we are not taking as a base of comparison the situation that characterized most of the period 1956–67:[19] rigid import controls and stop-go cycles, together with the prospect of further massive import substitution. The question is, How much additional efficiency and growth would result from the suggested steps? Many of the once-and-for-all gains that were to be reaped from post-1967 policies, such as fuller utilization of existing capacity, have already been mostly captured. There remain gains to be realized by a more efficient allocation of investment and other resources, which could offset declines in the growth rate arising from the exhaustion of pockets of resource underutilization. Much depends on how the rest of the world reacts to the expansion of new Colombian exports, and how such a reaction limits possible gains from international specialization. Suppose domestic policy and international circumstances allow resources now engaged in the most inefficient import-substituting activities, amounting to (say) 7 per cent of the GNP, to move toward new export activities during the next ten years. Suppose further that domestic resource costs per dollar earned or saved are on average twice as much in the former as in the latter activity. Those resources, once devoted to exporting, should generate a net gain of 7 per cent of GNP, which may be taken as an upper estimate on potential static gains.

It may be noted that given the conventions and practice of national accounting, some of the static gains may not even be reflected in GNP. Switching a civil servant with a given salary from reviewing license applications to rural teaching will not affect GNP, at least for a long time. Psychic gains and losses in dealing with or wielding bureaucratic power go unrecorded. And so on. But even if possible unrecorded net gains are taken into account, the elimination of import controls should not be expected to revolutionize either the efficiency, the growth, or the style of the Colombian economic system. Note that the comparison is not with an ideal textbook situation, but with what seems likely given world market realities limiting international specialization, and given Colombian political realities limiting the elimination of distortions benefiting one or another special interest. There is little point to supposing that the Colombian export share in GNP could reach Puerto Rican or Hong Kong levels, or that the Colombian economic system could be freer of static distortions than those of Italy or Japan.

TRADE POLICIES, FOREIGN EXCHANGE AVAILABILITY, AND GROWTH

In earlier chapters, I emphasized how balance-of-payments difficulties hampered Colombian growth, particularly during 1956–67. As shown in Table 8-5, gross investment in machinery and equipment, including transport, still relies heavily on imports. During the late 1950s the new steel mill in Paz del Río put a dent in that imported share; the impact of the start of automotive production can also be detected in 1971–72. Throughout, less dramatic and probably more efficient light manufacturing industries have also helped to expand the share of domestically produced machinery and equipment.

After the collapse of dollar coffee prices in the late 1950s, the constant-price share of GNP devoted to gross investment in machinery and equipment fell from an average of 12.6 per cent during 1950–56 to 7.7 per cent during 1957–69. Only during 1970–72 has that share risen in a sustained but unspectacular manner to an average of 8.3 per cent of GNP. While no detailed data are available on investment allocation, it is known that in the 1950s considerable investment was made in social overhead capital and other projects quite intensive in imported machinery and equipment; examples include the already mentioned steel mill and the Atlantic railroad. Thus, the drop in the GNP share devoted to gross investment in machinery and equipment reflects exogenous changes in investment allocation as well as balance-of-payments stringency.

It may be seen in Table 8-6 that investment in construction, its considerable year-to-year fluctuations smoothed in the table, behaved more stably than machinery and equipment capital formation; its direct and indirect import components are much lower than those of the latter category. Note that all the percentages presented in Table 8-6 have been computed from data expressed

TABLE 8-5

Share of Imports in Gross Investment in Machinery and Equipment Including Transport, 1950–54 to 1971–72
(underlying data in constant 1958 prices)

	Share		Share
1950–54	93.7%	1963–66	76.2%
1955–56	93.6	1967–70	73.4
1957–58	84.8	1971–72	67.8
1959–62	82.7		

SOURCE: BdlR-CN.

TABLE 8-6

Gross Capital Formation, 1950–54 to 1971–72

(per cent of GNP at market prices; underlying data in constant 1958 prices)

	Gross Capital Formation	Buildings, Other Construction, and Improvements	Machinery and Other Equipment	Net Change in Inventories
1950–54	22.3	9.3	12.0	1.1
1955–56	25.7	10.9	14.2	0.6
1957–58	20.8	10.0	7.1	3.7
1959–62	20.2	9.8	8.3	2.1
1963–66	19.2	8.6	7.8	2.8
1967–70	19.3	10.3	7.3	1.6
1971–72	20.7	10.1	8.3	2.4

SOURCE: BdlR-CN.

TABLE 8-7

Financing of Gross Capital Formation, 1950–54 to 1971–72

(per cent of GNP at market prices; underlying data in current prices)

	Gross Capital Formation	Private Savings	Public Savings	Net Capital Inflow
1950–54	16.1	11.9	4.1	—
1955–56	18.2	12.0	4.5	1.7
1957–58	19.6	15.7	4.6	−0.7
1959–62	19.9	14.9	3.8	1.2
1963–66	18.8	12.6	3.4	2.8
1967–70	20.9	12.0	6.1	2.8
1971–72	22.1	12.4	5.1	4.6

SOURCE: BdlR-CN.

in constant 1958 prices. It is instructive to compare these figures with those in Table 8-7, where capital formation and its financing are shown, as before, as GNP shares, but with the underlying magnitudes in current prices. While 1950–56 investment ratios in Table 8-6 exceed those of later periods, in Table 8-7 the opposite is recorded.

At an accounting level, the discrepancy is mostly explained by the evolution of the implicit prices of machinery and transport equipment relative to the GNP deflator. As shown in Table 8-8, a remarkable rise in the relative prices of these capital goods occurred after 1955–56; given Colombian depen-

TABLE 8-8

Implicit Price Deflators for Gross Investment, 1950–54 to 1971–72
(divided over implicit price deflator for GNP at market prices; 1958 = 100)

	Buildings, Other Construction, and Improvements	Transport Equipment	Machinery and Other Equipment	Imported Machinery and Equipment
1950–54	97.9	54.7	49.8	47.7
1955–56	96.0	51.8	50.3	48.1
1957–58	97.3	87.4	85.7	84.2
1959–62	110.8	81.9	89.7	85.0
1963–66	118.2	76.2	84.5	80.1
1967–70	117.0	92.6	101.2	101.6
1971–72	117.0	99.8	99.1	106.0

SOURCE: BdlR-CN. As suggested by the 1957–58 row, there was a sharp increase in the relative prices for machinery and equipment between 1957 and 1958.

dence on imports of these goods, such a rise can readily be traced back to a similar increase in the real import exchange rate, as can be seen by comparing the last column of Table 8-8 with data in Table 4-8.[20] After peaking in 1958, both relative prices fell, until new devaluations and the crawling peg brought them back to about their 1958 levels during the late 1960s and early 1970s.

The economic explanation for the sharp rise in the relative prices of machinery and equipment during 1957 and 1958, and their high levels thereafter, is in the deterioration of the balance of payments, which was first triggered by the collapse of dollar coffee prices. Such worsening of Colombian terms of trade meant a loss in the effectiveness of the mechanism through which the country transformed its savings into tangible machinery and equipment. Coffee, at that time the indirect but major supplier of nonconstruction capital goods, suffered an exogenous drop in dollar prices, equivalent to a productivity loss in the machinery and equipment industry in a closed economy. A similar phenomenon has been recorded for another Latin American country, Argentina, but for an earlier period.[21] An increase in the real exchange rate for imports as well as for nontraditional exports may thus be viewed as a way of adjusting to the decline in efficiency of the traditional indirect way of obtaining machinery and equipment, by rationing available foreign exchange more stringently in the short run, and by encouraging recourse to new direct and indirect sources of machinery and equipment in the long run.

While the real evolution of capital formation is best measured at constant prices, the burdens involved in achieving a given savings rate should be measured at current prices, as in Table 8-7. In an aggregate, ex post sense, it can be seen that the demand for all investment goods was shown to be inelastic by the post-1956 increase in relative prices;[22] a larger share of GNP was saved domestically (except during 1963–66) after the rise in capital goods relative prices than before. The paradoxical increase in national savings at a time of severe balance-of-payments and growth crises during 1957–58 is astonishing. It is noteworthy that national savings during the prosperous years of 1971–72 stood at 17.5 per cent of GNP, substantially below the 20.3 per cent rate achieved during the "blood, sweat, and tears" years of 1957 and 1958. Contrasting all of 1967–72 with 1950–56, the saving and capital inflow rates emerge as follows:

	1950–56	1967–72
Private savings	12.0%	12.1%
Public savings	4.2	5.8
Net capital inflow	0.4	3.4
Gross capital formation	16.7	21.3

Increases in the rates of public saving and capital inflow account for almost all of the increase in the current-price rate of capital accumulation.

Even allowing for possible changes in the structure of investment allocation, it would be difficult to credit the 1967–72 acceleration in GNP growth to a higher rate of capital formation. Assuming a one-year average gestation period for investments, and comparing constant-price rates of gross capital formation with GNP growth rates, the marginal capital-output ratio (MCOR) for 1951–55 is 4.08; for 1956–67, 4.81; and for 1968–72, 3.22. The sharp drop in MCORs between 1956–67 and 1968–72 contrasts with the more sluggish evolution of the aggregate investment rate, which for 1950–54 is 22.3 per cent; for 1955–66, 20.9 per cent; and for 1967–71, 19.7 per cent.

Before 1968, there were not only severe restrictions on the importation of capital goods, but also erratic stop-go fiscal and monetary policies, with expansionary binges being followed by restrictive policies. Austerity in fiscal and monetary matters, when applied, did help the balance of payments, but at the cost of slowing GNP expansion and generating excess capacity even in sectors where direct and indirect demand for imported inputs was small, such as construction. Excess capacity during 1956–67 was due not so much to a lack of key imported inputs paralyzing whole factories, but to fiscal and monetary policies which were not *steadily* expansionary because of fear—a well-founded fear—that balance-of-payments problems would result. Selective measures that would have allowed differential expansion depending on import intensity were difficult to implement beyond gross aggregation levels.

As the balance-of-payments situation improved after 1967, fiscal and monetary policy (supported by the crawling peg) could avoid the violence of previous stop-go spasms. But by 1972–73, further encouraged by booming world demand, macro policies may have become overly expansionary, in the sense that they could not be sustained. At any rate, since 1967 excess capacity was steadily put to use, whether or not it relied on imported inputs. Thus, new exports at one end tapped resources that had been less than fully used before, in a vent-for-surplus fashion, while expansive aggregate domestic demand had a similar effect on all nonexporting activities. Without the rising foreign-exchange earnings,[23] however, such a scenario would not have been possible. In other words, given the exogenous dollar coffee price, the implicit 1956–67 "plan" not only contained static inefficiencies but was also internally inconsistent. A GNP growth rate of, say, 6 per cent per year required import values greater than the exchange earnings arising from old and new exports. And given Colombian parameters the required imports could not all be replaced by domestic production within the required time span.

The higher *and* steadier post-1967 growth must have also encouraged an investment process more efficient than that undertaken under the stop-go gyrations of earlier years. How much this contributed to lowering the MCOR, however, is a moot point.

It is likely that to sustain the GNP growth rates registered since 1967 the constant-price investment coefficient, particularly that in machinery and equipment, will have to continue its upward climb and at a faster rate. The long-run benefit of breaking the foreign-exchange bottleneck, i.e., allowing a larger inflow of imported capital goods and a higher investment rate, will then become easier to identify than was the case during 1967–72, when the short-run benefits described above predominated. Compared with earlier years, Colombia now has a more diversified base for capital formation. Its indirect sources of machinery and equipment, e.g., exports, as well as its own direct output of those goods, look sturdier than in, say, 1956. A more general diversification of the Colombian productive structure and, thus, a greater capacity to transform, make policy tools potentially more effective in handling possible exogenous shocks and in maintaining both balance-of-payments and macroeconomic equilibrium. A higher rate of capital formation combined with a more efficient allocation of investment should lead to changes in the Colombian growth pattern less ambiguous than those noted earlier in this chapter for 1967–73.

In discussing the links between trade policies and growth in this section, I dealt exclusively with variations on the foreign-exchange-gap model and with short- and medium-term macroeconomic management, an approach which some may find overly "Keynesian." While emphasizing the importance of these effects for the Colombian case, I do not intend to deny the existence of possible links between trade policies and other dynamic effects that influence growth over the long run. But hard evidence on these matters is scanty. Leonard Dudley,[24] in a study of 25 import-substituting industries in the Colombian metal products sector during 1959–66, found important learning effects, explaining half of substantial productivity gains, particularly in casting, forging, and stamping. Whether or not import-substituting activities generate larger learning effects than exporting ones, however, is a moot point. There is anecdotal evidence showing that some firms (e.g., in textiles) are remarkably X-efficient and innovative whether they devote themselves to import substitution *or* to exporting, as are Germans with alternative socioeconomic systems. It will be recalled from Chapter 6 that as of 1971 major exporting firms still relied heavily on domestic sales. When the exporting experience becomes longer, and more differentiated from domestic sales, greater possibilities for exploring contrasts in behavior between exporting and import-substituting firms may become possible.

TRADE POLICIES, INCOME DISTRIBUTION, AND EMPLOYMENT

The use of one policy instrument or a cluster of closely related ones may bring a community closer to achieving several policy targets simultaneously. Such happy circumstances, however, are rare. In the recent upsurge of export optimism in Colombia as well as in other developing countries, there has been a tendency to suppose that switching from policies emphasizing import substitution to those giving greater incentives to exports will not only promote efficiency and growth, but will also significantly improve income distribution and accelerate the growth of employment in modern (or "truly productive") activities. This supposition is usually based not just on the observation that important control mechanisms associated with import substitution disproportionately benefit the powerful and the rich, but it also rests on appeals to a two-factor version of the Stolper-Samuelson theorem. For developing countries the latter emphasizes plentiful labor and scarce capital with or without downward wage rigidity. How much of an improvement in income distribution or employment can be expected from export-promoting policies, however, is usually not specified.

In earlier chapters, I argued that Colombian import controls and the protective system in general do appear to reinforce income inequality, regional disparities, and industrial concentration. The protective system has also encouraged a large number of capital-intensive projects. A policy package that eliminates import controls while encouraging exports could, however, generate new rents even as it destroys those associated with import substitution. Furthermore, the elimination of import controls would still leave a multitude of similar mechanisms through which the rich and powerful could take advantage of state power to buttress and further their position.[25] Imperfections in domestic capital markets, to give one fashionable example, are as large a source of inequality as import controls. Thus, focusing just on the protective system can give a misleading impression of the true sources of inequality, confusing a symptom for the cause of the disease, which, as noted by many Colombians, lies in the excessive economic and political power held by privileged minorities. It is debatable whether the economic and political power such minorities may lose from the abolition of import controls is greater that the power gains that would accrue to, say, cattle, cotton, and sugar landowners from their expanding exports.

In earlier chapters, evidence was presented on the characteristics of the new Colombian minor exports. Such limited data suggest that, at the very least, one would want to expand the usual two-by-two Heckscher-Ohlin trade model to a three-by-three one to analyze the impact of trade policies on income distribution and employment. On the input side, land or natural resources must be added to labor and capital, while nontradable goods (or the subsistence sector) must be added to importables and exportables. In the expanded model, applications of the Stolper-Samuelson theorem will become more difficult and ad hoc. But more fundamentally, it was seen earlier that the emerging trade pattern of Colombia cannot be explained only by a simple or expanded Heckscher-Ohlin model. Some "unusual" trade flows can be explained by reference to domestic policies, for example, Colombian trade with other members of the Latin American Free Trade Association (LAFTA). In addition, other trade theories, such as vent-for-surplus, the product cycle, and those emphasizing location, are helpful in explaining particular aspects of Colombian foreign trade. In the literature, there is no systematic exploration, either theoretical or empirical, of the implications of those positive trade theories for *functional* income distribution, much less for family income distribution or for the income of the poorest half of the population.

If a given export expansion can be explained by a vent-for-surplus model, the name of the distributional game will be pure rents. Who gets them depends on who owns the rent-yielding assets. If such assets are relatively homogeneous and compact in location, they can be grouped under one label, "land," and a Heckscher-Ohlin model could be good enough to explore links between trade and distribution, as in the Argentine case. In Colombia, these assets are less homogeneous, ranging from sugar land in the Cauca Valley to mineral deposits scattered over the whole country. One crop or mineral may be a heavy user of labor inputs, but others may not, depending on the technological characteristics of the production functions of the different staples, and the socioeconomic conditions in the region. Nevertheless, the 1972–73 boom in dollar prices of minor rural exports has highlighted one Argentine-like way of viewing a mechanism linking greater openness of the economy with a worsening of income distribution: as land prices rose because of the boom in those exportable goods, the prices of foodstuffs grown for domestic consumption, using somewhat similar land, also rose—in many cases ahead of money wages.

For exports of manufactured products the product cycle theory emphasizes the technological status of a commodity, i.e., whether it is new or old and standardized. Whether it is labor- or capital-intensive is of secondary importance. The cement exported from the Colombian Atlantic coast, for example, is a standardized good, benefiting in that case also from locational advantages; its capital intensity is not a major barrier to its competing in the Caribbean area. Flat glass is exported from Medellín, in spite of both capital intensity and locational disadvantages.

A switch, speaking in relative terms, from import substitution to export promotion could improve income distribution in countries such as Colombia or could worsen it. And the change attributable to trade policies could be quantitatively important or negligible. No simple model could give us answers to these alternatives, and the detailed information needed for confident projections is not available.

Much the same can be said regarding the possible impact on employment, although there is reason to be more optimistic here, at least for the urban sector. While the link between trade policies and income distribution has much to do with the structures of the import-competing versus exporting sectors, and relatively little to do with the over-all growth rate, it may be conjectured that the opposite is likely to be the case for urban employment. The impact of different growth rates on income distribution, ceteris paribus, is ambiguous, but is almost surely positive for urban employment. Even if it is feared that import liberalization may destroy labor-intensive handicrafts without generating a compensating expansion in labor-intensive exports, a higher GNP growth rate made possible by the relaxation of the foreign-exchange bottleneck is likely to have a net positive impact on urban employment creation. Over the longer run, of course, this could feed back positively on income distribution. The picture for rural employment is more complex, and much depends on what incentives are generated for changes in land tenure, and on the robustness of the subsistence sector.

To clarify these uncertainties it would be helpful to have for marginal import-competing and exporting activities direct and indirect input requirements of such things as natural resources, unskilled and other labor, imported machinery and equipment, and other capital goods. Disaggregation of activities would clearly have to go beyond that available in the Colombian input-output table, which has one row and column for the whole rural sector. It might then be possible to compare, for example, the direct and indirect factor use of refined sugar with that of "refined cotton," i.e., textiles, which now are excessively dichotomized as exports of primary products versus exports of manufactures.

But even at the level of first-round or direct effects, additional information of a kind not found even in fairly disaggregated input-output tables seems necessary to predict factor use. Factor proportions in a given Colombian industry appear to differ markedly by firm size. It thus becomes important to know whether large or small firms are carrying out marginal import substitution or exportation. It is also relevant to investigate whether, as seems likely on average, large firms participate more in tradable goods sectors (both exportables and importables) than in the sector producing nontradable goods and services. Some idea of the variability in factor use according to size of firm in the Colombian manufacturing sector is given in Table 8-9, on the assumption that differences in average labor productivity reflect, at least partly, differences in factor use. In this table it is indicated, for example, that the variation in average productivity of firms employing between 50 and 100 persons in all the standard industrial classifications is not so different from the variation in average labor productivity of firms producing paper and paper products but differing among themselves in size. It is suggested that the information gained about factor use from knowing that a given firm produces tobacco or rubber products is useful but limited unless size of firm also is specified. How much of this variability is due to heterogeneous output under the standard industrial classifications and how much is due to differences in factor use in the production of "identical" goods is another moot point, given available data. Only finer disaggregation according to both output and size can settle that issue. Similar considerations could be made regarding the rural sector, for which Albert Berry has documented substantial differences in *land* productivity according to farm size. Important distinctions in factor use and technology exist especially between small subsistence farms and large commercial ones producing the same crop.[26]

Colombia has made great strides since World War II in expanding its internal transport network. The abrupt geography of the country, however, still segments domestic markets for goods and services. Ideally, then, the consequences of export expansion or import substitution for regional factor markets and internal migration should be examined, a task not feasible with available data.

During a period of transition from policies emphasizing import substitution to those promoting exports, as 1967–72 undoubtedly was, most exporting firms also sold substantially, and predominantly, to the domestic market. As late as 1973, a group of large firms accounting for 42 per cent of registered manufactured exports of that year were reported to have sold 90.8 per cent of

TABLE 8-9

Value Added per Employed Person in Colombian Manufacturing, 1967

	Average (thous. 1967 pesos) (1)	Stand. Dev. (2)	Coeff. of Variation (col. 2 div. by col. 1) (3)	No. of Industries or Firm Categories Included (4)
According to size of firm (no. of persons):				
1–14	29.1	18.4	0.63	25
15–19	38.1	47.7	1.25	24
20–49	42.1	34.6	0.82	25
50–99	47.0	28.1	0.60	25
100–199	64.6	48.5	0.75	25
200 and over	81.3	79.3	0.98	24
All manufacturing (average and deviation across 25 industrial classifications)	63.0	58.6	0.93	25
According to industrial classification:				
Food	59.6	18.1	0.30	6
Beverages	94.8	58.4	0.62	6
Tobacco products	91.0	132.8	1.46	6
Textiles	32.5	8.6	0.26	6
Clothing and footwear	22.9	6.1	0.27	6
Printing and publishing	35.3	16.1	0.46	6
Pharmaceuticals and related products	68.9	33.1	0.48	6
Furniture and fixtures	19.6	6.1	0.31	6
Rubber products	75.6	88.7	1.17	6
Ceramic products	17.5	6.2	0.35	6
Nonelectrical appliances	28.9	10.0	0.35	5
Electrical appliances	44.2	11.9	0.27	6
Motor vehicles	37.2	25.0	0.67	6
Wood and products	23.5	6.6	0.28	6
Paper and products	50.6	25.2	0.50	6
Leather and products	34.2	15.7	0.46	6
Chemicals other than pharmaceuticals	88.2	34.0	0.39	6
Petroleum and coal products	158.7	98.7	0.62	5
Nonmetallic mineral products	31.2	15.8	0.51	6
Basic metal products	77.2	22.5	0.29	6
Metal products	33.7	13.4	0.40	6
Mechanical machinery	30.6	6.1	0.20	6
Electrical machinery except appliances	43.6	20.6	0.47	6
Transport equipment	30.3	8.1	0.27	6
Other	40.8	11.6	0.28	6
All manufacturing (average and deviation across 6 firm-size categories)	46.3	20.1	0.43	6

Notes to Table 8-9

SOURCE: Basic data obtained from IBRD, *Economic Growth of Colombia: Problems and Prospects,* November 1, 1970, vol. IV, App. 1, Table II. This is the complete document on which the World Bank publication listed in Table 8-3 was based. It should be noted that the averages shown for each firm-size or industrial category are the unweighted averages obtained from the relevant subgroups, which already involve some averaging. Thus, they can be expected to differ from the (more exact) averages shown in Table 8-3. The first line of this table, for example, was computed as follows: Using the average value added per employee of firms having 1 through 14 employees in each of the 25 industrial categories, the average for all industrial firms of that size (29.1) was obtained, and its standard deviation (18.4) computed. For all manufacturing in the seventh row of the table, averages for the value added per employee in each of the 25 industrial categories (including all sizes of firms within that category) were used in the same fashion.

their output in the domestic market.[27] Many of these firms used underutilized capacity to produce exports. Thus, a given export expansion may have a widely varying first-round impact on factor use depending on whether attention is directed to the short run or the long, and depending also on what assumptions are made about firm behavior. Putting to use excess installed capacity for sales abroad could involve a marginal capital use per unit of output much lower in the short run than in the long. Contrary to what is likely to happen in import substitution, new smaller firms may plunge into exporting as the export drive becomes consolidated, once the larger firms have shown that Colombian output can compete internationally and establish an export infrastructure. Or smaller firms may become associated with larger export firms in increasing numbers as subcontractors, an evolution that has also occurred in the import-competing sector. In short, the factor use observed during the early stages of an export drive may be significantly different from that observed at more mature stages of export expansion, in a pattern different from that observed during corresponding stages of an import substitution drive.

The calculation of indirect effects on factor demands and other general equilibrium effects are also difficult accurately to trace out. The complementary or indirect services required by different types of export and import-substituting activities could vary substantially. For example, the export of a staple like coal will need complementary capital-intensive services, such as transportation by railroads or trucks to take the product to harbors, quite different from the needs of carnation exports or those generated in duty-free zones.

As was noted in Chapter 1, Berry and Urrutia have shown that as of the mid-1960s the distribution of Colombian personal income was highly unequal; in their calculations for 1964, the Gini coefficient was 0.57.[28] Furthermore, they find that a period of worsening distribution began in the 1930s and continued until around the mid-1950s, not only over-all but in both urban and rural sectors. From the mid-1950s until the mid-1960s, the evidence they

TABLE 8-10

Labor Share in GDP, 1950–54 to 1971–72

(per cent)

	Agriculture and Livestock	Manufacturing	Construction	Commerce	Transport	GDP
1950–54	35.9	29.2	73.5	18.3	36.4	35.9
1955–58	31.3	33.5	71.9	18.3	36.9	35.7
1959–62	32.1	35.6	71.8	18.6	44.0	37.4
1963–66	33.2	37.6	74.4	18.3	47.8	39.3
1967–70	30.9	40.2	79.4	21.0	45.3	40.4
1971–72	27.6	40.7	77.3	17.1	47.0	40.1

SOURCE: BdlR-CN. Percentages were computed using data at current prices and measured at factor cost.

examined suggests a moderate over-all improvement and an improvement in urban distribution but a continued worsening of the distribution in agriculture. They add that there is some tentative evidence that the latest episode of fast growth, between 1967 and 1973, may have been characterized by a deterioration in the position of the urban employed worker, although the exact causes for such deterioration are unclear. Some of this effect may have been compensated for by a decrease in unemployment, however. They conclude that the challenge now facing Colombia is in avoiding an increase in inequality in the future as economic growth accelerates.

Changes in the labor share of GDP provide a crude, but available, index of recent changes in income distribution. It may be seen in Table 8-10 that in 1971–72, by which time the post-1967 policies had become well established, there was either an end or a reversal of the upward trend in the manufacturing and over-all wage shares that had started after 1955–58. The plunge in the rural wage share suggests that the new commercial crops use less labor than the old staple, coffee, or the subsistence sector. By 1972, the wage share was 26.5 per cent in agriculture and livestock, 40.2 per cent in manufacturing, and 39.4 per cent for the whole GDP.

Scattered evidence[29] suggests that open unemployment rates in the four largest Colombian cities peaked in 1967, and have been declining ever since. As in other developing countries, however, the openly unemployed in Colombia are typically young people, nonheads of families, and others who can afford to be in that situation. Those at the bottom of the income scale usually have some kind of employment, and there is no evidence on whether demand for their services has expanded substantially since 1967.

Both a priori considerations and available post-1967 evidence cast doubt on the power of further import liberalization by itself significantly to alter Colombian income distribution and employment patterns. It is particularly doubtful that further import liberalization would do much for or against those in the bottom half of the income scale, say, during the next ten years or so. Indeed, it is conceivable that continued encouragement of modern mechanized rural activities oriented toward foreign markets could further damage the prospects of landless farmers and *minifundistas* for obtaining family-sized farms. It should be recalled that about 45 per cent of the Colombian active population is still engaged in rural activities and that a good share of the poorest part of the nation is to be found there. Unless other policies are adopted, the encouragement of commercial, export-oriented farming could worsen land and income distribution in the countryside, and by absorbing parts of the subsistence sector, it could actually generate disguised rural or urban unemployment. It would not be the first time in history that such a thing has happened.

TRADE AND FINANCIAL POLICIES
AND NATIONAL AUTONOMY

While income distribution and employment data are scarce, at least the concepts involved are in principle quantifiable. "National autonomy" is a vaguer concept, but of no less importance to those responsible for framing international trade and financial policies in Colombia and elsewhere. As measured by the proportion of imports of goods and services in GDP, the openness of the Colombian economy rose from 13.0 per cent during 1963–66, to 14.0 per cent during 1967–70, and to 15.6 per cent in 1971–72.[30] Has this trend been accompanied by a significant change in the degree of control of Colombians over their own economy? What will be the impact of further liberalization and openness on such control?

The post-1967 expansion has been characterized not only by a remarkable diversification in the goods exported, but also by a continuing diversification of geographical trade partners, visible also in imports. The extent of the geographical diversification may be seen in tables 3-8 and 4-10. It was also noted earlier, in chapters 2 and 6, that the participation of foreign-owned enterprises in minor exports, while important, particularly for manufactured products, is less than that of domestic firms, and probably less than the participation of foreign firms in the most dynamic import-substituting activities. It would indeed be dangerous for the political viability of export promotion if the production or merchandising of new exports fell predominantly under the control of foreign enterprise. Dissatisfaction with protectionist policies was boosted as a greater share of those firms most critical to the success of import substitution turned out to be foreign owned.

Vulnerability to external cycles and pressures has been reduced not only by geographical and product diversification, but also by the establishment of preferential arrangements with middle-income countries at a similar stage of industrialization. The Andean Common Market may be viewed partly as insurance against a collapse of world markets. If such an event occurs, import substitution at the Andean level could go into high gear partly to offset the collapse of export drives. Had Latin America had such arrangements in 1929, the industrialization of the 1930s and 1940s would in all likelihood have been faster and more efficient. Andean and wider Latin American integration schemes also afford some insurance against possible commercial and financial blockades and could facilitate access to specific raw materials. Ecuador and Venezuela, both Colombian neighbors and members of the Andean group, are blessed by ample oil deposits, while other Andean partners have rich stores of minerals.

Year-to-year percentage changes in total export dollar earnings for 1968–72 compared with 1963–67 already show not only a higher average growth rate (8.19 per cent versus 2.42 per cent) but also a lower average absolute deviation from the mean of the more recent period (5.97 per cent versus 8.11 per cent).

Trade is only one aspect of Colombian links with the international economy, and trade liberalization will typically be accompanied by larger gross flows of capital as well as special services, such as technology. A case can be made that international markets for technology and capital are less diversified and competitive than those for most goods, thus posing a potential threat to the autonomy of countries relying too heavily on them without defensive mechanisms. Such mechanisms, of course, can also be used to obtain better bargains. For these reasons, Colombian authorities are likely to retain present controls and registration procedures for transfer of technology and capital flows, particularly direct foreign investments, even if they eliminate import controls. In some cases the greater competitive pressures put on import-competing firms, many of them foreign owned, by the elimination of import controls, plus realistic exchange rates, will reduce the importance of keeping detailed tabs on such matters as overinvoicing of imported inputs and fake royalty payments abroad. This should make for greater efficiency of controls over transactions involving monopoly power originating abroad, rather than wasting effort dealing with monopoly power created by misguided domestic protectionism.

The presence of both capital and technological inflows raises the possibility of excessive reliance on foreigners. The effect could be to weaken local efforts and reduce the capability of Colombia for long-run autonomous development. The flabby performance of recent Colombian private and public savings, at a time of fast growth *and* substantial capital inflow, documented earlier in this chapter, suggests that such a concern may not be misplaced, even if it is difficult to say much more on the subject for a single country.

More, however, can be said on different types of capital flows. Non-concessional long-term capital is now available to Colombia mainly in two forms: as direct foreign investment (DFI) and as sales abroad of Colombian debt. The former type, as is well known, comes as a package of technology, management, marketing, and capital. The same Decree Law 444 of 1967 that consolidated the framework for a crawling peg and export promotion also established firm controls over DFI, later reflected in the celebrated Resolution 24 of the Andean group. The fears of the international financial press notwithstanding, DFI has continued flowing into Colombia. Indeed, and somewhat disappointingly, the allocation pattern of such investment since 1967 has been about what it was before. It may be seen in Table 8-11 that chemicals, refineries, rubber, and plastics, heavily oriented toward import substitution, have continued attracting about one-third of DFI. The same source given in that table indicates little change in the geographical origins of DFI: the United States still accounts for about half, with the shares for Switzerland, France, Japan, and the Federal Republic of Germany showing an increase after 1967.[31]

As with other semi-industrialized or resource-rich developing countries, Colombia discovered during the early 1970s that it could obtain substantial sums from "arm's length" world capital markets. During 1973, for example, Colombia was reported to have borrowed $170 million in the Eurocurrency market.[32] This source of funds, although expensive, provides a healthy alternative to both DFI and the more traditional forms of borrowing from multilateral intermediaries, such as the IBRD and the IADB, as well as to concessional bilateral finance. Borrowing from either the Eurocurrency market or other foreign capital markets carries costs and risks not associated with borrowing from the IBRD and the IADB, but could involve less sacrifice of national control over investment decisions.[33] As with any form of foreign borrowing, of course, it bears careful controlling, both at the level of individual loans and in the aggregate.

As measured by the traditional indicators, e.g., service payments on the whole external public debt as a percentage of exports of goods and nonfactor services, the Colombian debt burden remains moderate. It stood at 15.5 per cent in 1965–66, at 12.7 per cent in 1967–70, and at 13.5 per cent in 1971–72.[34] So long as exports maintain their dynamism, the Colombian capacity to borrow in private markets should be quite good, potentially strengthening the position of the country vis-à-vis multilateral intermediaries and bilateral donors.

On the whole, it is doubtful that the gradual post-1967 liberalization trend has substantially changed Colombia's capacity for autonomous decision making; on balance, the net change seems to be, if anything, toward greater effective national control over the domestic economy. Aided also by trends in

TABLE 8-11

Structure of Accumulated Direct Foreign Investment in Colombia
(per cent of total)

	As of January 1, 1967	Accumulated Investment from January 1, 1967, Through December 31, 1972
Foodstuffs, beverages, and tobacco	6.8	3.7
Textiles, clothing, and leather products	4.0	3.8
Wood products and furniture	0.3	4.1
Paper, printing, and publishing	8.9	2.7
Chemicals, refineries, rubber, and plastics	31.8	33.3
Nonmetallic minerals	5.1	2.6
Basic metals	1.6	1.2
Metal products, machinery, and equipment	11.3	12.7
Other manufacturing	0.6	0.4
All manufacturing	70.3	64.4
Finance, insurance, real estate, and related services	11.4	24.4
Commerce, hotels, and restaurants	11.4	6.5
Mining (except petroleum)	2.7	1.4
Transport and communications	2.4	0.8
Agriculture, livestock, and fishing	0.9	0.9
All other	0.8	1.6
Total	100.0	100.0
Total value, millions of U.S. dollars	$429.1	$111.0

SOURCE: BdlR-IAGJD, 1972, p. 122. Data refer to the registered and accumulated value of investments except those in petroleum. Registered value underestimates the value of assets owned and controlled by foreign investors.

the world economy, policymakers are able to consider more options than they could have realistically faced, say, around 1965. On the other hand, the greater openness of the economy demands a more careful coordination of different policy tools, such as monetary, fiscal, and exchange-rate policies, than was necessary when both Colombia and the Atlantic world had less complex and interrelated economies, as during the 1950s.

SOME FINAL REMARKS

The gradualist trade and payments policies followed since 1967 have impressive achievements to their credit. By placing balance-of-payments management on a routine basis, they permitted a more efficient and faster over-all growth rate, which appeared out of reach during 1957–66. A remarkable expansion of exports, aided by a booming world economy, confounded export pessimists. The improved balance-of-payments and growth performance also defied gloomy predictions about the unique post-1967 Colombian approach to liberalization made by perspicacious foreign observers as late as 1971.[35] As noted by several Colombian analysts, the relaxation of the foreign-exchange bottleneck and the removal of periodic exchange crises from the front pages have given policymakers the option of turning their attention to the *really* serious problems in the Colombian economy—poverty, underemployment, income distribution, and national autonomy—areas in which the impact of trade and payments policies is indirect and weak or uncertain.

Further import liberalization, beyond the stage reached in mid-1974, and a reorganizing of the export promotion system could, if properly managed, and with the right world market conditions, consolidate and expand the post-1967 gains in efficiency and growth. But a good case can be made that other reforms, complementing those in the area of foreign trade and payments, are likely now to have a larger payoff, particularly in the area of income distribution. These would include a profound tax reform, involving stiffer land taxes, expansion of public expenditures in education and health, and a liberalization of the domestic capital market, either by giving a greater role to market-influenced interest rates or by lending and borrowing policies of a nationalized banking and financial system that imitated ideal competitive solutions. The relaxation of the foreign-exchange constraint has focused attention once again on the need to expand local (private and public) savings if the over-all growth rate is to be increased, or even maintained, since the marginal capital-output ratio registered in recent years is unlikely to persist. A less distorted internal capital market may help somewhat in this area.

While avoidable balance-of-payments crises have not distracted policymakers in recent years, a similar superficial issue has re-emerged, especially in 1973 and 1974. During those years overly expansionary fiscal and monetary policies, including financial reforms boosting construction, led to an overheating of the economy which, coupled with exogenous increases in the world dollar price level, resulted in severe inflation. Among other things, such inflation has endangered the crawling peg policy, undertaken since 1967 amidst declining inflationary rates. The policymaker, in particular the new reformist administration inaugurated August 1974, is forced to give first priority to a macroeconomic management issue which lacks positive long-run

structural effects but which if left unattended could have negative consequences. In some respects the anti-inflation struggle should accelerate the
trend toward more efficient trade policies, as in the case of the dismantling of
import controls. However, such a struggle also encourages export controls, so
that even as the old prohibited and prior-license import lists disappear or
shrink, similar ones appear on the export side. And the temptation remains to
slow down the crawling peg as a way of fighting inflation.

In retrospect, the Colombian experience vindicates the case for gradual-
ism in import liberalization which went pari passu with export expansion. It
was not necessary to dismantle the protective system before that export
expansion could be generated. The wisdom of avoiding shock treatments
while keeping control over macroeconomic management policies remains
relevant for anti-inflationary policies.

Even as Colombian policymaking has gained in sophistication, trends in
the world economy have imposed upon it the need for further improvement,
particularly in the areas of macroeconomic and balance-of-payment management. As Colombian links with world trade and financial markets multiply, for
example, problems long familiar to policymakers of industrialized countries,
such as the coordination of monetary and foreign-exchange policies, will claim
greater attention from Colombian authorities. The Colombian crawling peg
during most of 1967–74 was basically used to eliminate wide divergences
between local and external inflation; expectations about the pace of the crawl
were fairly stable and on the whole were confirmed by actual experience.
Under these circumstances the crawling peg has not performed the isolating
role a more freely fluctuating rate is supposed to achieve. Therefore, domestic
monetary policy cannot have the autonomy it could have under a truly flexible
rate system. Furthermore, the confused and disturbed state of the world
economy during 1974 indicates that Colombian exchange-rate policy will have
to deal not only with disturbances originating inside the country, but also with
those issuing from an increasingly erratic world market.

It would therefore be a mistake to interpret import liberalization and
rationalization of the system of protection as a retreat from planning in the
foreign sector. Such steps in fact are a part of the search for a more efficient
planning of international trade and finance policies.

NOTES

1. These rates of growth or decline are obtained by fitting trend lines, as in tables 1-1 and 1-2.

2. In Table 1-2, GDP growth rates are shown only for 1950–56 and 1967–72. Preliminary
statistics indicate a GDP growth rate of 7.0 per cent for 1973. See *Coyuntura Económica,* April
1974, p. 5. UNECLA estimates place the GDP annual growth rate at 5.2 per cent during 1945–50

and at 4.2 per cent for just 1947–50. The UNECLA estimates can be found in DANE-BME, no. 226, May 1970.

3. See Richard Caves, "Export-led Growth and the New Economic History," in J. N. Bhagwati et al., eds., *Trade, Balance of Payments and Growth: Papers in International Economics in Honor of Charles P. Kindleberger* (Amsterdam: North-Holland, 1971), especially pp. 419–438.

4. Trend growth rates and deviations somewhat different from those shown in tables 8-1 and 8-2 are obtained when the dummy variable t_2 for the six years 1967–72 is given values of 1, 2, . . . , 5, 6 (instead of 18, 19, . . . , 22, 23), leaving t_1 as before. Using this alternative procedure, for example, the following results are obtained (standard errors in parentheses), which may be compared with those in tables 8-1 and 8-2:

	Trend	Deviation
All agriculture	3.05	0.96
	(0.17)	(0.63)
All livestock	3.57	1.51
	(0.22)	(0.81)
All manufacturing	6.07	0.19
	(0.11)	(0.42)
Industrial manufacturing	6.83	−0.22
	(0.15)	(0.56)

5. Thomas L. Hutcheson, "Incentives for Industrialization in Colombia" (Ph.D. diss., University of Michigan, 1973).

6. Ibid., App. B, pp. 147–148.

7. The theoretical rationale for linking effective rates of protection to either import-substitution ratios or sectoral growth rates has been questioned by Jagdish Bhagwati, "Tariff Protection and Industrialization in Nigeria: A Comment," *Bangladesh Economic Review,* forthcoming.

8. Other case studies are reported in Daniel Vargas and Eduardo Wiesner, "Las Exportaciones y el Empleo; Una Perspectiva para Colombia," mimeographed (Bogotá: FEDESARROLLO, November 1971). There is little mystery in these DRC results: typically one starts with labor-intensive exports selling at world prices and compares them with heavily protected activities whose output sells domestically at prices twice or more those in world markets. The further contribution made to the gap in DRCs by differences in cost structure and guesses about shadow input prices is usually quite small.

9. The 1962 Colombian development plan included export targets for 1970, which were revised by the IBRD during 1962. Those projections, made in millions of current U.S. dollars, can be compared with actual 1970 figures, as follows:

	Colombian Plan	IBRD Estimates	Actual 1970 Exports
Registered exports, total	$827	$700	$736
Coffee	405	340	467
Crude oil	167	167	59
Bananas	43	43	18
Cotton	39	40	35
Tobacco	⎫	15	7
Sugar	173	5	15
Other	⎭	90	135
Nonregistered exports	30	30	59

The projections are from IBRD, *An Appraisal of the Development Program of Colombia,* Report WH-119a, June 21, 1962, Annex I, pp. 5 and 11. Actual 1970 data are from Chapter 2, above. Actual registered minor exports in 1970 exceeded the IBRD projections by 9 per cent, but fell short of the ambitious targets of the development plan by 18 per cent.

10. See Francisco E. Thoumi, "Evolución de la Industria Manufacturera Fabril 1958–1967," DANE-BME, March 1971, p. 60.

11. David Morawetz, "Import Substitution, Employment and Foreign Exchange in Colombia: No Cheers for Petrochemicals," mimeographed (Harvard Development Advisory Service, September 1972). Morawetz adds: "In Colombia petrochemicals received more government finance and support than any other industrial sector in the 1960s. For example, in 1969 chemicals and petrochemicals participated 40 percent in the portfolio of the largest government industrial development agency (IFI) and received 25 percent of all credits and refinancings granted by the government's Private Investment Fund (FIP), in spite of the fact that it generated only 8 percent of industrial production and employment" (p. 1).

12. For an early analysis of this industry see Bernard E. Munk, "The Colombian Automotive Industry: The Welfare Consequences of Import Substitution," mimeographed (AID, August 1968). In that paper Munk was pessimistic about cost reductions in this industry even assuming Andean integration.

13. Speculative holdings of importable-goods inventories were emphasized by Alberto Roque Musalem, but from a balance-of-payments and macroeconomic perspective. See his *Dinero, Inflación y Balanza de Pagos: La Experiencia de Colombia en la Post-Guerra* (Bogotá: Talleres Gráficos del Banco de la República, 1971), particularly Chapter I.

14. See Francisco E. Thoumi, "The Utilization of Fixed Industrial Capital in Colombia: Some Empirical Findings," mimeographed (IBRD, December 1973).

15. See Carlos F. Díaz-Alejandro, "The Andean Common Market: Gestation and Outlook," in R. S. Eckaus and P. N. Rosenstein-Rodan, eds., *Analysis of Development Problems: Studies of the Chilean Economy* (Amsterdam: North-Holland, 1973), pp. 293–326. See also David Morawetz, "Economic Integration Among Less Developed Countries with Special Reference to the Andean Group" (Ph.D. diss., Massachusetts Institute of Technology, 1972).

16. Current tax revenues of the national government reached 9.8 per cent of GDP in 1970, but fell to approximately 9.0 per cent by 1973, contributing to a large fiscal deficit and a deteriorating, inflationary situation during 1973 and 1974. See *Coyuntura Económica,* April 1974, p. 124 and pp. 133–134.

17. During 1974 the U.S. Treasury charged Colombia with "dumping" carnations in the U.S. market, giving as evidence the CAT received by those exporters. It will be recalled that the CAT has been in effect since 1967; its creation was widely celebrated by U.S. AID officials.

On September 26, 1974, the Colombian government announced a sharp reduction in the CATs granted to exporters. Among the reasons given for such a move was the recent imposition by the United States of countervailing duties on some Colombian exports. Colombia also announced that GATT-approved exemptions from sales taxes would now be granted to exporters. As sales taxes burden luxury goods more than necessities, it was argued that such a step would reduce pressure on the cost of living of the poorest Colombians. The government also argued that a high CAT was stimulating fake export invoicing, notably on clothing and on emeralds, rubies, and other precious stones. Skinning the CAT is expected to increase public revenues by about P900 million. The government indicated that it expects eventually to lift all export prohibitions.

18. The best proxy for the price ratio of tradable goods to nontradables may be an average EER relative to Colombian wages for unskilled labor deflated by comparable wages abroad. Data for this were not available for the whole period under study. Even this measure, of course, neglects to take into account changes in the terms of trade.

19. Such a base was taken in Díaz-Alejandro, "Andean Common Market," p. 326.

20. National accounting procedures may overemphasize somewhat the link between the real

import exchange rate and the relative prices of machinery and equipment by neglecting to account fully for changes in import premiums at times of balance-of-payments turbulence. Changes in import duties on capital goods, however, have been small. It will also be recalled that major industrial corporations import their machinery and equipment directly.

21. See Carlos F. Díaz-Alejandro, *Essays on the Economic History of the Argentine Republic* (New Haven: Yale University Press, 1970), especially Essay 6. For a long time 1950 was the base year for Argentine national accounts expressed in constant prices. In that year, relative prices of all Argentine investment goods reached a peak, as did Colombian ones in 1958. Researchers using Argentine and Colombian constant-price data for cross-country comparisons have therefore frequently marveled at the high investment coefficients and extraordinary marginal capital-output ratios of the two countries. Contrary to the Argentine experience, Colombian implicit prices for the two major commodity-producing sectors have evolved comparatively undramatically relative to the GNP deflator, as follows (1958 = 100):

	Agriculture and Livestock	Manufacturing		Agriculture and Livestock	Manufacturing
1950–54	99.0	109.3	1963–66	96.9	106.0
1955–56	104.3	103.5	1967–70	94.3	97.6
1957–58	102.7	101.0	1971–72	95.5	97.2
1959–62	96.2	103.6			

22. Some model builders have speculated about such an elasticity. See W. M. Corden, "The Effects of Trade on the Rate of Growth," in Bhagwati et al, eds., *Trade,* Chap. 6, especially pp. 126–131.

23. Without the rise in minor and coffee exports it is doubtful whether Colombia could have expanded its foreign debt and attracted other types of capital to the extent realized since 1967.

24. Leonard Dudley, "The Effects of Learning on Employment and Productivity in the Colombian Metal Products Sector," mimeographed (University of Montreal, September 1973).

25. The statement stands, of course, whether the country is developed or underdeveloped. Without import controls (but with milk subsidies!), the 1973–74 Watergate matter in the United States showed some of the many channels through which private interests can manipulate state power. The Matesa scandal in Spain was in fact related to export-promotion schemes.

26. See R. Albert Berry, "Land Distribution, Income Distribution and Productivity," Chapter IV of a forthcoming Yale Economic Growth Center book on the Colombian rural sector. Berry indicates that the labor-land ratio may vary by as much as five to ten times between the two ends of the technology spectrum, a range associated with size of farms, in a crop such as corn.

27. See FEDESARROLLO, *Encuesta Industrial,* June 1974, pp. 7–8. In 1972 these firms had sold 92.7 per cent of their output domestically.

28. R. Albert Berry and Miguel Urrutia, *Income Distribution in Colombia* (New Haven: Yale University Press, forthcoming), Chap. 12.

29. Here I follow (again!) unpublished estimates of R. Albert Berry, as well as FEDESARROLLO, *Coyuntura Económica,* various issues.

30. Both imports of goods and services and GDP (at market prices) are measured at current prices. The percentages will thus reflect changes in the relation between the average import exchange rate and the GDP deflator. For earlier years, the corresponding percentages are as follows: 1950–54, 12.9; 1955–56, 13.5; 1957–58, 14.8; and 1959–62, 14.3.

31. A good share of the registered DFI gives as its home base countries such as Panamá, Curaçao, the Bahamas, Luxembourg, and Liechtenstein, making further precision as to geographical origins spurious. Some of these countries, incidentally, are also notorious smuggling centers. It appears that Colombia was hurt more by having stalled on the enforcement of Andean rules than if the country had acted at once. The debate over the constitutionality of Andean rules during 1972

seems to have led to a slowdown in DFI inflow. But once Decision 24 was firmly in place, DFI picked up vigorously. See *Business Latin America,* September 25, 1974, p. 310.

32. See *IMF Survey,* June 3, 1974, p. 165.

33. In the articles listed below, I have argued the thesis that DFI, particularly in the form it took during the 1950s and 1960s, is an unsatisfactory mechanism for promoting international interdependence: "Direct Foreign Investment in Latin America," in Charles P. Kindleberger, ed., *The International Corporation; A Symposium* (Cambridge: The M.I.T. Press, 1970), pp. 319–344; "The Future of Direct Foreign Investment in Latin America," in Stephen E. Guisinger, ed., *Trade and Investment Policies in the Americas* (Dallas: Southern Methodist University Press, 1973), pp. 3–28; and "North-South Relations: The Economic Component," *International Organization,* Winter 1975, pp. 213–241. As they gain in bargaining power, one may expect countries such as Colombia and Mexico to tie their regulations over DFI to the treatment received by their emigrating labor (or their labor-intensive exports) in the home countries of foreign investors.

34. As reported in World Bank/IDA, *Annual Report,* 1974, p. 87. The corresponding 1972 percentages were 22.2 for Argentina, 13.4 for Brazil, and 23.5 for Mexico.

35. See chapters 7 and 8 in Richard R. Nelson, T. Paul Schultz, and Robert L. Slighton, *Structural Change in a Developing Economy; Colombia's Problems and Prospects* (Princeton, N.J.: Princeton University Press, 1971). Although their study was published during 1971, background research was carried out mainly during the difficult years of 1967 and 1968. Nelson and Slighton, who themselves called my attention to the pessimism of the indicated chapters, consider that they underestimated the influence of the younger Colombian economists and the rapidity with which an export lobby with political clout would be created.

Appendixes

Appendix A

Definition of Concepts and Delineation of Phases

DEFINITION OF CONCEPTS USED IN THE PROJECT

Exchange Rates.

1. *Nominal exchange rate:* The official parity for a transaction. For countries maintaining a single exchange rate registered with the International Monetary Fund, the nominal exchange rate is the registered rate.

2. *Effective exchange rate (EER):* The number of units of local currency actually paid or received for a one-dollar international transaction. Surcharges, tariffs, the implicit interest forgone on guarantee deposits, and any other charges against purchases of goods and services abroad are included, as are rebates, the value of import replenishment rights, and other incentives to earn foreign exchange for sales of goods and services abroad.

3. *Price-level-deflated (PLD) nominal exchange rate:* The nominal exchange rate deflated in relation to some base period by the price level index of the country.

4. *Price-level-deflated EER (PLD-EER):* The EER deflated by the price level index of the country.

5. *Purchasing-power-parity adjusted exchange rate:* The relevant (nominal or effective) exchange rate multiplied by the ratio of the foreign price level to the domestic price level.

259

Devaluation.

1. *Gross devaluation:* The change in the parity registered with the IMF (or, synonymously in most cases, de jure devaluation).

2. *Net devaluation:* The weighted average of changes in EERs by classes of transactions (or, synonymously in most cases, de facto devaluation).

3. *Real gross devaluation:* The gross devaluation adjusted for the increase in the domestic price level over the relevant period.

4. *Real net devaluation:* The net devaluation similarly adjusted.

Protection Concepts.

1. *Explicit tariff:* The amount of tariff charged against the import of a good as a percentage of the import price (in local currency at the nominal exchange rate) of the good.

2. *Implicit tariff* (or, synonymously, tariff equivalent): The ratio of the domestic price (net of normal distribution costs) minus the c.i.f. import price to the c.i.f. import price in local currency.

3. *Premium:* The windfall profit accruing to the recipient of an import license per dollar of imports. It is the difference between the domestic selling price (net of normal distribution costs) and the landed cost of the item (including tariffs and other charges). The premium is thus the difference between the implicit and the explicit tariff (including other charges) multiplied by the nominal exchange rate.

4. *Nominal tariff:* The tariff—either explicit or implicit as specified—on a commodity.

5. *Effective tariff:* The explicit or implicit tariff on value added as distinct from the nominal tariff on a commodity. This concept is also expressed as the effective rate of protection (ERP) or as the effective protective rate (EPR).

6. *Domestic resources costs (DRC):* The value of domestic resources (evaluated at "shadow" or opportunity cost prices) employed in earning or saving a dollar of foreign exchange (in the value-added sense) when producing domestic goods.

DELINEATION OF PHASES USED IN TRACING THE EVOLUTION OF EXCHANGE CONTROL REGIMES

To achieve comparability of analysis among different countries, each author of a country study was asked to identify the chronological development of his country's payments regime through the following phases. There was no presumption that a country would necessarily pass through all the phases in chronological sequence.

Phase I: During this period, quantitative restrictions on international transactions are imposed and then intensified. They generally are initiated in response to an unsustainable payments deficit and then, for a period, are intensified. During the period when reliance upon quantitative restrictions as a means of controlling the balance of payments is increasing, the country is said to be in Phase I.

Phase II: During this phase, quantitative restrictions are still intense, but various price measures are taken to offset some of the undesired results of the system. Heightened tariffs, surcharges on imports, rebates for exports, special tourist exchange rates, and other price interventions are used in this phase. However, primary reliance continues to be placed on quantitative restrictions.

Phase III: This phase is characterized by an attempt to systematize the changes which take place during Phase II. It generally starts with a formal exchange-rate change and may be accompanied by removal of some of the surcharges, etc., imposed during Phase II and by reduced reliance upon quantitative restrictions. Phase III may be little more than a tidying-up operation (in which case the likelihood is that the country will re-enter Phase II), or it may signal the beginning of withdrawal from reliance upon quantitative restrictions.

Phase IV: If the changes in Phase III result in adjustments within the country, so that liberalization can continue, the country is said to enter Phase IV. The necessary adjustments generally include increased foreign-exchange earnings and gradual relaxation of quantitative restrictions. The latter relaxation may take the form of changes in the nature of quantitative restrictions or of increased foreign-exchange allocations, and thus reduced premiums, under the same administrative system.

Phase V: This is a period during which an exchange regime is fully liberalized. There is full convertibility on current account, and quantitative restrictions are not employed as a means of regulating the ex ante balance of payments.

Appendix B

Principal Dates and Historical Events in Colombia

September 1931: The gold standard was suspended. Widespread exchange controls and trade restrictions were introduced.

April 9, 1948: The assassination of Jorge Eliécer Gaitán, leader of the Liberal party, provoked wild urban riots, and was followed by rural violence, which lasted well into the 1950s.

December 1948: Exchange restrictions were revised.

July 10, 1950: Exchange restrictions were revised. A new protectionist tariff was adopted during 1950.

March 20, 1951: Except for a prohibited import list of some 1,200 specified luxury or locally produced items, practically all licensing restrictions on imports were removed, leaving only a prior registration procedure for permitted imports. Basic exchange rates depreciated from 1.95 to 2.50 pesos per U.S. dollar. Multiple exchange rates were considerably simplified, but some still remained as a result of the application of exchange taxes and a mixed effective rate for coffee exports.

August 1, 1952: An export voucher system introduced for minor exports; vouchers, which were negotiable, could be used to import previously prohibited items.

September 6, 1952: The house of Carlos Lleras Restrepo, Liberal party leader, set on fire, marking a further intensification of Liberal-Conservative rivalry.

June 13, 1953: General Gustavo Rojas Pinilla assumed the presidency, with the backing of the armed forces and of a good share of public opinion.

February 19, 1954: The prohibited import list was eliminated. Throughout most of 1954 a gradual relaxation of import and exchange restrictions took place, but by October some restrictions had been reintroduced. In February a de facto ceiling of 3.50 pesos per U.S. dollar was established for the rate applicable to minor exports.

March 1954: Colombian coffee reached 99 U.S. cents per pound in international markets; by August it was down to 67 cents.

June 1954: Restrictions on imports of many basic food staples produced locally were reintroduced.

August 1954: A backlog of commercial arrears owed to foreign suppliers began to be noticeable. In October the granting of exchange for import payments was made contingent upon arrival of the merchandise in Colombia, and prior import deposit requirements were brought up from the 10–30 per cent range to a range of 20–60 per cent. Stamp taxes were also raised.

February 16, 1955: Imports were reclassified and subjected to ad valorem stamp taxes, as follows:

	Per Cent	Description
Preferential	3	Raw materials for essential industries
Group I	10	Other raw materials and essential products
Group II	30	Essential durable and semidurable goods
Group III	80	Less essential goods
Group IV	100	Specified nonessential goods
Prohibited	—	Luxury goods

May 13, 1955: A broad free market was introduced. Imports in groups II, III, and IV and most nontrade transactions were shifted to new free-market rate (from official rate). By December 31, 1955, the free-market rate reached 4.2 pesos per U.S. dollar, compared with 2.5 pesos for the official rate.

April 1956: Import deposit requirements were almost doubled.

November–December 1956: Import restrictions intensified; commercial arrears continue to grow. The list of prohibited imports extended drastically. An exchange certificate market replaced the free market. The fluctuating rate of exchange certificates reached 6.5 pesos per U.S. dollar by December 31, 1956; that market showed great instability.

May 10, 1957: Rojas Pinilla was ousted; a provisional government was formed. The Liberal and Conservative parties agreed on a sixteen-year pact, the National Front.

June 1957: A stabilization program adopted to arrest inflationary pressures
and restore payments equilibrium. A Superintendency of Imports was
created to review import license requests; a prohibited list, a restricted
list, and a free group were maintained. Some liberalization of import
restrictions took place. A new, simplified exchange system was introduced. A new certificate market was put into operation, together with a
free market. Both consolidated sharp devaluations; on December 31,
1957, the fluctuating certificate rate was 5.4 pesos per U.S. dollar, while
that for the free market was 6.2 pesos. The quotation for the certificate
rate was theoretically determined at auctions held by the Bank of the
Republic. Most commercial arrears were settled by the end of 1957. The
net effect of the exchange reforms of June 1957 was, however, detrimental to the rate applicable to minor exports, which were switched from the
free to the new certificate market. Progressively tighter advance import
requirements registered since June 1957. The term "certificate" refers to
the legal fiction that the documents obtained in such a market referred not
to foreign exchange, but to a certificate issued by the central bank and
backed by dollars.

March–April 1958: The exchange system was modified; negotiable exchange
certificates were no longer issued against the proceeds of exports, whose
rate was then pegged at 6.1 pesos per U.S. dollar (less the appropriate
export tax), although periodic changes in this and other pegged rates were
contemplated, in principle.

August 7, 1958: Alberto Lleras Camargo was inaugurated as President, following his election in May.

January 16, 1959: New changes in the exchange and payments system. A new,
more favorable rate was established for minor export proceeds, which
was to vary in line with fluctuations in the free-market rate.

May 1959: A more comprehensive customs tariff with higher and less uniform
import duties was introduced.

February 1960: The Treaty of Montevideo was signed, creating the Latin
American Free Trade Association. The treaty entered into force in June
1961. Colombia officially joined in September 1961.

April–May 1960: Minor devaluations were made in the official buying and
selling rates, but the spread between the official and free rates widened.
The official rates were rigidly pegged, at 6.7 pesos per U.S. dollar, while
the free rate underwent sharp fluctuations.

January 13, 1962: The Colombian government requested that the Committee
of Nine of the Alliance for Progress study and report on its first General
Economic and Social Development Plan. During January all export taxes
were eliminated.

August 7, 1962: Guillermo León Valencia was inaugurated as President, following his election in May.

September 1962: Virtually all imports were made subject to prior license. The liberalization trend of 1959–61 was reversed during 1962. Tariff changes during 1962 also stressed import substitution.

September 1962: The International Coffee Agreement was signed, after two years of negotiation. It began to operate in 1964.

November 1962: Early in the month merchandise included in the import free list and the prior licensing list was transferred temporarily (for six weeks) to the prohibited list. On the twentieth of the month, the "auction" rate was allowed to depreciate from 6.7 to 9.0 pesos per U.S. dollar. A free market was maintained; at the end of December 1962 the rate in that market was 11.1 pesos per U.S. dollar.

December 1962: New free and prior-license import lists were issued.

January 11, 1963: The Bank of the Republic began pegging the free-market rate, at 10 pesos per U.S. dollar.

September 1963: The powers of monetary management were transferred to the new Monetary Board, whose majority was made up of cabinet ministers.

July 17, 1964: The Monetary Board was given legal authority to change the certificate system and the auction rate.

October 25, 1964: The Bank of the Republic ceased pegging the free-market rate. By December 31, 1964, the free-market rate had reached 12.8 pesos per U.S. dollar. Minor exports continued receiving the free-market rate.

December 1, 1964: Serious consideration was given to new devaluation, but political resistance proved too great. Import licensing became stricter; the free import list was eliminated.

June 30, 1965: The exchange rate for minor exports, previously equal to free market, was pegged at 13.5 pesos per U.S. dollar. The free-market rate climbed above 19 pesos in July and August. Pressures for a new devaluation persisted.

September 1965: A number of imports were freed from licensing requirements, if paid for at the new "intermediate" official exchange rate of 13.5 pesos per U.S. dollar; others remained subject to licenses, but obtained a "preferential" rate of 9 pesos. Plans for further import liberalization were announced. The official buying rate for coffee exports was raised from 7.7 pesos to 8.5 pesos.

October 1965: Progressive reductions of advance import deposits were started; reductions continued on schedule until August 1966, when the original plan was stretched in time. That schedule had called for the elimination of prior import deposits twenty months after October 1965.

November 1965: More imports were transferred to the "intermediate" exchange rate and freed from licensing requirements.

January 1966: A third list of liberalized imports was issued.

February–March 1966: Three further lists of liberalized imports were issued.

July–August 1966: All imports were placed under the intermediate rate of 13.5 pesos per U.S. dollar; most imports were freed of licensing requirements. The free exchange market continued for some invisibles and capital transactions; the free rate *appreciated* between September 1965 and mid-1966.

August 7, 1966: Carlos Lleras Restrepo was inaugurated as President, following his election in May.

Last quarter of 1966: The New York coffee price fell from 50 cents a pound during the first quarter of 1966 to 45 cents during the last quarter of 1966.

November 29, 1966: All imports again required to have prior licenses; operations in the free exchange market suspended. The free market was replaced by the capital market, with the rate pegged at 16.3 pesos per U.S. dollar. President Lleras Restrepo rejected pressures from the IMF and foreign creditors to devalue. All Colombian residents were required to declare foreign-exchange holdings to the Exchange Control Office. Price controls were imposed.

January 27, 1967: Previous import deposit rate requirements brought up to only 40 per cent below their level in September 1965 and further raised on February 9, 1967, to about September 1965 levels.

March 22, 1967: Decree Law 444 was published, restructuring the whole field of exchange and foreign trade. It set up a ("crawling") exchange certificate market rate and a capital market rate. Import control regulations were maintained. Detailed and rigorous regulations were also established over direct foreign investment.

Post-November 1967: Concern was expressed about the (temporary) slowdown in the upward crawl of the major (certificate) exchange rate.

May 1968: The free import list regained some significance.

June 1968: The capital and certificate exchange rates were unified.

August 22–24, 1968: His Holiness Pope Paul VI visited Colombia.

December 1968: INCOMEX replaced the Superintendency of Foreign Trade.

February 1969: Previous import deposit rates, generally lowered during 1968, were further reduced.

June 11–13, 1969: President Carlos Lleras Restrepo visited the United States. Lleras-Nixon discussions led to the elimination of "additionality," which sought to link disbursement of U.S. aid to *additional* Colombian imports from the United States.

September 1969: A sharp upswing in dollar coffee prices started.

October 22, 1969: The Andean Pact entered into force.

January 14, 1970: New regulations for free trade zones within Colombia were established.

March 16, 1970: The import free list, comprising about 100 tariff items, was expanded by 51 tariff items.

April 7, 1970: Thirty-five tariff items were shifted from the prohibited to the prior list.

April 14, 1970: Import taxes and prior import deposits were abolished in Colombian trade with Chile and Peru for 169 tariff items in the LAFTA Common List. Shorter lists also went into effect for Bolivia and Ecuador.

July 7, 1970: Industrial and commercial free zones were created in Buenaventura and Palmaseca.

August 7, 1970: Misael Pastrana Borrero was inaugurated as President, following his election in April.

September 1970: Further expansion of the import free list by 63 tariff items; for 1970 as a whole items in the free list accounted for about 25 per cent of reimbursable imports. Throughout the year many items were also switched from the prohibited to the prior license list, and advance import deposit requirements were lowered.

October 15, 1970: The CAT waiting period was reduced from twelve to nine months.

January 1971: Tariffs and advance import deposits were lowered for unassembled automotive vehicles and parts. Other advance import deposits also were lowered.

February 1971: Several items were moved from the prohibited to the licensing list, and from the licensing to the free list.

May 1971: Further reduction in prior import deposits. Maximum rate was set at 100 per cent (lowered from 130 per cent).

June 1971: New regulations were established for the free trade zones of Barranquilla, Buenaventura, and Palmaseca.

June 1971: The exchange rate applicable to oil transactions was raised from 9 to 20 pesos per U.S. dollar.

June 1971: The Andean Investment Code was put into effect by decree. That decree was declared invalid by the Supreme Court in December 1971.

September 1971: Congress again authorized the Executive to reform the tariff system.

September 1971: Further reductions in advance import deposits.

October 1971: The waiting period between customs clearance of imports and the reimbursement of advance import deposits was reduced from ninety to eighty-five days.

December 1971: The CAT waiting period was reduced from nine to three months (for manufactured or processed exports) and to six months for other minor exports.

February 26, 1972: As the first step in an over-all tariff reform, the rates of import duty for some 800 items were altered; tariffs were raised by five or ten percentage points on most items while the rates on many others were reduced. Many of the reduced rates were raised again in April, May, and June.

February, March, April, 1972: The advance import deposit rates for a wide range of goods was further reduced.

July 5, 1972: Import duties on a number of inputs used in domestic industries were reduced.

July 18, 1972: All technical service contracts as well as trademarks, patents, and licensing and royalty agreements with foreign firms were required to have both the prior approval of the Exchange Office and authorization by the Royalty Commission.

July 19, 1972: The 85-day waiting period between customs clearance of current imports and the return of advance import deposits was eliminated.

November 1972: Further reductions were made in the advance import deposit requirement.

December 1, 1972: Certain measures for the protection of domestic manufacturing were provided. Public sector purchases were to be directed primarily to domestic industrial products.

December 30, 1972: Import duties on 569 tariff items were increased by an average of three to four percentage points to adapt the Colombian customs tariff to the minimum external tariff of the Andean group.

January 1, 1973: Following persistent reports of irregularities, a reduction in the CAT for emeralds from 15 to 12 per cent was implemented.

February 20, 1973: The coverage of the free list reached about 43 per cent of 1972 reimbursable imports.

February 28, 1973: All advance deposit rates were reduced to no more than 10 per cent.

March 29, 1973: The CAT for agricultural exports was reduced from 15 to 13 per cent.

May 11, 1973: A new type of advance import deposit was introduced.

July–August, 1973: Several export restrictions were introduced.

July 1973: INCOMEX offices, including import control records, were destroyed by fire.

August 14, 1973: All items in the prohibited import list were transferred to the prior licensing list.

September 29, 1973: Further CAT reductions were announced for several products.

October 3, 1973: Advance import deposits were raised to a minimum rate of 35 per cent.

November 20, 1973: Lists of permitted exports, of prohibited exports, and of those requiring prior approval were established by INCOMEX.

January 1, 1974: The valuation basis for exports under the Vallejo Plan was changed from total export value to value added. Further CAT reductions were implemented.

March 1974: A large number of import duties were reduced.

June 1974: Nearly half of reimbursable imports were included in the free list.

August 7, 1974: Alfonso López Michelsen was inaugurated as President, following his election in April.

September–October, 1974: Using emergency powers, the new administration decreed an important tax reform and introduced other economic measures, including the near elimination of CATs.

November 1974: Delays in the processing of import requests were reported. The trend toward import liberalization seemed to have halted.

Appendix C

Abbreviations

BdlR: Banco de la República (central bank). BdlR-CN denotes the national accounts (*Cuentas Nacionales*) published by the bank; BdlR-IAGJD, the bank's annual report, *Informe Anual del Gerente a la Junta Directiva;* BdlR-RdBdlR, the bank's monthly statistical bulletin, *Revista del Banco de la República.*

BNM: Brussels Tariff Nomenclature.

CAT: Tax credit certificates given to minor exporters (*certificados de abono tributario*).

CEDE: Development Research Center at the University of Los Andes, in Bogotá (Centro de Estudios sobre Desarrollo Económico).

DANE: National Statistical Office (Departamento Administrativo Nacional de Estadística). DANE-BME denotes its monthly statistical bulletin, *Boletín Mensual de Estadística;* DANE-AGDE, its statistical yearbook, *Anuario General de Estadística;* DANE-ADCE, its foreign trade yearbook, *Anuario de Comercio Exterior.*

FEDESARROLLO: A private Bogotá research foundation specializing in development problems (Fundación para la Educación Superior y el Desarrollo).

GDP: Gross domestic product.

GNP: Gross national product.

IADB: The Inter-American Development Bank.

IBRD: The International Bank for Reconstruction and Development (the World Bank).

IFI: An agency of the Colombian government in charge of promoting industrial development (Instituto de Fomento Industrial).

IMF: International Monetary Fund. IMF-IFS denotes the fund's monthly statistical bulletin, *International Financial Statistics;* IMF-AROER, its *Annual Report on Exchange Restrictions;* IMF-DOT, its monthly and annual publication, *Direction of Trade;* IMF-BOPY, its *Balance of Payments Yearbook.*

INCOMEX: An agency of the Colombian government in charge of supervising foreign trade (Instituto Nacional de Comercio Exterior). The import control mechanism is a major part of INCOMEX.

LAFTA: The Latin American Free Trade Association.

PROEXPO: The export promotion fund (Fondo de Promoción de Exportaciones), also part of INCOMEX.

SITC: Standard international trade classification.

UA: Publication edited by Miguel Urrutia and Mario Arrubla, *Compendio de Estadísticas Históricas de Colombia* (Bogotá: Universidad Nacional de Colombia, 1970).

UNECLA: United Nations Economic Commission for Latin America. UNECLA-SB denotes the commission's *Statistical Bulletin for Latin America;* UNECLA-DANE, the statistical appendix to UNECLA's major study of Colombia, reprinted in DANE-BME, no. 226 (1970), pp. 115–189.

UNFAO: United Nations Food and Agricultural Organization. UNFAO-PY denotes its *Production Yearbook;* UNFAO-TY, its *Trade Yearbook.*

UN-YOITS: United Nations *Yearbook of International Trade Statistics.*

USAID: Agency for International Development of the United States government. Also referred to as AID.

USGPO: United States Government Printing Office.

Index